TRANSFORMATION

AMERICA'S JOURNEY TO DARKNESS

The
Bible Nation
Society

Transformation: America's Journey to Darkness
First Edition 2001
Second Edition 2016

ISBN-10: 0692812806

The Bible Nation Society
BibleNation.org

Layout & Design by Josh Levesque

Cover Photo "America In Chains"
Created by Steven Von Worley

All Scripture quotations are exclusively from the King James Version

To my son Robbie, thank you for making fatherhood such a joy. May you have the opportunity to live in a Christian America.

CONTENTS

1. THE CULTURE WAR

2. A CHRISTIAN NATION

3. THE WAR ON LIFE

4. THE WAR ON LAW

5. THE WAR ON EDUCATION

6. THE WAR ON MARRIAGE

7. THE WAR ON FAMILY

8. THE WAR ON MORALITY

9. THE WAR ON FREEDOM

10. THE WAR ON FAITH

11. THE WAR ON ENTERTAINMENT

12. FIGHTING THE CULTURE WAR

TITLES IN ITALICS CONTRIBUTED BY DR. DOUG LEVESQUE

INTRODUCTION

DR. DOUG LEVESQUE

TRANSFORMATION

INTRODUCTION

This classic book *Transformation, America's Journey To Darkness* written in 1995 by Dr. Phil Stinger, shocked the Christian world for its forthright assessment describing the downward spiral of American culture, politics and religion. The notion that the United States of America was demonstrably racing toward decline was received like a bitter pill that upset the stomach of a lackadaisical church. Christian academia was not ready for it. Charismatic leaders were critical of its perceived negativity. Despite the criticism it sold out. Now, twenty one years later, in 2016 it seems an even greater and prophetic telling of a dark and downward journey. It's medicine still seems distasteful, but now is sought after by church leaders and academics alike with less distaste. Its' diagnosis and Biblical treatment of our national ailments is being sought after with an amazing freshness. Perhaps there is a respite for America, for a season at least. No real reversal is possible without an understanding and acceptance of where we went wrong. No corrective process can be initiated without taking a hard look at the Scriptural map of proper national navigation.

Dr. Stringer and I humbly re-submit this book to you with the hopeful expectation that you will be moved to action, and share its insights with others. He has graciously asked me to offer edits, updates and additions. I have happily complied. We are both unashamedly Bible believing Christians, preachers, patriots, and optimists. However, we are in agreement that without the church's repentance and the culture's revival to a righteous direction, the journey toward darkness will continue. The Bible does paint a picture of such dark directions for society. It foretells of yet another cultural wrong turn as in the days of Noah and of Lot, when nothing but a crash and burn scenario may be in order. At critical times like those foretold in the Bible, the wrathful outcomes of flood, fire and brimstone became imminent and there was only one option...escape. For Noah and his family an ark was prepared. For Lot and his family a marathon to a mountain cave was called for. Today, for the increasingly disparate Christian minority in America we remind our readers to "remember Lot's wife." The current surge of American populism and election elation may be short lived. Use this time wisely.

Staying on track and keeping to the proper course will become increasingly difficult and certainly costly to churches and Christians. No counterfeit maps will help, and no shortcuts should be offered. Only a determined and obedient faith like that of Noah, "By faith Noah…" will see us through the darkness of American decline or take us to a true American resurgence. Modern new evangelical personalities are selling a path of compromise. As popular culture redefines "values" and embraces "religious pluralism", pseudo Christian populists are selling out the Gospel and it's force for personal and societal change in order to remain "relevant" to an increasingly pagan culture. Modern Simonry attempts to be "missional" and speak the language of a wicked culture by replacing hard truth with soft voices and even softer services. The transformation of the Biblical message of sin and salvation through Jesus Christ into the dangerous gospel of "serve humanity" and fight for social justice was predicted in the 1995 edition of this book. This 2016 edition does not seek to say "told you so", but reiterates the warning, updates the issues and personalities, and unmasks the current charades. Vigilance is our goal.

If you feel an anti-christian wind blowing across our land, this book validates that spiritual unease and offers hope that you are not alone in that soulful sense. If you are skeptical of such spiritual subversion, read on and be persuaded that all is not well. We point our joyful fingers in the direction of a celestial city, not made with hands but very real nonetheless. We look for a city whose builder and maker is God. We strain our spiritual eyes for a shining city on a hill that our founders saw and sought to copy as the very best in earthly living. The blueprint of the United States was and should remain that Biblical ideal. We do not balk at Jesus Christ as our King, for the government will be upon his shoulders, but until then let us keep referring to the same blueprint of Scripture for our national and cultural foundations. This is not a Kingdom Dominion Ideal so prominent within Republican circles. Christ will establish His reign Himself. America has never been perfect, but it had a sense of what perfection was. Today, the transformation of decline redefines that good proposition into a new Babylon concept, a satanic offer of the sublime, a "darker is better" theory. We agree with Isaiah and prophesy with him, "Woe unto them that call good evil and evil good!"

Turn and face the darkness!

INTRODUCTION

TRANSFORMATION

1
THE CULTURE WAR

TRANSFORMATION

CULTURAL WARFARE

*"Beware lest any man spoil you through philosophy
and vain deceit, after the tradition of men, after the
rudiments of the world, and not after Christ."*
(Colossians 2:8)

The term "Culture War" has become common in describing contemporary American life and politics. Robert P. Dugan, Jr. (National Association of Evangelicals) said: "We are in the midst of raging Kulturkampf, a cultural war to determine the ways of thinking, living, and behaving that define a society."

The following two statements are from Dr. James Dobson's book *Children at Risk:*

> *Nothing short of a great Civil War of values rages today throughout North America. Two sides with vastly differing and incompatible world views are locked in bitter conflict that permeates every level of society . . . Let me put it in another way. Children are the prize to the winners of the second great Civil War. Those who control what young people are taught and what they experience—what they see, hear, think, and believe—will determine the future course for the nation.*

A Culture War exists when two or more different cultures compete to be the mainstream in a society. A Culture War may be cold (when the conflict is a strong clash of values or ideas), or hot (a civil war of violent force for control). For the most part, the American Culture War has been cold (though more and more liberals are calling for government harassment of Christians).

The Scripture warns that those who oppose Christianity and Christian culture will want to draw people away from their faith and values. Colossians 2:8 says, "Beware lest any man spoil you through philosophy and vain deceit, after the tradition of men, after the rudiments of the world, and not after Christ."

This passage begins with the strongest possible word of warning—

19

BEWARE. This is a very strong warning with very serious consequences for failure to take this warning seriously.

This is the very important warning: There are people who want to "spoil" your spiritual life—ruin your faith, values, and doctrine. The reasons for this obsession on their part will be covered in the next three chapters. Nevertheless, make no mistake about it, these people do not want to just be free to live in personal rebellion against Christian truth. They want to lessen their feelings of personal guilt by involving as many people in their non-Christian lifestyle as possible. This is why they are waging a Culture War against Christian values, against Christian morality, and against America's historic Christian culture.

THE BATTLEFIELD OF THE CULTURE WAR

It should be remembered that it is often hard to persuade adults to change their culture. Because of this, the primary targets of the war against Christian values are children and teenagers.

The Culture War is fought in many areas in the United States:

- The American news media often reports events and evaluates them from a non-Christian (or even anti-Christian) perspective.
- The public school system is full of non-Christian ideas taught as facts to American young people.
- The entertainment media often provides TV programs, movies, and music that promote non-Christian values.
- In the political arena, many politicians campaign against Christian values (and a few openly campaign for them). Many politicians desperately try to find a way to appear to be in the middle.
- Many government bureaucrats use local, state, and federal programs to promote non-Christian values or to hinder historic Christian values.

The Culture War shows up in:

- National political campaigns
- Situation comedies
- School board meetings

- The federal tax code
- Adoption policies
- Health care and abortion proposals
- Television and radio talk shows
- Political primaries
- News coverage
- Foreign policy
- Endless other areas of American life

It should be noted that in spite of all the propaganda to the contrary, the Culture War is not something that has been declared by Christians. Most Christians simply want to be left alone to spend time with their families and build their churches. Historic Christian values were already in place in America. Those opposed to such values had to declare the Culture War.

After three decades of a cold culture war against Christian values, large numbers of Christians are finally starting to defend their much assaulted way of life. This self-defense has brought a vicious attack upon Christians from those who have been at war with Christian values. In a June, 1994, column, Cal Thomas comments on these criticisms:

Susan Estrich, who managed Michael Dukakis' 1988 presidential campaign, accused 'religious extremists' of coming out of the closet and beating the system. That used to be called democracy before what ought to be called the pagan left decided that only people who think as they do are entitled to hold office.

These vicious scare tactics aside, most people have awakened to the fact that something has gone dreadfully wrong in America. We won the Cold War, but we have lost the Culture War. More people fear guns and drugs in the schools and on the streets than they do someone who might say a prayer over the public address system.

A warning to the pagan left comes from a CNN-USA Today-Gallup survey, which reports that most Americans prefer a president with strong morals to one with compatible political views.

The pagan left smears conservative Christians by conjuring up images of snake handlers and the like because it knows it has lost the issues. It raises the specter of imposed morality, but cannot defend its imposed morality, which has produced, according to the Census Bureau, the highest divorce rate in the world, the highest teen pregnancy rate, the most abortions, the highest percentage of children raised in single-parent homes, the highest percentage of violent deaths among the young, and a male homicide rate that is five times greater than any other developed country except Mexico.

Is the pagan left suggesting that the imposition of some of the Christian rights's morality would be worse than this?

PHILOSOPHY

Colossians 2:8 refers to four methods that will be used to "spoil" (wage a Culture War against) Christianity. The first is philosophy. Although the term philosophy makes most people think of a formal class in college, the word actually refers to the "love of learning." While that may sound positive rather than negative, it deserves a closer look. Learning is not automatically good. Learning the wrong information is damaging.

The attitude of our day is that the mere amount of information communicated can be the solution to all of our problems, regardless of the content of the information communicated. For example, in the early 1960's Americans were shocked at a two percent teen pregnancy rate. Americans were told that only a massive sex education program could solve this "crisis." Despite the howls of protest, the American people tolerated huge government programs to communicate information about sexual relationships. This information was taught in the schools and elsewhere. Tragically, however, much of the information communicated came from a non-Christian, non-moral perspective. After 30 years, billions of dollars, and hundreds of programs, the teen pregnancy rate has risen to 22 percent. The mere "love of learning" has not solved the problem, but rather has made it worse.

Our society is filled with examples of the same approach. Parents, concerned about the modern scourge of drugs, have tolerated hundreds of new so-called anti-drug programs in the schools. However, many of these programs teach young people, "It is up to you whether or not you use drugs." This is the moral equivalent of a program citing statistics about teen violence and then telling teens, "It is up to you whether or not you participate in drive-by shootings." While some programs, like "Just

Say 'NO'" have actually helped, many drug programs have actually made matters worse.

The same is true with some counseling and therapy programs. When someone gets into trouble today they are automatically referred to counselors for therapy without knowing what they are going to be taught in therapy.

It is interesting to watch those "modern" politicians, educators, and entertainers who have been teaching American young people that there are no absolute values. The same politicians, educators, and entertainers are now decrying the epidemic of teen violence. Yet what are those violent teens doing but living as if there were no absolute values? Our "modern leaders" have communicated their "philosophy" all too well.

VAIN DECEIT

This passage also gives warning that Christian values can be "spoiled" by "vain deceit." Vain deceit is asserting as true that for which you can offer no evidence. You simply assert a principle that men in rebellion against God desperately want to believe is true. You assume that is must be true, you offer no evidence, and you attack anyone who asks questions or requires evidence. You then act as if your principle has been proven, and you expect everyone else to act accordingly. Tragically, many careless Christians will accept the "vain deceit" around them and adjust their thinking accordingly.

The following are twenty examples of statements based upon "vain deceit" that are common in the United States today:

- The United States was founded upon principles of secular neutrality.
- You cannot legislate morality.
- All cultures are equal.
- A fetus is only a mass of tissue in the mother's womb.
- Abortion is a constitutional right.
- Man is the highest form of animal.
- Fossils are scientific evidence for the theory of evolution.
- Homosexuality is genetic.
- Spanking is child abuse.

23

- Sexual activity by unmarried teenagers is inevitable.
- Christians are all interested in imposing their values on everyone.
- Preaching against homosexuality is a hate crime.
- Homosexuals never recruit.
- Christianity opposes women.
- The continued existence of our planet is threatened by American industry.
- Our diversity has made us great.
- Poverty is the root of all crime.
- Consuming alcohol until you are drunk is a disease.
- It does not make any difference whether there is a father in the home or not.
- It is bigotry to prefer one religion to another.

Every year, billions of taxpayer dollars are spent on programs based upon these assumptions, yet the problems they are supposed to solve only get worse.

TRADITION OF MEN

Colossians 2:8 also warns of people having their faith be "spoiled" by the "tradition of men." Traditions of men are principles of vain deceit that have been repeated so often, and for so long, that they have been absorbed into a culture. The religion of the Pharisees had been spoiled just this way. "But in vain do they worship me, teaching for doctrines the commandments of men." (Matthew 5:19)

Christians must be very careful to scrutinize their thinking and to make sure that the principles by which they live are based on the Scriptures and not on tradition. This is the basis for the process of Christian growth called "renewing your mind" (Romans 12:1-2, Ephesians 4:23, Colossians 3:10).

RUDIMENTS OF THE WORLD

In Colossians 2:8, we are also warned that evil men will want to "spoil" our Christian faith after the rudiments of the world. Rudiments is a word that refers to the basics, essentials, or fundamentals. The essence of man's sinful nature is its selfishness. The world refers to those systems of men based upon the selfishness of man's sinful nature. When anyone appeals to the inherent selfishness of men as the basis for electing a politician, approving a policy, or promoting wickedness, they are appealing to the rudiments of the world.

Rather than appealing to the moral self-discipline that the Word of God and Spirit of God can produce in the hearts of men, most modern leaders appeal to the worst in man. As a result, our culture is fast becoming characterized by rebellion against God and all the human tragedy that is the result of this rebellion.

NOT AFTER CHRIST

The last phrase of Colossians 2:8 gives us an infallible standard by which to discern the attempts of men to spoil our faith. "And not after Christ" is the standard by which we recognize the philosophy of men, the vain deceit of the human heart, and the traditions of men. The standard of Christ-centered thinking is what separates us from the rudiments of the world.

Christians must learn to be careful, Biblical, and Christ-centered in their thinking. They must learn to ask, "Where did this idea come from?" They must learn to be on guard against those that would spoil their faith, morals, and doctrine.

CULTURAL REBELLION

"And even as they did not like to retain God in their knowledge,
God gave them over to a reprobate mind, to do those things which
are not convenient." (Romans 1:28)

Romans chapter one describes the process by which an individual rebels against God. When enough individuals in a culture rebel against God, the whole culture can be said to be in rebellion against God. Most cultures in the history of the world fit into this category.

Notice in this passage the bolded references which demonstrate what all people know. The problem is not a lack of knowledge about the Creator God and what His existence implies, but simply rebellion against that truth. Romans 1:16-32:

16 *For I am not ashamed of the gospel of Christ: for it is the power of God unto salvation to every one that believeth; to the Jew first, and also to the Greek.*
17 *For therein is the righteousness of God revealed from faith to faith: as it is written, The just shall live by faith.*
18 ***For the wrath of God is revealed from heaven*** *against all ungodliness and unrighteousness of men,* ***who hold the truth in unrighteousness;***
19 ***Because that which may be known of God is manifest in them; for God hath shewed it unto them.***
20 ***For the invisible things of him from the creation of the world are clearly seen, being understood by the things that are made, even his eternal power and Godhead; so that they are without excuse:***
21 ***Because that, when they knew God,*** *they glorified him not as God, neither were thankful; but became vain in their imaginations, and their foolish heart was darkened.*
22 *Professing themselves to be wise, they became fools,*
23 *And changed the glory of the uncorruptible God into an image made like to corruptible man, and to birds, and fourfooted beasts,*

and creeping things.

24 Wherefore God also gave them up to uncleanness through the lusts of their own hearts, to dishonour their own bodies between themselves

*25 **Who changed the truth of God into a lie**, and worshipped and served the creature more than the Creator, who is blessed for ever. Amen.*

26 For this cause God gave them up unto vile affections: for even their women did change the natural use into that which is against nature:

27 And likewise also the men, leaving the natural use of the woman, burned in their lust one toward another; men with men working that which is unseemly, and receiving in themselves that recompence of their error which was meet.

*28 **And even as they did not like to retain God in their knowledge,** God gave them over to a reprobate mind, to do those things which are not convenient;*

29 Being filled with all unrighteousness, fornication, wickedness, covetousness, maliciousness; full of envy, murder, debate, deceit, malignity; whisperers,

30 Backbiters, haters of God, despiteful, proud, boasters, inventors of evil things, disobedient to parents,

31 Without understanding, covenantbreakers, without natural affection, implacable, unmerciful:

*32 **Who knowing the judgment of God**, that they which commit such things are worthy of death, not only do the same, but have pleasure in them that do them.*

The Founders of our country, writing in the Declaration of Independence, referred to the Creator God as a "self-evident truth."

CREATION DEMANDS A CREATOR

The principle is simple: Creation demands a Creator. Because we are created beings, we are accountable to our Creator. To be independent and unaccountable, we would have to create our own universe which would then operate under our own rules.

Little children grow up naturally understanding this. (That is one reason they are so much easier to win to Christ than adults.) About the time an individual reaches the teenage years, it is possible to try and hide from the truth about a Creator God (the truth that, according to the Scriptures, you already know). In fact, if this is going to happen, it usually happens during the teenage years. People become uncomfortable about the concept of God when they feel clear guilt about their sin. So, the old nature simply hides from the truth and begins to imagine other answers than the truth of the Creator God for the great questions of life.

These made-up answers may include a concept of a god or gods, but they always let man off the hook for his sin. They either explain away sins as righteous acts, or they create an easy way for man to atone for his own sins.

II Peter 3:5-7 refers to the same thought process. Even though all scientific evidence points to the whole earth having once been covered by water, men imagine their own explanations (some quite bizarre) to explain these facts and mock at the idea of a universal flood:

*5 For this they **willingly are ignorant of**, that by the word of God the heavens were of old, and the earth standing out of the water and in the water:*
6 Whereby the world that then was, being overflowed with water, perished:
7 But the heavens and the earth, which are now, by the same word are kept in store, reserved unto fire against the day of judgment and perdition of ungodly men.

The fact of the universal flood reminds man of a Creator God who exercises judgment. So, men in rebellion against God conveniently ignore the facts and imagine other answers. Romans 1:21 clearly describes this process, "Because that when they knew God, they glorified him not as God, neither were thankful, but became vain in their imaginations, and their foolish heart was darkened."

Many Biblical passages refer to the process of man using his imagination to try to escape from the truth of the Creator God and judgment.

Genesis 6:5 (describing conditions right before the flood), "And God saw that the wickedness of man was great in the earth, and that every imagination of the thoughts of his heart was only evil continually."

Jeremiah 7:24, "But they hearkened not, nor inclined their ear, but walked in the counsels and in the imagination of their evil heart, and went backward, and not forward."

Perhaps no passage on this subject is better known that Psalm 2:1, "Why do the heathen rage, and the people imagine a vain thing?"

Paganism is based upon religious ideals and myths from the evil imaginations of men.

The religions of the world, from Baal worship, to Hinduism, to the principles of Buddha, to modern day blind faith in evolution, are simply the products of the imagination of men in rebellion against God. In their desperation to find excuses for the behavior that makes them feel guilty men will put their faith in the most incredible ideas.

Blind faith in the theory of evolution requires men to believe that some primordial ooze (which came from rapidly spinning gases) evolved into simple-celled organisms, which evolved into sea creatures, then into fish, then into amphibians, then to reptiles, then to small mammals, then to primates, then to cave men, then to modern man. This is supposed to be science (factual truth). If you ask questions, you are told about millions of intermediate stages, billions of years, possible mutations, and changing atmospheric conditions. This is exactly the kind of teaching that Christians are warned about in I Timothy 6:20-21:

> *O Timothy, keep that which is committed to thy trust, avoiding profane and vain babblings, and oppositions of science falsely so called: Which some professing have erred concerning the faith. Grace be with thee. Amen.*

Romans 1:22 clearly refers to these thought processes by declaring, "Professing themselves to be wise they became fools."

The Founders of our country understood that they were creating a nation based upon the truth of a Creator God. Even the most casual reading of the Declaration of Independence makes that clear. The culture that stemmed from this new nation was based upon the truth of the Creator God. There were always individuals who followed the process of rebellion described in Romans 1, but they were always on the fringe of society. Since the 1960's, rebellion against the truth of the Creator God has been more organized, has involved more people, and has pushed itself into the mainstream of American society.

Just as Romans 1:17-20 makes it clear that men have no excuse for not knowing the truth of the Creator God, Romans 1:23 makes it clear that men try to transfer God's glory to His creation, " . . . and changed the glory of the uncorruptible God into an image made like to corruptible man, and to birds, and fourfooted beasts, and creeping things." Men in rebellion toward the Creator God seem much more comfortable worshiping animals, forces of nature, idols of wood and stone, men, and governments than worshiping God. All of these false gods can be explained in such a way as to justify man's sin. Any reminder of the truth of the Creator God makes sinful men feel guilty.

CONSEQUENCES OF IGNORING THE CREATOR

When men hide from the truth of a Creator God, there are no rational grounds left for a moral code. Men ask the questions:

Who is to say what is right or wrong?
Who is judge?
What makes any one person's opinion better than anyone else's?

When the Creator God is left out of the discussion, there is no answer to these questions. As a result, God gives man up to the whims and imaginations of his sinful nature. Romans 1:26 states is this way, "For this cause God gave them up to uncleanness." Left to the old sinful nature, humans devise rationalizations for using the bodies of others to satisfy their own lusts (moral impurity).

This process causes men to separate sexual relationships from their spiritual and social purpose. Only their physical nature is retained. Sexual relationships take on the same character as recreational sports—except there are consequences from which human beings cannot escape. Out-of-wedlock pregnancies, venereal disease, loss of self-respect, AIDS, and an exploding welfare system all stem from the failure of men to follow God's moral code.

Rather than admit that their moral code does not work, rebellious men blame others, no matter how illogical or ridiculous their statements may be.

- Homosexual activists blamed President Reagan and President Bush because homosexual behavior spread AIDS;
- Former Clinton administration Surgeon General Joycelyn Elders blamed churches that preach morality for the failure of her policies;
- Self-proclaimed black community spokesmen blamed Daniel Patrick Moynihan for simply pointing out what out-of-wedlock births were doing to the black community.

The fact is, God's moral code was given to us for a good reason. Sexual relationships are given by God to be part of the marriage covenant. When they are part of the marriage covenant, they bring joy and happiness to the marriage partners, propagate the human race, strengthen society, and are actually a spiritual experience.

When sexual relationships are practiced in rebellion to God, they hurt both participants and society in general. Romans 1:24 puts it this way, "Wherefore God also gave them up to uncleanness through the lusts of their own hearts, to dishonour their own bodies between themselves:"

The Bible is very clear in describing God's moral code. "For God hath not called us to uncleanness, but unto holiness." (I Thessalonians 4:7) Liberals are fond of criticizing the sexual moral code laid down in Scripture. They accuse this moral code of being harsh, judgmental, and repressive.

GOD'S MORAL CODE

God's Word provides five primary sexual prohibitions:

- Prohibition against fornication (including premarital sex as well as all other sex sins)—Deuteronomy 22:28-29; I Thessalonians 4:3; Acts 15:29; I Corinthians 6:18, 7:2, 10:8; and Ephesians 5:3.
- Prohibition against adultery—Exodus 20:14, Leviticus 20:10.
- Prohibition against incest—Leviticus 20:11-12, 14, 18-21; Deuteronomy 27:20, 22-23; and I Corinthians 5:1.
- Prohibition against homosexuality—Leviticus 20:13; Romans 1
- Prohibition against bestiality—Leviticus 20:15-16; Deuteronomy 27:21.

The Lord also warns against the thought patterns that lead to such behavior. Matthew 5:27-28:

> *Ye have heard that it was said by them of old time, Thou shalt not commit adultery: But I say unto you, That whosoever looketh on a woman to lust after her hath committed adultery with her already in his heart.*

The Lord also condemns the attitudes which justify immorality (see the Bible passages which warn about lasciviousness, wantonness, licentiousness, uncleanness, and reprobation). All of these terms imply a lack of self-control and moral restraint.

Just think what our culture would be like if everyone took God's moral code seriously. There would be no child molestation or rape, and sexually transmitted diseases like AIDS and chlamydia would eventually vanish. Women would no longer have to fear being treated as mere sex objects. Unwed pregnancies would be nonexistent. Untold billions of dollars would be saved from welfare payments no longer needed. Divorce rates would plummet. Guilt would no longer shatter young teenagers' self-respect. There would be no demands for abortion, pornography, or prostitution.

In Romans 1:25, God sums up the problem of those who are living in rebellion: "Who changed the truth of God into a lie, and worshipped and served the creature more than the Creator, who is blessed for ever. Amen."

As bad as this picture has been painted, it only gets worse. When men free themselves (hide) from the idea of a Creator God, no way can be found to put moral limits of human behavior. Since no one can answer the question of what is wrong, individuals drift farther and farther into perverse behavior. This leads man into the ultimate form of rebellion towards God—homosexuality.

Characteristics of a Culture in Rebellion Against God

Homosexuality is the ultimate form of rebellion against God. It involves not only rebelling against the principles of God but against the very body that God created. Homosexual acts involve using the body in ways for which it was never designed by the Creator God.

Romans 1:26-27 says:

For this cause God gave them up unto vile affections: for even their women did change the natural use into that which is against nature: And likewise also the men, leaving the natural use of the woman, burned in their lust one toward another; men with men working that which is unseemly, and receiving in themselves that recompence of their error which was meet.

This passage makes several points clear about homosexuality:
- Homosexuality is a "vile affection" (not a genetic trait but an evil desire).
- Homosexual desires occur after God has abandoned a rebellious person to the evil imaginations of the sinful nature.
- Homosexuality is "against nature."
- Homosexuality is based upon lust which "burns" out of control (hence, homosexuals have many sex partners).

Since the body was never designed for homosexual acts, there is punishment for homosexual behavior in what the behavior itself does to the human body.

There will be much more about this in a later chapter. In summary, homosexual behavior is the ultimate form of rebellion against God and is destructive to those who participate in homosexual acts.

Rebellious humans do not want to remember the truth of the Creator God. It stirs up painful feelings of guilt. Because of this, God allows them to try and live as if there was no God.

Romans 1:28, "And even as they did not like to retain God in their knowledge, God gave them over to a reprobate mind to do those things which are not convenient." Ephesians 4:17-19 covers the same ground:

This I say therefore, and testify in the Lord, that ye henceforth walk not as other Gentiles walk, in the vanity of their mind, Having the understanding darkened, being alienated from the life of God through the ignorance that is in them, because of the blindness of their heart: Who being past feeling have given themselves over unto lasciviousness, to work all uncleanness with greediness.

The Bible makes it clear that the result of this attitude toward life is not "convenient." This approach to life simply does not work. It leads people to catastrophe instead of joy. There is pleasure in sin for a season; the price tag is always too great. The problems that plague modern American life come about precisely because of the new paganism and rebellion against God. Romans 2:29-31 lists activities which are sin and are not convenient. These activities bring sorrow upon the individuals who engage in them. They bring destruction upon the culture that is characterized by them. They accurately describe much of American culture today.

Unrighteousness

Americans have been told for a generation that there are no absolutes of right and wrong. Unfortunately, too many Americans got the message, and they are starting to live as if there were no absolutes. Unrighteousness has become the rule rather than the exception.

Fornication

(referring to sexual sins): Such sins are no longer relegated to the red light districts and back alleys of society but have become more open, tolerated, and even promoted. Everyone is asked to pay for the consequences of immoral living. In a society where we are told that it is none of our business what our neighbor does, we are told that it is our responsibility to help pay for the consequences.

Wickedness

(referring to any sin that extends from the selfishness of human nature): In a society where restraint and morality were once the highest appeal of society, rights (regardless of the consequences to others) have now become the most important focus of society.

Covetousness

(refers to the insatiable desire of the old nature; to focus on self): A casual glance at modern advertising or a study of statistics about personal debt shows how clearly covetousness has replaced thrift, saving, and responsible living in America.

Maliciousness

(refers to the attitude of enjoying seeing pain in the lives of others): The rise of vandalism and random violence extends from the growth of maliciousness in American society.

Envy

"Class warfare" and the "politics of envy" have become such a part of the American political scene that articles and whole books have been written on these topics.

Murder

The United States has the highest murder rate of any industrialized nation in the world. (This is without even counting abortion.) In some American cities, murder has become a daily occurrence.

Debate

America has always been famous for having a wide variety of public spirited debates on an endless number of subjects. However, public debate in the U.S. has never been so "mean-spirited." Never have there been so many calls for limiting free speech by the political and religious left.

Deceit

Old-timers in America often long for the time when a man's handshake was his bond. This is not true anymore. Con artists, cheats, and phony companies are things for which everyone must watch out. The lack of public trust for politicians indicates the American public realizes how many elections have been won by deceiving the American people

Malignity

(refers to bad character): The state of politicians in America indicates how much the American attitude towards character has changed. Formerly, politicians were expected to be examples of morality and integrity. Now, people who bring up character issues in politics are attacked as being part of the "lunatic fringe."

Whisperers and Backbiters

(both words refer to gossips, busy-body people who enjoy saying sensational things about people, even if they are not true): National Enquirer-type tabloids have become a multi-billion dollar industry in the United States. The spirit of "back-biting" has resulted in many sensational interviews in magazines and on TV and radio. The American public eats it up. "Gossip rags" play a more important role in American life than serious journals.

Haters of God

Public displays of hatred toward God by homosexual activists and Satanists have never been more prominent in America. Attacks on churches and preachers (the visible representatives of God) have increased at an incredible rate. Blaming the Christian concept of God for all of America's social ills has never been more fashionable among politicians and the news media than it is now.

Despiteful

(refers to the attitudes of anger and bitterness that cause people to direct anger and malicious actions toward those against whom they are bitter): Commentators from all political persuasions have mentioned the mean-spiritedness of current American life.

Proud, Boasters

(refers to the attitude of lifting yourself, in your own opinion, above those around you): In politics, sports, and everyday life, humility is an almost unheard-of trait.

Inventors of Evil Things

(refers to the ability of human nature to create situations that promote and spread evil among people): The pornography industry, the use of popular music to promote Satanism, suicide, moral impunity, and the endless attempt to introduce nudity and pornography into mainstream television illustrates the attention being given to "inventing evil things" in American life.

Disobedient to Parents

(refers to the attack on the Biblical role of parents in guiding their children): From Hillary Clinton's famous quotes comparing parental control over children to slavery and concentration camps, to the modern psychological counseling models that reject parental authority, parental authority in America is being challenged. For many parents of teenagers, the biggest challenge they face is trying to deal with their teens. Nevertheless, if God has no authority, how can mere parents have any authority? The natural teenage impulse toward rebellion has been magnified by the spirit of the day.

Without Understanding

(refers to an inability to even understand basic moral questions): I Timothy 4:2 refers to people whose conscience has been seared with a hot iron (in other words, their conscience is incapable of feeling). Moral principles that were once taken for granted in America now seem foreign to many Americans. This is illustrated by the legal and political controversy over teaching abstinence (moral purity) in the public schools.

Covenant Breakers

(refers to breaking official agreements and contractual obligations): America's courts are full of court cases over real and alleged covenant breaking. However, the form of covenant breaking that influences American life most is divorce. Marriage is a legal contract before man and should be a sacred covenant before God. Yet almost 48% of American marriages end in divorce. This break up of such a high percentage of American homes has more influence on day-to-day life in America than any political or government program.

Without Natural Affection

(refers to the lack of the natural human bonds that develop in a society or individual life influenced by the concept of the Creator God): Several examples are obvious in American life. An expectant mother should naturally be filled with love and excitement about the new life sheltered within her womb. Yet, every year in America, over one million mothers choose to have that life destroyed. As previously mentioned, the natural love between a husband and wife is lacking in so many homes that almost one half of all marriages end in divorce. Children should have a natural love and affection for their parents, yet parent-child relations are often strained in the United States. The job of taking care of elderly parents is more and more being passed over from children to government.

Implacable

(refers to being incapable of being persuaded): The number of repeat offenders in the prison system gives testimony to the number of hardened hears that cannot be influenced. It might also be noted that no matter how much evident there is that the policies of the new paganism are destructive, some leaders still insist that the problem is that America is not pagan enough.

Unmerciful

(refers to lacking the ability to feel mercy for others): Again, the abortion crisis illustrates this problem, as does random violence, and the growing menace of child abuse in our country.

The depth of this corruption in the lives of individuals is illustrated by their attitude toward the most evil members of society. It seems that the pain and sting of guilt are lessened when you can point to someone who is worse than you. Capitalizing on this, many rock music stars have purposely presented themselves as horribly perverted and corrupt (sometimes they really are, sometimes it is just an act to promote sales). The attention paid to such people as Madonna, Michael Jackson, and Marilyn Manson shows how this principle works. The honor and respect given to violent criminals illustrates the depth of rebellion against God in our society.

As Senator William L. Armstrong asks in the foreword to Winning the New Civil War:

What is the profit to America if we have endless economic prosperity, computers, and a hundred channels of television in every home, new cars, boats, glamorous vacations, and more . . . if our families are shattered, our children are corrupted; if we forget or throw away the values and traditions that are the soul of America; or worst of all, if we Christians fail to honor Jesus Christ?

It is time for Americans to face how serious the problems in our society are and where they really originate. America's challenge is a spiritual one, though it has social, moral, and political ramifications. The solutions are spiritual, though they have social, moral, and political significance.

A civil war of values, of ideals, and of moral principles is occurring in America today. A Culture War for the future of American civilization is taking place. This war will be won or lost (depending on your perspective) in the next few years—in your lifetime! The results of this war will be as significant as the results of the War for Independence. What an exciting and challenging time to live!

2016
Facebook & The Modern Culture War
Dr. Doug Levesque

While the defined culture war continues, it is growing nastier and the consequences are reverberating past the church, past the home and into every individual person's psyche. It is harder today to shield oneself or one's family from the vileness of the fight for American society. With the rapid progress and widespread use of the smart phone, powerful words, images and media are pervasive. Around the clock targeting of children and teen "interests" put nuanced rhetoric from warring parties in front of the mold-able minds of future generations. Competing voices pound the digital appetites of millions of hand-held devices persuading the masses of cultural do's and don't's, redefining cultural taboos and frontiers. If governance and law sit upon the culture, and culture rests upon religion, then the most powerful pulpits ever created are Facebook, Twitter and YouTube. They are the new tools with which to rule, govern and influence. Compared to thirty years ago, the culture war battlefields of today are more formidable and more rapidly affected.

Cultural contests used to be held on campus commons and in newspaper opinion pages. These avenues of battle were slow moving and able to be controlled or countered. But today's "social media" is the new sounding board where hundreds of millions of young and old alike seek information, inspiration and encouragement. It is an identity shaping weapon where adolescent status is confirmed, collegiate sense of acceptance is determined, and young professionals turn for direction and counsel for their future. For new parents, Facebook is often a greater moral compass than the Bible, and for new political idealists, it is where they garner courage. Preachers like to say that either you pray to Google and Facebook, or you put your face and faith in the Holy book - the Bible.

Facebook deifies self, offering the potential to create oneself in the "cloud" of universal likes. The Bible deifies Jesus Christ and warns not to take of the forbidden fruit that Satan offered with the false promise that "ye shall be as gods." That original garden battlefield is now an ethereal one, giving every user a power to preach or "share" their self centered message.

While new technologies have the potential to be used for Gospel promotion and affecting the culture for good, increasingly they are used to consolidate power with a keystroke. A grand sort of political correctness has been placed in the hands of Facebook owner Mark Zuckerberg, who has the subtle power of determining social behavior and rhetoric. Small groups and hidden huddles may be created in order to converse outside of public purview or plan secret actions, but Gospel work is done tangibly and out in the open.

If just a few of the technological elites decide to isolate certain ideas, corral certain speech, or ban certain opinions, then BOOM, a digital block becomes a powerful weapon. Biblical and cultural opinions about homosexuality, social norms, and the nature of God or evil can be elevated or destroyed, shaped or banned. In the ocean of ideas that affect the American culture, the Bible voice is marginalized while the approved algorithms of whimsical neo pagan tides ebb and flow ceaselessly shaping intellectual content to Zuckerberg's approval. The culture war seems to be being fought by millions when it is really in the hands of fewer demagogues.

Consider the following headlines after the 2016 presidential election:

- "Barack Obama says Facebook's fake news problem is creating 'dust cloud of nonsense'" (Nov. 8, 2016 - International Business Times)
- "Here's Why Facebook Is Partly to Blame for the Rise of Donald Trump" (Nov. 10, 2016 - Fortune.com)
- "ZUCK TO THE FUTURE Mark Zuckerberg 'feeling hopeful' about America under Donald Trump" (Nov. 10, 2016 - The Sun)

Jasper Hamill's article in the Sun newspaper quotes Zuckerberg in response to the election as saying, "I thought about all the work ahead of us to create the world we want for our children." Apparently Zuckerberg perceives his cultural war "work" as creating a world he wants. He is further quoted, "This work is bigger than any presidency and progress does not move in a straight line." That sounds like a Luciferian line straight out of the garden with snake like movement to boot. And again, "[This] work will take long term focus and finding new ways for all of us to work together, sometimes over decades." It became quickly evident whose side the Facebook founder was on, and while that might excite Trump enthusiasts, it should also be a warning to the power of social media and smart phone phenomenon in the culture war. If Facebook might push a close Presidential election race one way or the other, what else might it determine?

THE CULTURE WAR

TRANSFORMATION

2
A CHRISTIAN NATION

RELIGION & CULTURE

"For the weapons of our warfare are not carnal, but
mighty through God to the pulling down of
strongholds." (2 Corinthians 10:4)

ISRAEL'S SPIRITUAL CYCLE

The history of the Old Testament nation of Israel is a never-ending cycle which goes something like this:

- Israel is blessed by God and pledges faithfulness.
- The next generation is seduced by the religions of the gods of the Canaanites.
- Israel rebels against God.
- Israel is judged until it repents and is delivered.

The stories of the Judges, the United Monarchy, and the Divided Monarchy read like a broken record.

At first glance it is puzzling to see how the nation of Israel could keep making the same mistakes over and over again. Nevertheless, it should be remembered that the Canaanite gods represented an entire culture of self-indulgence and child sacrifice! Man's sinful nature found great sympathy with the Canaanite way of life, just as it rebelled against the culture of self-discipline, responsibility, and morality connected with the worship and laws of Jehovah.

The children of Israel were warned in the strongest possible terms to avoid the worship of other gods.

- "Thou shalt have no other gods before me." (Exodus 20:3)
- "Thou shalt not bow down thyself to them, for I the Lord thy God am a jealous God." (Exodus 20:5)
- "Make no mention of the name of other gods, neither let it be heard out of thy mouth." (Exodus 23:13)

- See also Genesis 35:2; Leviticus 19:4, 26:1; Psalms 16:4, 44:20, 59:8, 79:6, 81:9, 97:7; Isaiah 42:17; Joel 3:12; Jonah 2:8; Micah 5:15; Habakkuk 1:16; and many others

The children of Israel has been specifically warned about the false gods and wicked culture of Canaan (Leviticus 18:25-30 and Deuteronomy 18:9-14). In fact, the Lord was so concerned about the influence of false Canaanite gods and their self-indulgent wicked culture that Israel (in one of the most highly criticized events of the Old Testament) was ordered to exterminate the Canaanite tribes! It was possible for Canaanites to turn to the true God and be accepted in Israel (see the stories of Rahab and Ruth), or they could flee Canaan. Nevertheless, Israel was not to ignore the threat their violent and immoral culture represented. Unfortunately, Israel never obeyed God's instruction and was constantly tempted to the lifestyle of the Canaanites.

Some of the most prominent Canaanite gods were:

- **Baal**—of the Philistines (known as Merodach by the Babylonians). Baal, known as the "lord of Heaven," was worshiped by both ritual immorality and child sacrifice (II Kings 16:7, 21:6). These acts were supposed to cause Baal to bestow prosperity upon his worshipers.
- **Ashteroth**—goddess of the Philistines (known as Ishtar in Babylon and Venus in Greece). Ashteroth was worshiped by ritual immorality; both men and women paid temple prostitutes for their immoral acts. Ashteroth would then bless the crops and grant fertility to the women (who could then keep the children or sacrifice them to Baal as they chose). Consumption of alcohol was also part of the worship ceremonies.
- **Chemosh**—national god of the Moabites. Chemosh was especially worshiped by child sacrifice, primarily the offering of a first-born son (II Kings 3:26-27). Contrast this with Christian teaching. Humans must offer their first-born son to satisfy the power of Chemosh; Jehovah offered His only begotten Son to satisfy His sense of holiness for us.
- **Molech**—national god of the Ammonites (also known as Milcom). Molech was worshiped by offering children as burnt sacrifices--

47

the children of Israel were especially warned about the religion of Molech (Leviticus 18:20-21 and 20:2-5). David has often been criticized for making the Ammonites pass through the fires of their own brick-kilns as he conquered Ammon (II Samuel 12:30-31). But it should be remembered that these were the same brick-kilns in which they had burned their children. This punishment, harsh as it was, was just.

- **Dagon**—another god of the Philistines, considered to be half man-half fish. Dagon was worshiped by drunkenness and acts of violence and rape against non-Philistines. It was the statue of Dagon that was destroyed when the Ark of the Covenant was placed in the same building with it (I Samuel 5).

RELIGION DETERMINES CULTURE

Religion, then as it is now, was more than just idle theological speculation. Religion determined culture. The Canaanite religions were designed to conform to the sinful nature of man. Religious excuses were designed for drunkenness, violence, and all forms of immorality. Child sacrifice was given religious and cultural justification. This appealed to the self-indulgent. After all, providing the resources, care, time, and training for infants is a great burden to the self-centered (and a great privilege to the God-centered).

Paganism is not confined to the ancient religions of Palestine. In the 2000's in the United States of America, a new paganism is obvious. There are those leaders and groups who demand government approval and support for their immoral activities and government protection from any natural consequences. Acts of immorality and violence are worshiped just as sincerely (if not as formally) in some segments of our society as they ever were in ancient Palestine. Legalized abortion (the most technologically sophisticated method of child sacrifice) has made it possible for 35 million human beings to be sacrificed to god of "choice."

A non-stop Culture War raged between the false gods of the Canaanites and the truth of Jehovah. Prophets (true and false) thundered their message and individuals made their decisions. Open warfare broke out. We do not live a theocracy today. Our Culture War is not to be decided by acts of violence (though more and more violence is being directed at Christians). Ours is a Culture War of ideas--God-centered values versus the self-indulgence of the new pagans.

> *"For the weapons of our warfare are not carnal, but mighty through God to the pulling down of strongholds; Casting down imaginations and every high thing that exalteth itself against the knowledge of God and bringing into captivity every thought to the obedience of Christ" (II Corinthians 10:4-5).*

As the United States abandons its Christian culture, the role of paganism is becoming more and more open in American life. The June 21, 1993, issue of Christianity Today carried a full-page ad for Sadigh Gallery. Included among the many idols of gods and goddesses available from the Gallery were statues of Baal and Ashteroth.

Today you can order a child's coloring book entitled "The Many Faces of the Great Mother." The first picture for children to color is the goddess Ashteroth.

In the fall of 1993, the Girl Scouts of America changed their oath of allegiance, lessening the emphasis upon God. One of the stated reasons was to make it easier for girls from pagan families to join the Girl Scouts.

Watchword, a publication of the American Baptist Churches printed an article which told of a woman being made to feel better about an abortion. She had been praying to God asking him to remove her feelings of guilt. A friend suggested she pray to the mother goddess who would approve of her "sacrifice."

In November, 1993, the World Council of Churches sponsored a "Re-Imaging Conference." There more than 2,000 women declared their liberation from Christian orthodoxy. They offered prayers to the goddess Sophia (alternately described as the goddess of wisdom and the goddess of lesbianism). This was followed by another such conference in Dallas that included prayers to Sophia and representations of witchcraft and Hinduism. This conference also concluded that there is no sin, that it is blasphemy to call God "He," and that the doctrine of the Trinity is an attack upon women.

In the basement of the United Nations building is the United Nations Society for Enlightenment and Transformation. This society provides an outlet for uniting pagan and occult groups to influence the world.

The Olympics have always featured some of the trappings of paganism.

However, the 1994 Winter Olympics carried these trappings much further. Prayers to Zeus and honor given to Vettas (spirits worshiped by Vikings) were given special prominence. According to CBS, worshiping Vettas is just another way of expressing concern about the environment.

The opening ceremonies for the 1996 Summer Olympics in Atlanta were replete with references to pagan gods, including ritualistic dances to "summon" the gods of the world's five major cultures to be present during the games. A replicated temple of Zeus was also included, with honor given the pagan ancient Olympic games which have served as the pattern for the modern Olympiad.

There is a growing "politically correct" movement to limit children's Halloween costumes for fear that modern witches will be offended. Columnist Mike Roydo reported receiving this letter from a witch (November 3, 1993):

You ask why should we be sensitive to the feelings of witches? My reply: Witchcraft or WICCA is a legitimate, nature-based religion practiced by many people both in America and abroad, and should be accorded the same respect as Christianity, Islam, Buddhism, etc. The witch portrayed today at Halloween is the Goddess in her crone aspect. She   signifies the dying year and the wisdom that comes with age. It was only after the onset of Christianity that the Pagan Wise-woman became a figure of fear and hatred. So there is, as you can see, a very good reason to be sensitive to the feelings of witches like myself.

The U.S. Army has redesigned its chaplain's crest. The cross and the Jewish Star of David have been removed and replaced with pagan symbols of nature worship. Many, many more examples could be given. Paganism is moving mainstream in America.

In Psalm 106:34-42, the Lord described the influence of paganism upon Israel:

34 They did not destroy the nations, concerning whom the LORD commanded them:
35 But were mingled among the heathen, and learned their works.
36 And they served their idols: which were a snare unto them.

37 Yea, they sacrificed their sons and daughters unto devils,

38 And shed innocent blood, even the blood of their sons and of their daughters, whom they sacrificed unto the idols of Canaan; and the land was polluted with blood.

39 Thus were they defiled with their own works, and went a whoring with their own inventions.

40 Therefore was the wrath of the LORD kindled against his people, insomuch that he abhorred his own inheritance.

41 And he gave them into the hand of the heathen; and they that hated them ruled over them.

42 Their enemies also oppressed them, and they were brought into subjection under their hand.

AMERICA'S CHRISTIAN HERITAGE

"Righteousness exalteth a nation: but sin is a reproach
to any people." (Proverbs 14:34)

THE EARLY PRESIDENTS

The early Presidents involved in the founding of the United States all made clear their recognition of the role of Christianity in the establishment of this country.

George Washington took his first oath of office on April 30, 1789. As he took the oath, his hand rested upon the Bible. When he was done, he kissed the King James Bible and reverently said, "So help me God." Every President since—except one—has also sworn this vow to God.

In the Washington Memorial Chapel in Valley Forge hangs a copy of this prayer by George Washington:

Almighty God; we make our earnest prayer that thou wilt keep the United States in Thy holy protection; that Thou wilt incline the hearts of the citizens to cultivate a spirit of subordination and obedience to the government; and entertain a brotherly affection and love for one another and for their fellow citizens of the United States at large. And finally that Thou wilt most graciously be pleased to dispose us all to do justice, to love mercy, and to demean ourselves with that charity, humility, and pacific temper of mind which were the characteristics of the Divine author of our blessed religion, and without a humble imitation of whose example in these things we can never hope to be a happy nation. Grant our supplication, we beseech Thee, through Jesus Christ our Lord. Amen."

On July 2, 1776, John Adams declared to Congress:

"The second day of July, 1776, will be the most memorable epoch in the history of America, to be celebrated by succeeding

generations as the great anniversary festival, commemorated as the day of deliverance by solemn acts of devotion to God Almighty from one end of the Continent to the other."

For Adams, Independence Day would not only be a patriotic holiday but also a religious one. He also wrote, "The general principles on which the Fathers achieved independence were . . . the general principles of Christianity."

On March 6, 1799, President Adams called for a National Day of Fasting and said in part:

As no truth is more clearly taught in the Volume of Inspiration, nor any more fully demonstrated by the experience of all ages, than that a deep sense and a due acknowledgement of the growing providence of a Supreme Being and of the accountableness of men to Him as the searcher of hearts and righteous distributor of rewards and punishment are conducive equally to the happiness of individuals and to the well-being of communities . . . I have thought proper to recommend, and I hereby recommend accordingly, that Thursday, the twenty-fifth day of April next, be observed throughout the United States of America as a day of solemn humiliation, fasting, and prayer; that the citizens on that day abstain, as far as may be, from their secular occupation, and devote the time to the sacred duties of religion, in public and in private; that they call to mind our numerous offenses against the most high God, confess them before Him with the sincerest penitence, implore His pardoning mercy, through the Great Mediator and Redeemer, for our past transgressions, and that through the grace of His Holy Spirit, we may be disposed and enabled to yield a more suitable obedience to His righteous requisitions in time to come; that He would interpose to arrest the progress of that impiety and licentiousness in principle and practice so offensive to Himself and so ruinous to mankind; that He would make us deeply sensible that "righteousness exalteth a nation, but sin is a reproach to any people." (Proverbs 14:34)

Thomas Jefferson was the author of the draft of the Declaration of

Independence. He also wrote, "Can the liberties of a nation be secure when we have removed the conviction that these liberties are the gifts of God?"

James Madison is often called the Father of the Constitution. He, along with Jefferson, was considered a great champion of religious freedom. Both promoted the concept of the First Amendment on the grounds that Christianity would be more likely to flourish if left unhindered by government. Nevertheless, Madison obviously never considered his ideas on religious freedom as "secular neutrality." As President, in both 1812 and 1813 he called for National Days of Prayer (stating in both cases that compliance was voluntary.)

LATER PRESIDENTS

Over the years, other American Presidents have demonstrated an understading of Biblical principles that created the American culture and system of government.

John Quincy Adams declared that our Founding Fathers "connected in one indissoluble bond the principle of civil government with the principles of Christianity."

Andrew Jackson: "Go to the Scriptures . . . the joyful promises it contains will be a balsam to all your troubles;" and, "[That Book . . . is the rock on which our republic rests."

Woodrow Wilson: "America was born a Christian nation. America was born to exemplify that devotion to the elements of righteousness which are derived from the revelations of Holy Scripture."

Calvin Coolidge: "The foundations of our society and our government rest so much on the teachings of the Bible that it would be difficult to support them if faith in these teachings would cease to be practically universal in our country."

Franklin Roosevelt described the United States as "the lasting concord between men and nations, founded on the principles of Christianity." He also said, "We cannot read the history of our rise and development as a nation without reckoning with the place the Bible has occupied in shaping the advances of the Republic . . ."

In a 1947 letter to Pope Pius III, Harry Truman said, "This is a Christian nation." He also wrote: "The fundamental basis of this nation's law was given to Moses on the Mount. The fundamental basis of our Bill of Rights comes from the teaching we get from Exodus and St. Matthew, from Isaiah and St. Paul. I do not think we emphasize that enough these days. If we do not have the proper fundamental moral background, we will finally wind up with totalitarian government which does not believe in rights for anybody but the state."

Dwight D. Eisenhower wrote: "The Bible is endorsed by the ages. Our civilization is built upon its word. In no other book is there such a collection of inspired wisdom, reality, and hope."

These statements must come as a shock to most of the American news media which seems to believe that the mere mention of God, the Bible, or religion by a political candidate threatens the very existence of religious freedom in America. This must also come as a shock to the Hollywood community that seems to believe that any statement about religion or morality by a President (or other national leader) constitutes establishing a state church.

SUPREME COURT RECOGNITION

Throughout our national history the Supreme Court has often recognized our Christian heritage.

In 1811 (People v. Riggles), the Supreme Court declared, "We are a Christian people."

In 1892, (Church of the Holy Trinity v. United States), the Court declared:

> *Among other matters note the following: The form of oath universally prevailing, concluding with an appeal to the Almighty; the custom of opening sessions of all deliberative bodies and most conventions with prayer; the prefatory words of all wills, "In the name of God, Amen;" the laws respecting the observance of the Sabbath, with the general cessation of all secular business, and the closing of courts, legislatures, and other similar public assemblies on that day; the churches and church organizations which abound in every city, town, and hamlet; the multitude of charitable organizations existing everywhere under Christian auspices; the gigantic missionary associations, with general*

support, and aiming to establish Christian missions in every quarter of the globe. These, and many other matters which might be noticed, add a volume of unofficial declarations to the mass of organic utterances that this is a Christian nation.

In 1931, the Supreme Court Justice George Sutherland reviewed the 1892 decision and stated, "We are a Christian people."

In 1952, the liberal Supreme Court Justice William O. Douglas declared, "We are a religious people and our institutions presuppose a Supreme Being" (Zorech v. Clauson).

Every session of the Supreme Court begins with this statement, "God save the United States and this honorable Court" and with prayers.

Supreme Court Justice David J. Brewer (1890-1910) used to present a lecture entitled "The United States, A Christian Nation." It said in part:

This Republic is classified among the Christian nations of the world. It was so formally declared by the Supreme Court of the United States. In the case of Holy Trinity Church v. United States, 143 U.S. 471, that Court, after mentioning various circumstances added, "These and many other matters which might be noticed, add a volume of unofficial declarations to the mass of organic utterances that this is a Christian nation." Nevertheless, in what sense can the United States be called a Christian nation? Not in the sense that Christianity is the established religion, or that people are in any manner compelled to support it. On the contrary, the Constitution specifically provides that "Congress shall make no law respecting an establishment of religion, or prohibiting the free exercise thereof." Neither is it Christian in the sense that all citizens are either in fact or in name Christians. On the contrary, all religions have free scope within our borders. Nor is it Christian in the sense that a profession of Christianity is public service, or essential to recognition either politically or socially. In fact, the Government as a legal organization is independent of all religions

Nevertheless, we constantly speak of the republic as a Christian nation—in fact, as the leading Christian nation of the world. This popular use of the term has significance. It is not a mere creation of the imagination. It is not a term of derision but has substantial basis—one that justifies its use.In 1989, Supreme Court Justice Sandra Day O'Connor stated that our nation was founded upon a Christian heritage. This was greeted with howls of protest.

CONGRESS

The Congress has routinely acknowledged our Christian heritage in countless proclamations and decrees. As recently as 1982, the Congress declared that 1983 would be the Year of the Bible and said:

The Bible, the word of God, has made a unique contribution in shaping the United States as a distinctive and blessed nation . . . Deeply held religious convictions springing from the Holy Scriptures led to the early settlement of our Nation . . . Biblical teaching inspired concepts of civil government that are contained in our Declaration of Independence and the Constitution of the United States (Public Law 97-280, 96 State. 1211, approved October 4, 1982).

OTHER RECOGNITIONS

Our nation's Christian heritage has been recognized and encouraged in a wide variety of ways by our government. In 1814, Francis Scott Key wrote the poem, "The Star-Spangled Banner." This was later put to music and in 1931, the Congress adopted this as our national anthem. Its fourth verse reads:

O thus be it ever when free men shall stand
Between their loved homes and war's desolation!
Blest with victory and peace may the heaven rescued land
Praise the Power that hath made and preserved us a nation!
The conquer we must
When our cause it is just
And this be our motto:
"In God is our trust."

And the star-spangled Banner
In triumph shall wave

O'er the land of the free
And the home of the Brave.

In 1892, Baptist pastor Francis Bellamy wrote the Pledge of Allegiance to the American Flag:

I pledge allegiance to the flag of the United States of America.
And to the Republic for which it stands, one nation under God,
indivisible, with liberty and justice for all.

In 1945, the Congress adopted this pledge as the official pledge to the flag, but they left out the two words "under God." In 1954, at the request of President Eisenhower, the Congress adopted the original wording of the pledge.

In 1865, the Congress voted to add the phrase "In God We Trust" to our coins. This action came in response to a request from Secretary of the Treasury Salmon P. Chase, who said in part, "No nation can be strong except in the strength of God or safe except in His defense. The trust of our people in God should be declared on our national coins."

A phrase from Leviticus 25:10 is on the base of the Liberty Bell: "Proclaim liberty throughout the land unto all the inhabitants thereof."

GOVERNMENT BUILDINGS

America's Christian heritage is constantly referenced in the buildings and architecture of our government institutions. The Ten Commandments hang on the wall of the Supreme Court building above the chair reserved for the Chief Justice.

The phrase "In God We Trust" is inscribed over the raised platform in the House of Representatives. It is also found on the wall of the Senate Chamber. In the Capitol Rotunda is the figure of the crucified Christ.

Micah 6:8 and Psalm 19:1 are quoted on the walls of the Library of Congress.

On the cap of the Washington Monument is the phrase "Praise Be to God." On the walls of the stairwell are numerous Bible verses.

THE GREAT SEAL

The Great Seal of the United States includes the phrase, "God has smiled on our undertaking." Under the seal is the phrase "This nation under God."

LIBERAL REACTION

In spite of all this, the religious left and the news media act as if any mention of a spiritual heritage for our nation is a brand new idea invented by uneducated religious fanatics. Liberals are not used to the idea of advancing a political agenda by persuasion. Their programs can only be instituted by taking away people's freedoms. They often seem unaware that any other approach exists. As a result, they consistently misjudge the motives and methods of anyone who seeks to understand, explain, or continue America's Christian heritage.

The greatness of the American republic was created by an understanding of Christian principles of government. The nature of the American republic was successful because of the Christian culture that formed American life. Our future can only be as prosperous if we return to those principles, and if there is a revival of Christian culture in our society.

AMERICA'S CHRISTIAN CULTURE

"If the foundations be destroyed, what can the righteous do?" (Psalm 11:3)

It is clear that the Founders of our country understood that the system of government and the institutions of government they were putting into place were based on the Christian culture that was mainstream American life in the colonies.

John Adams wrote, "Our Constitution was made only for a moral and religious people. It is wholly inadequate to the government of any other."

Noah Webster wrote, "The moral principles and precepts contained in the Scriptures ought to form the basis of all our civil constitutions and laws."

Patrick Henry said, "It cannot be emphasized too strongly or too often that this great nation was founded, not by religionists but by Christians, not on religions but on the gospel of Jesus Christ."

MULTI-CULTURALISM

A few years after the founding of the United States, preacher Jedediah Morse, considered the father of American geography wrote: "Whenever the pillars of Christianity shall be overthrown, our present republican form of government, and all the blessing that flow from them, must fall with them." Nevertheless, for the last 40 years, multi-culturalism, a companion myth to secular neutrality, has been moved and pushed to the forefront of American life.

Multi-culturalists proclaim that all cultures are equal and demand that all of our educational programs be adjusted accordingly. Political candidate and commentator Pat Buchanan created a firestorm when he declared, "Our culture is superior. Our culture is superior because our religion is Christianity, and this is the truth that makes men free." A parade of media figures, TV comics, and Democrat and Republican politicians immediately declared that statement to be bigotry and pledged their loyalty to multi-culturalism.

ARE ALL CULTURES EQUAL?

Is the ancient Canaanite culture of Baal-worship and child sacrifice really equal to the Christian concept of loving parents?

Is the ancient Shawnee tradition of burning captives at the stake really equal to the Christian concept of forbidding government the option of "cruel and unusual punishment"?

Is the ancient Aztec practice of human sacrifice really equal to the Christian concept of the sanctity of human life?

Is the ancient Hindu concept of suttee (throwing the wife on the funeral pyre of the husband) really equal to the Christian concept of comforting the widows and orphans in their affliction?

Is the Viking concept of plunder really equal to the Christian concept of charity?

The list of examples could go on and on. Of course, it can be pointed out that professing Christians have, at times, done terrible things. Nevertheless, when a Christian plunders, he does so in rebellion against his religion. When an ancient Viking (or modern socialist) plunders, he does so in obedience to his religion and cultural teaching.

Every American—Christian, Jew, Moslem, atheist, or pagan—enjoys the fruits of America's Christian culture. It is tragic that so many now take it for granted. America has been tolerant previously because it has been Christian.

THE RESULTS OF MULTI-CULTURALISM

Many Americans take for granted the incredible freedom, prosperity, and blessings that all Americans share (even those who deny their origin.) Modern multi-culturalism seeks to divide America into fragmented segments by focusing on our differences instead of focusing on the great commitment to freedom that once united all Americans. As Indianapolis Mayor Stephen Goldsmith said (while holding up a coin with the Latin phrase E Pluribus Unum), "'One out of many' We used to talk about the melting pot, but we do not talk about the melting pot much anymore. We talk about differences. Too much pluribus, I guess, and not enough unum." Modern multi-culturalism seeks to replace tolerance (permitting everyone to follow their own values as long as they do not use force upon their neighbors) with pluralism (the exalting of all values to an equal place in society). However, the motive for proclaiming multi-culturalism does not seem to be promoting freedom but, rather, the gaining of power—raw power. As Robert Royal (Intercollegiate Review, Spring, 1992) writes:

> *Despite its widespread currency, the term multi-culturalism remains a murky concept. In theory, it suggests a substantive pluralism, a quintessential modern American culture of cultures in which no voice predominates—save the voice that says no voice shall predominate. Nevertheless, in fact, as it is widely used on campuses and at other cultural venues, multi-culturalism means promoting certain elements in the American mix—primarily black, Hispanic, feminist, and homosexual elements—while demoting what is thought of as a white, male, heterosexual monolith. Multi-culturalism, properly understood then, has little to do with culture or cultures, and quite a lot to do with special interest politics.*

America is increasingly being divided into factions where self-proclaimed leaders can exercise influence and authority and gain wealth. Pulitzer Prize winning historian David J. Boorstin writes:

> *The menace to America today is in the emphasis on what separates us, rather than on what brings us together . . . I am wary of the emphasis on power, rather than a sense of community. The separate groups in our country are concerned about their power—whether it be black power or white power—the power of any particular group. I think the notion of a hyphenated American is un-American. I believe there are only Americans. Polish-Americans, Italian-Americans, or African Americans are an emphasis that is not fertile.*

A person may object to America's historic Christian culture, but to deny its existence is to live in a liberal fantasy world. For the first 190 years of our nation's history, America's culture was already Christian. For the last 40 years a "Culture War" has been taking place between those who want to replace our Christian culture and those who want to conserve it.

Radicals may criticize America's historic culture, but their criticisms must be put into perspective. It is true that there has been poverty in Christian America. Nevertheless, what is considered poverty in America is middle-class living or better in much of the non-Christian world.

It is true that slavery was an inconsistency in America's Christian heritage. Writing about slavery, Thomas Jefferson said, "Indeed, I tremble for my country when I reflect that God is just and that His justice cannot sleep forever." However, the United States bears the unique distinction of being the only nation in the history of the world where a majority fought a civil war that ended with a minority being given their freedom.

Feminists may chafe at the idea that our historic culture assigns different roles to men and women, but they should take note of how women are treated in non-Christian countries. Because women are usually physically weaker, they are consigned to lesser roles in most countries. Try espousing the ideals of women's liberation in a Communist, Moslem, Hindu, or Buddhist country. In our Christian past, womanhood was exalted to an ideal in the United States.

As our historic American culture disintegrates, life in America is undergoing drastic changes. We cannot agree on the basic principles to be taught in our school systems. Our courts have no clear foundations upon which to make decisions; our juries have no common consensus for delivering verdicts. Factions in our society compete with one another for privileges and dollars from government programs.

Politicians pit groups of Americans one against another. Violence and crime run rampant. As our people struggle with the answers to our modern dilemma, two completely different sets of answers are presented.

Those whose primary faith is in government seek more government control. They envision a common culture stemming from a wise, all powerful government. On the other side of the "Culture War" are those who seek a return to America's historic Christian culture. They believe our problems extend from the collapse of this culture. This controversy is over whether or not America should be a Christian nation.

IS AMERICA A CHRISTIAN NATION?

Controversy rages in political, legal, and educational circles. Nevertheless, before you can answer the question, you must define what you mean by this statement. The phrase, "America is a Christian nation," could have several possible meanings. It could mean:

1. When America was founded, a majority of its Founders were nominal Christians.
2. When America was founded, a majority of its Founders were practicing Christians.
3. A majority of Americans are nominal Christians today.
4. A majority of Americans are practicing Christians today.
5. Christianity is the religion officially established by our Federal Government.
6. The American system of government was shaped and formed by the Christian world view.
7. American culture is shaped by the Christian world view.

The first and third possibilities are obviously true. The fourth and fifth possibilities are obviously not true, while the second is debatable. The sixth obviously was true, but the system is certainly in a process of change from those principles upon which it was founded. Tragically, the seventh was true, but certainly it is not true any longer.

Conservative Jewish columnist Don Feder said it well:

I observed with sad amusement the furor several years ago when a hapless conservative leader declared that America was a Christian nation, inciting the intense agitation of a near hysterical establishment. By this, he was not suggesting that the United States either had or required an official religion, comparable to the Church of England, or that the machinery of government should be harnessed to the propagation of religious dogma.

His statement was a recognition of certain historical/social realities: that America was founded by individuals inspired by the Biblical world view, that most Americans at least pay lip service to those concepts, while many still order their existence by the same, that our national survival depends on the triumph of those values whose proponents are locked in a fierce competition with their opposite number.

The establishment can rest easy. Thanks to its good offices, this is no longer a Christian (or Judeo-Christian) nation. More's the pity. The paganizing of America, a process commenced in the [1960's] (but whose intellectual antecedents can be traced back decades) is already well advanced.

Upon this simple foundation from our Christian culture are our institutions of government and society based:

We hold these truths to be self-evident that all men are created equal, that they are endowed by their Creator, with certain unalienable rights, that among these are life, liberty, and the pursuit of happiness.

Nevertheless, as Psalm 11:3 says, "If the foundations be destroyed, what can the righteous do?" As the foundation of our Christian culture has faded, so has our respect for human life (which is based upon the self-evident truth of creation). As our historic Christian culture has been swept away, so has our liberty (to be replaced with dependence upon big government).

A Culture War rages in the United States to determine whether the last vestiges of our Christian culture will be swept away, or whether there will be a return to our foundations.

2016
America 6.0 - The Latest Edition
Dr. Doug Levesque

The question now is, are we still a Christian nation? How do we remain so? Another view of American history may be helpful in answering these questions. America's journey toward darkness is not new. It may be speeding up, or approaching the darkest of days, but the battle for the direction of the United States has been raging for hundreds of years. Since before July 4, 1776, a culture war was evident. In fact, several revolutions can be recognized in our history. They are sometimes equated with our national growth or military wars, but they are recognizable shifts in American society. How we have viewed ourself and governed our nation has been through a number of editions. We are currently at the far extent of our uniquely Christian identity and expression. We are in yet another release of American culture and governance. Let's express it as America 6.0.

Like a software giant's constant upgrading and release of new versions of their product, so has American culture transitioned away from its Godly heritage toward a more humanistic rendition. At least five editions can be generally noted. These editions might not agree with historians epochs of American history or legal scholars degrees of jurisprudence; however, there is a recognizable correlation. After all, the culture rides upon the spiritual war that Christians fight by using Biblical armor and weaponry. Here is a rudimentary yet reasonable breakdown of these editions of American culture:

Edition	Power Struggle	Dates	Cultural Results
America 1.0 Infancy	Colony vs. Nation	1607 to 1776	Bible culture = Independence

America 2.0 Childhood	State power vs. Federal power	1776 to 1865	Enlightenment culture = Washington D.C.
America 3.0 Adolescence	Regional Power vs. Colonial power	1865 to 1918	European culture = League of Nations
America 4.0 Adulthood	Liberating Power vs. Consolidating Power	1918 to 1945	Empire culture = United Nations
America 5.0 Maturity-Prime	Super Power vs. Relegated Power	1945 to 2016	Babylonian culture = Globalism-G10
America 6.0 Old Age-Decline		2016 to Present	

Some will balk at this timeline and observation. Offense might be taken as to the concept of 2016 bringing in a new edition of American culture, a culture of death, weakness and decline. At every stage of development Christians fought cultural battles. Consider each edition's "bugs":

1.0 Liberty v. Licentiousness

After the Revolutionary War freedom of the press, religion, speech and assembly was a two edged sword that liberated Biblical thought but also unchained deism, Masonry, and atheism, as well as pride, personal ambition and greed. The evil seeds of self interest were fought against by every pulpit, but a micro culture of spiritual rebellion was watered in shadows of wantonness.

2.0 Faith v. Reason

After the Civil War, the federation of power rested increasingly in the nation's capitol called the District of Columbia. Christians were not comfortable with the mythological goddess being personified with the head of government but were satisfied with the term Washington D.C. as an honor to their first and revered president. Reason and enlightenment fought for the culture and sounded, well, reasonable, but Christians recognized the terms as Satanic counterfeits for "reject the Bible as authoritative".

3.0 Restraint v. Decadence

Following the Great War, America was on par with every other European nation and a recognized colonial power. This new found strength created a hormonal surge that defined a new cultural battlefield. Would we continue as a culture with a lust for success or exercise a Scriptural restraint? Would we follow a chase for wealth, or would we discipline ourselves toward righteousness?

4.0 Evangelism v. Exploitation

World War Two put the United States and it's culture as second to none. Gen. MacArthur called for missionaries to come minister to Asia. Some responded with compassion, but the greater culture wanted to exploit markets. After all, we had spilled blood to stop tyrants and open doors to American influence. American goods or American goodness was a difficult balance to maintain. The baby boomers that came from this era fought a culture war that likened America to Rome.

5.0 Responsibility v. Self Centeredness

The Cold War was actually very hot. Korea, Vietnam, and the Middle East have all been hot spots for the U.S. A very hot culture war was also initiated around 1968 when the sexual revolution, divorce, rock and roll, and television spread like wildfire. An age of rebellion has put a spiritual battle between self and the Savior on the front of American society. Christians have fought, won and lost in this era. Public prayers, evolution, abortion and homosexuality have overrun the walls of fortress America.

6.0 Light v. Darkness

In an age where pseudo-Christian churches and personalities preach and practice an unholy and unbiblical form of religion, the very definitions of right and wrong, light and darkness are being questioned. Our culture war is now for the clear meanings of Jesus, salvation, gospel, evil, faith, and Heaven. Some are oblivious to this battle. Others have seemingly gone mad and now fight for religious pluralism. Pluralism attempts to lower the true faith into an equal footing with all other opinions, making it a crime to exalt Christ over any other idea.

This journey toward darkness must still be fought. The year 2016 may be a respite, or it may bring forth a final and ultimate battle for religious liberty and Christian culture in America.

Face the darkness in whatever form it comes Fight the darkness whoever carries its' banner. Forsake the darkness however it restates its' false promises.

TRANSFORMATION

3
THE WAR ON LIFE

TRANSFORMATION

THE BIBLE AND ABORTION

"It is he that hath made us and
not we ourselves." (Psalm 100:3)

Professor L.R. Agnew of the UCLA School of Medicine relates the story of when he posed this question to his students:

Here is the family history. The father has syphilis. The mother has tuberculosis. They have already had four children. The first one is blind, the second one died. The third child is deaf. The fourth also has tuberculosis. The mother is pregnant with her fifth child. The parents are willing to have an abortion if you decide they should. What do you think?
Most of the students decided on abortion.
"Congratulations! You have just murdered Beethoven."

It is a common claim that the Bible does not say anything about abortion. While the word abortion is never used, the Bible teaches many truths that made God's view of abortion very clear.

The Scriptures are clear that God is the giver of life. In Deuteronomy 32:18, the children of Israel were rebuked for forgetting the God that formed them. Jacob declared unto Rachel that it was God who had refused to use her womb to bring about new life (Genesis 30:2). Later the Scripture says that God remembered her and "opened" her womb. It was the Lord who shut Hannah's womb and the Lord who opened it. In Samuel 1, David declared that the Lord had given him life in his mother's womb. In Psalm 127:7, the Psalmist wrote, "Lo, children are an heritage of the LORD: and the fruit of the womb is his reward."

The Scripture also clearly teaches that men receive the gift of life from the action of God. "The spirit of God hath made me, and the breath of the Almighty hath given me life." (Job 33:4). This is more than just a natural process.

Human life began when God shaped Adam in His own image and breathed into him the breath of life. "And the LORD God formed man of

73

the dust of the ground, and breathed into his nostrils the breath of life; and man became a living soul." (Genesis 2:7).

This life is transmitted from generation to generation in an unbroken chain that links Adam and Eve with every child conceived in the mother's womb. When the father's sperm and the mother's ovum unite, another human being is formed. This developing baby, still sheltered in the mother's womb, is a human life as surely as a fully developed adult.

THE SANCTITY OF LIFE

Being created in the image of God gives life its sanctity—its sacredness. This reflection of the image of God (and the image of the parents) begins when life starts in the womb. To arbitrarily destroy life at any point is to kill that which God has made in His own image.

The Bible is clear that God considers the unborn baby to be a human being. Under the God-given civil law of Old Testament Israel, if men took the life of an unborn baby, they were to pay for that life with their own. Exodus 21:22-25:

If men strive, and hurt a woman with child, so that her fruit depart from her, and yet no mischief follow; he shall surely be punished, according as the woman's husband will lay upon him; and he shall pay as the judges determine. And if any mischief follow, then thou   shalt give life for life, Eye for eye, tooth for tooth, hand for hand, foot for foot,   Burning for burning, wound for wound, stripe for stripe.

The principles are clear. If physical violence causes a pregnant woman to deliver her baby prematurely, the baby was to be examined. If no physical harm was done to the child, the person responsible would pay a financial settlement for the problem he had caused. If physical damage had been done to the baby, the culprit was to pay for the shedding of innocent blood. This passage makes it clear that the life of the unborn baby was equal in importance to the life of the adult. The Bible makes this truth clear in other ways. Isaiah 49:1, "Listen, O isles, unto me; and hearken, ye people, from far; The LORD hath called me from the womb; from the bowels of my mother hath he made mention of my name."

THE HUMANITY OF THE UNBORN

Webster's Dictionary defines being human as having human form or attributes. Can anyone suggest that the developing baby does not have human form or attributes? Certainly the body exists in human form. It is not a rock, a vegetable, or an animal. The developing baby in the mother's womb is a human being with all the potential of any other human being at any stage of development.

It is also clear in the Scriptures that God deals with the baby as an unborn person. Jeremiah 1:5, "Before I formed thee in the belly I knew thee; and before thou camest forth out of the womb I sanctified thee, and I ordained thee a prophet unto the nations." Galatians 1:15 (speaking about Paul), "But when it pleased God, who separated me from my mother's womb, and called me by his grace."

In Psalm 139:13-16 the Holy Spirit, through David, clearly declares David's personhood while he was in his mother's womb and the activity of God in forming his physical body:

13 For thou hast possessed my reins: thou hast covered me in my mother's womb.
14 I will praise thee; for I am fearfully and wonderfully made: marvelous are thy works; and that my soul knoweth right well.
15 My substance was not hid from thee, when I was made in secret, and curiously wrought in the lowest parts of the earth.
16 Thine eyes did see my substance, yet being unperfect; and in thy book all my members were written, which in continuance were fashioned, when as yet there was none of them.

It is clear that Jeremiah, Paul, and David were "precious" while in the womb. The same is true of John the Baptist. The Scriptures declare that as Mary shared the good news of the coming of the Messiah with her cousin Elisabeth, unborn babe, John, "leaped in her womb" (Luke 1:41-44). The Bible also declared that John was filled with the Holy Ghost even from his mother's womb (Luke 1:15).

It is interesting to note that brephos, the Greek word translated baby (referring to an unborn baby in Luke 1), is also used to describe Jesus in the manger (Luke 2:16) and Timothy as a child learning the Scriptures (II Timothy 3:15). The Scripture makes no distinction between an unborn baby, a recently born baby, or an infant in the first learning stages.

ISSUES OF PERSONHOOD

Tragically, men sometimes make the mistake that personhood can be granted or taken away by human government. The Nazi position on the Jews, the United States Supreme Court decision about blacks (the Dred Scott case concerning slavery), and the modern Roe v. Wade case about abortion are three primary examples. Nevertheless, personhood is clearly granted by God and men must recognize it—not presume to determine it.

The importance of the personhood of the baby is clear from the terms people use in reference to pregnancy. When the termination of the life of an unborn baby is planned, the child is referred to as a "fetus" or "embryo." By contrast, when parents plan to keep the child the unborn baby is "my baby" or "my child." Did you ever hear anyone say, "I am going to have a little fetus," or "I am going to remove the little baby"? Our respect for human life may be affected by the circumstances, but our attitude does not determine human life.

In God's sight, the unborn baby is a jewel in His creation. A 12-week old unborn baby is only about 1-2 inches long, yet every organ of the human body and every attribute of a human being is already in place. How tragic that every 20 seconds in this country we tear babies such as these from the mother's womb and literally discard them. Every day 4,300 unborn babies are put to death, 25% of all American pregnancies, over one million a year.

The Scriptures are very clear that God condemns the shedding of innocent blood. Exodus 23:7, "and the innocent and righteous slay thou not: for I will not justify the wicked, that innocent blood be not shed in thy land." While God condemns the shedding of innocent blood, he allows the shedding of guilty blood in such cases as murder (Exodus 21:12), rape (Deuteronomy 22:25), and incest (Leviticus 18:6, 29). Every time an abortion takes place the blood of a living human being is shed. What crime has this unborn baby committed that justifies shedding its blood? The answer, clearly, is none. Every abortion sheds innocent blood.

The Scripture makes it clear that believers should do all that is in their power to protest the shedding of innocent blood and to rescue those who are "delivered to death." Proverbs 24:11-12 says:

If thou forbear to deliver them that are drawn unto death, and those that are ready to be slain; If thou sayest, Behold, we knew it not; doth not he that pondereth the heart consider it? and he that keepeth the soul, doth not he know it? and shall not he render to every man according to his works?

Abortion on demand is simply the sacrifice of unborn child to the whims of a selfish, irresponsible, and perverted parent. Ezekiel 16:20 declares that we bear our children unto the Lord. Luke 17:2 warns, "It were better for him that a millstone were hanged about his neck, and he cast into the sea, than that he should offend one of these little ones."

America is already under the judgment of God for violation the sanctity of human life (a principle upon which this nation was founded). As Jack Kemp said:

Every single year, there is the tragic silence of a million newborn cries that will never be developed; Potential we will never see; Books never authored; Inventions never made . . . the right to life is a gift of God, not a gift of the state.

Those who teach that the Bible approves of abortion plainly distort the Bible. Those who teach that the Bible has nothing to say on the subject ignore what is clearly taught.

The Bible is clear in teaching that an unborn baby is a living human being. The Bible does not distinguish between a baby still in the womb, and a newborn baby. The Bible is clear that conception is not solely a natural process, but it is a divine act of God. This is why every act of intercourse does not produce a baby. God treats babies in the womb as persons. Babies in the womb can experience emotions (the example of John the Baptist proves this). The Bible teaches that God is working in our lives both preparing us physically and for life while we are still in the womb. God absolutely prohibits shedding innocent blood, and He hates hands that shed innocent blood. (Proverbs 6:16-17).

Abortion cannot be reconciled with Christianity. The most serious advocates of abortion recognize that they are campaigning against basic Christian teaching. Malcolm Potts wrote in a 1970 issue of California Medicine Magazine:

It will become necessary and acceptable to place relative rather than absolute values on such things as human lives . . . This is quite distinctly at variance with the Judeo-Christian ethic and carries serious philosophical, social, economic, and political implications for Western society and perhaps for world society. The process of eroding the old ethic and substituting the new has already begun. It may be seen most clearly in changing attitudes toward human abortion. In defiance of the long held Western ethic of intrinsic and equal values of every human life, regardless of its stage, condition, or status, abortion is becoming accepted by society as moral, right, and even necessary. It is worth noting that this shift in public attitude has affected the churches, the laws, and the public policy rather than the reverse.

In no area is the Culture War between America's historic Christian culture and the new paganism seen more clearly than the debate over abortion.

TWELVE MYTHS OF ABORTION

"The spirit of God hath made me, and the breath of the Almighty
hath given me life." (Job 33:4)

As we have already seen, men in rebellion against God often justify their actions with ideas and myths that stem from the imagination of their evil hearts (Romans 1:21; Proverbs 6:18). In the discussion of abortion, this mythology is clearly seen. Statements that are obviously untrue are repeated again and again as if the frequency of their utterance could give them credibility. When anyone attempts to question or examine these statements, he is attacked viciously, as if the viciousness of the attack could disprove the substance of the question. In the next few chapters, we will examine 12 of the many myths of abortion.

MYTH 1

An unborn fetus is only a mass of tissue.

One pro-abortion pamphlet states, "A fetus is only a wad of cells adhering to the walls of a uterus—until these cells free themselves and become independent."

Many young women take comfort in the idea that their abortions only deal with removing tissue cells like removing a tumor or dead skin. But upon what rational examination is this based? More than one young woman had reported coming out from under the anesthetic early to be shocked at seeing fingers, facial parts, arms, and legs being dumped in the trash. Even a casual examination of fetal development disproves this myth.

- At conception, a new and totally different human being with 48 chromosomes (the same as any human) exists, having the capability of replacing his own dying cells.
- On the 13th day, the fetus is one-fourth of an inch long with a brain, human proportions, eyes, ears, mouth, kidney, liver, stomach, intestines, and a spinal cord and nervous system.
- By the 18th day, a heart in its early stages of development has

begun pumping its own blood.

- At six and one-half weeks, the skeleton is complete, and the first movements are made. The two-month-old fetus attains the ability to grasp objects, swim, hiccup, suck his thumb, and wakes up and sleeps with regularity.
- At the 11th week stage, all body systems are formed and at work. The fetus now breathes, swallows, is sensitive to pain, and is an independent individual. Present systems will grow and mature, but nothing new will develop in the body.
- The 16-week-old fetus has grown to five and one-half inches long. Toes and fingers have now formed, and facial features are clearly evident.
- "Quickening" is first felt at 18 weeks as the fetus, now active and energetic, flexes its muscles, punches, and kicks.
- By the 20th week, which represents the first half of the gestation period, babies are often born prematurely and alive.

By any standard, the unborn child is more than a tumor or a wad of tissue. If you simply believe in granting the "benefit of the doubt," abortion should be prohibited.

Every abortion stops a beating heart, ends the development of a unique DNA code, and sheds innocent blood. If a baby is only a "wad of cells" at conception, what process turns it into more than a wad of cells?

MYTH 2:

An unborn fetus cannot feel pain.

There is an obvious question to be asked in response to this myth: How do you know?

Unborn babies obviously experience sensations, respond to outside stimuli, recognize familiar voices, etc. It is only reasonable to assume that some sensations of pain occur in their development, according to the evidence gained by using ultrasound and fiber-optic cameras. By four months of development, babies are frowning, moving their lips, and grasping with their hands.

When you consider the methods used to cause abortion, it is clear that they are all an assault on, and a shock to, any trace of a nervous system.

There are several techniques used for inducing abortions, depending on the child's stage of growth in the womb. They are:

- Suction aspiration,
- Dilation and curettage,
- Dilation and evacuation,
- Prostaglandins,
- Salt poisoning,
- Hysterotomy,
- Partial-birth abortion,
- Fetal reduction, and
- RU 486.

Suction Aspiration

Suction aspiration abortion (or menstrual extraction if done early in pregnancy) is used in 95% of induced abortions. A powerful suction tube is inserted into the womb through the dilated cervix. This dismembers the body of the developing baby and tears the placenta from the uterus, sucking them into a container. These body parts are usually recognizable as arms, legs, the head, etc. Great care must be used to prevent the uterus from being punctured during this procedure. Uterine hemorrhage and infection can easily result if any fetal or placental tissue is left behind in the uterus.

Dilation and Curettage (D&C)

In this technique, the cervix is dilated or stretched to permit insertion of a loop-shaped steel knife in order to scrape the wall of the uterus. This cuts the baby's body into pieces and cuts the placenta from the uterine wall. Bleeding is sometimes considerable.

This method is used primarily during the seventh to 12th weeks of pregnancy and should not be confused with therapeutic D&C, done with a blunt curette for reasons other than undesired pregnancy.

Dilation and Evacuation (D&E)

Used to remove a child from the womb who is as old as 18 weeks, this method is similar to the D&C. The difference is that forceps are used to grasp part of the developing baby who already has calcified bones. The parts must be twisted and torn away, the placenta sliced away, and the bleeding is profuse.

Salt Poisoning

Otherwise known as "saline amniocentesis" or "salting out," this technique is used after 16 week of pregnancy when enough fluid has accumulated in the amniotic fluid sac surrounding the baby.

A needle is inserted through the mother's abdomen directly into the sac, and a solution of concentrated salt is injected into it. The baby breathes in, swallowing the salt, and is thereby poisoned. After about an hour, the child dies. The mother usually goes into labor approximately a day later, delivering a dead, burned, and shriveled baby. This is the second most common method of inducing abortion. It is outlawed in Japan and other countries because of inherent risks to the mother.

Prostaglandin

Prostaglandin are hormones which assist the birth process. Injecting concentrations of them into the amniotic sac induces violent labor and premature birth of a child usually too young to survive. Oftentimes salt or another toxin is first injected to assure that the baby will be delivered dead, since some babies have trauma of prostaglandin birth at this stage, and have been delivered alive. This method is usually used during the second half of the pregnancy. A self-administered prostaglandin suppository is also being developed for first trimester abortion. Serious side-effects and complications from prostaglandin use, including cardiac arrest and rupture of the uterus can be unpredictable and very severe. Prostaglandin is also used in conjunction with RU 486.

Hysterotomy

Similar to the Cesarean Section, this method is generally used if the salt poisoning or prostaglandin methods fail. Sometimes babies are born alive during this procedure which raises questions as to how and when the infants are killed and by whom. Some infants who are attended to after a hysterotomy have been known to survive and were subsequently accepted by their natural mothers or placed in adoptive homes.

This method offers the highest risk to the health of the mother. The risk of mortality from hysterotomy is two times greater than risk from D&E.

Partial Birth Abortions

A partial birth abortion is the killing of a baby seconds before birth. The abortionist turns the baby around and pulls the boy or girl out of the womb feet first. "Delivery" is stopped when just the top of the baby's head is the only part of the baby still within the birth canal. The abortionist uses scissors to puncture the back of the baby's head at the base of the skull, inserts a suction tube and sucks the baby's brains out. After the baby's head is collapsed, "delivery" is completed.

In 1996, a federal law called the Partial-birth Abortion Act was first passed by Congress. This bill was designed to outlaw this inhumane, barbaric assassination of defenseless babies. President Bill Clinton vetoed the measure saying that the mother's health was not considered. At full term, a normal birth would have much lower risk to the health of the mother. Efforts to override President Clinton's veto failed.

Fetal Reduction

"Selective Reduction of Multi-Fetal Pregnancy in the First Trimester" is the clinical name for a relatively new method of abortion.

As a result of widespread use of infertility drugs, multiple pregnancies (pregnancies where there are often as many as four to six, or even more, fetuses present) are increasingly common.

Doctors routinely recommend selectively reducing the number of fetuses by means of abortion. There are three main reasons for this as given by Dr. John C. Willke on his radio program, Life Issues:

- They say it's safer for the mother—(there is little evidence to support this).
- They say it increases the chance of survival of the remaining babies—(that is true).
- The third reason given is simply the parents don't want that many kids.

Dr. Willke continues, "Sometimes not only do they succeed in killing the 'extra' unwanted babies, but they end up losing them all."

The method of killing the unwanted babies involves literally selecting the ones to be sacrificed and injecting a poisonous drug directly into the heart. One wonders what possible process an individual could use to select which ones to kill and which ones to save.

Who can guarantee that such barbaric practices do not cause the unborn baby any pain?

RU 486

RU 486 (or Mifepristone) is literally abortion-in-a-pill. When taken between the fifth and seventh weeks of pregnancy (counting from the date of the last menstrual period), RU 486 blocks the vital nutrient hormone, progesterone, from reaching the rapidly developing fetus, literally causing it to wither and die. After this, prostaglandin is given to produce hard labor, causing the dead baby to be expelled from the womb.

Dr. John C. Willke states emphatically, "RU 486 kills a developing baby after his or heart has begun to beat." This dispels the common notion that RU 486 is a contraceptive as opposed to an abortifacient.

When used together, the RU 486-prostaglandin combination is effective 95% of the time. However, this is not without serious health risks. Contrary to popular myth:

- RU 486 is not more private or quicker than traditional abortions. As many as four office visits are required.
- RU 486 is not cheaper—it can be three-four times more expensive.
- RU 486 shows no signs of being "safer" for the mother.
- The RU 486 abortion method is no less painful. The suction method is very painful, but it is over quickly. With RU 486, the pain lasts a minimum of four hours.

MYTH 3:

Only the government can determine personhood.

Besides being contrary to the Bible and all semblance of logic, this is obviously not what the Founders of our country had in mind.

The Preamble to the Constitution, the paragraph that describes why the Constitution was created, states the following:

We the People of the United States, in Order to form a more perfect Union, establish Justice, insure domestic Tranquility, provide for the common defence, promote the general Welfare, and secure the Blessings of Liberty to ourselves and our Posterity, do ordain and establish this Constitution for the United States of America.

The Fifth Amendment says:

No person shall be . . . deprived of life, liberty, or property without due process of law.

The Declaration of Independence states:

We hold these truths to be self-evident, that all men are created equal, that they are endowed by their Creator with certain unalienable Rights, that among these are life, liberty, and the pursuit of Happiness.

The definition of posterity is "all future generations." To have future generations, we must have at some time persons in the making in embryo, in fetus, and in the child stage. If we do not, or all of these middle phases can be legally eliminated, we will not have future generations, and we will have violated one of the basic tenets of the Constitution. The decision to deprive our posterity of life has been made without "assistance of counsel for his (her) defense" and is in direct violation of both the Fifth and Sixth Amendments.

Abraham Lincoln, referring to slavery, discussed how the Declaration of Independence must be applied to all men, or it could not be guaranteed for any man. He said:

This was their majestic interpretation of the economy of the Universe. This was their lofty, and wise, and noble understanding of the justice of the Creator to His creatures. Yes, gentlemen, to all His creatures, to the whole great family of man. In their enlightened belief, nothing stamped with the divine image and likeness was sent into the world to be trodden on . . . They grasped not only the whole race of man then living, but they reached forward and seized upon the farthest posterity. They erected a beacon to guide their children and their children's children, and the countless myriads who should inhabit the earth in other ages.

He warned also of the danger we would face if we closed our eyes to the value of life in any category of human beings:

I should like to know if taking this old Declaration of Independence, which declares that all men are equal upon principle, and making exceptions to it continues, where will it stop? If one man says it does not mean a Negro, why cannot another say it does not mean some other man?

No government can be trusted with defining personhood. No matter what the Nazi government said about the Jews, they are still persons. No matter what the United States Supreme Court of the last century said about Negroes, they are still persons. That mistake led to the American Civil War. No matter what the modern Supreme Court says about unborn babies, they are still persons.

MYTH 4:

The vast majority of Americans support abortion.

Many polls have been taken covering the abortion issue. The answers you get depend primarily on how you ask the questions. If you ask Americans if they want all abortions banned, a clear majority says no. Many Americans feel that abortion in the aftermath of a rape, or when the mother's health is in danger, is legitimate. Much false information about these two situations exists. (Less than two percent of abortions are related to these causes.) However, if you ask Americans if they approve of abortion as a method of birth control, a clear majority also say no. If you ask Americans if they think that abortions should be taxpayer funded, an overwhelming majority are clearly opposed.

The issue of public support, however, is a false one. If a majority of people supported slavery, would that make it right? If a majority wanted to practice genocide against the Jews, would that make it right?

Our Founders wanted some clear laws that would protect minorities from the whims of the majority. They clearly determined that protecting the "right to life" was one of the unalterable purposes of government. The right to life is not based upon a majority decision; it is a God-given right.

MYTH 5:

The abortion issue is simply an issue of reproductive freedom for women.

Reproductive freedom deals with the subject of conception. Once you have conceived a child, you have already reproduced yourself. The subject of abortion has to do with how we will treat babies after reproduction has already taken place. There is no scientific reason to question that life begins at conception. Mayo Clinic geneticist Hymie Gordon testified, "I have never encountered in my reading—long before I became concerned with abortion, euthanasia, and so on—anyone who has argued that life did not begin at the moment of conception." There has been no argument about these matters.

Micheline Matthew Roth, a medical school professor at Harvard said:

In biology and in medicine it is an accepted fact that the life of any individual organism begins at conception. . . . No experiments have disproved this finding. So it is scientifically correct to say that an individual life begins at conception . . . and that this developing human is always a member of our species in all stages of life.

No matter how much mythology you may hear, this is not a women's freedom issue. Fully half of the babies aborted are women.

As the two popular bumper stickers put it: "Equal rights for unborn women" and "Abortion is the ultimate form of child abuse."

MYTH 6:

Abortion is a "separation of church and state" issue.

The myth is repeatedly quoted. The illogical premise is simply that, since opposition to abortion comes from religion, no law can be made restricting it. But religious principles also cause opposition to all other murders. Religious principles also lead to the opposition of incest, child molesting, theft, rape, and violence. Does anyone suggest that laws restricting these activities are a violation of separation of church and state? People cry that you cannot legislate morality, but the laws against murder are legislating morality. The truth is, it is not Christians who are trying to impose their will on others. The ultimate imposition of your will on other human beings is to dissect them or poison them and take away their right to life.

When liberals demand that everyone pay taxes to pay for other people's abortions, they are trying to impose their will on other people. When they demand that everyone "donate" tax moneys to provide school clinics and counselors to promote abortion, they are trying to impose their religious convictions on society as a whole.

MYTH 7:

Women have a Constitutional right to abortion.

During the discussion of the Human Life Amendment, the Religious Coalition for Abortion Rights ran this text in an ad:

> *Right now, the United States Senate is holding hearings on a Constitutional Amendment to outlaw abortion.*
>
> *This effort, backed by a handful of Senators, seriously threatens the religious freedom of every American.*
>
> *If they succeed, you will be forced to accept, as law, one narrow religious and moral belief—even if it is not your own, your church's, or your synagogue's.*
>
> *The Religious Coalition for Abortion Rights of New York State represents most of the country's major religions. We are organizations like the American Baptist Churches,   NYS,; the N.Y. Federation of Reform Synagogues; The Episcopal Church; the United Presbyterian Church, Synod of the Northeast; the United Church of Christ; and The United Methodist Church, whose positions on abortion you might not be aware of.*
>
> *We believe that abortion is an individual decision and, therefore, your God-given right. While we support a woman's choice to become a mother, we also support her choice   not   to. But most importantly, we feel no religious group has the right to use the power of politics to impose their beliefs on you.*
>
> *Yet this is precisely what the Constitutional Amendment would*

do. By outlawing abortion, it will rob you of the right to make your own personal decisions according to your own conscience.

By your support, of the Religious Coalition for Abortion Rights, we can work together to stop this small group from forcing you to practice what they preach.

Our country's most cherished unalienable right is being threatened: Freedom.

Planned Parenthood has stated that the passing of a "Human Life Amendment" would be the first time a Constitutional right was ever taken from the American people.

But an obvious question remains unanswered: Where in the Constitution is the right to abortion ever mentioned? To the contrary, our government was established to protect our right to life.

In order to support his pro-abortion Roe v. Wade decision, Justice Blackmun invented a "right to privacy" which is unmentioned in the Constitution and twisted it to refer to abortion. The "Constitutional right to abortion" exists only in a liberal fantasy world. It is only a product of their imaginations. It is found nowhere in the Constitution.

MYTH 8:

Abortion is too important a decision to be left up to the government.

In a free society, very few decisions are made by the government. The only legitimate roles for the government involve protecting the nation from foreign invasions and protecting individuals from having force exerted against them.

However, abortion is the ultimate expression of force against a helpless individual. Who is to defend those that are helpless from aggressive life-threatening forces?

Cultures may be judged in many ways, but ultimately, they will be judged by this: how did they treat the most helpless members of society?

Should it be a private decision whether or not to take a human life? Is child molestation too important a decision to be left up to the government? It should also be noted that abortions result in several potential health hazards for the mother.

Daniel J. Martin, clinical instructor at St. Louis University Medical

School said, "The impact of abortion on the body of a woman who chooses abortion is great and always negative. I can think of no beneficial effect of a social abortion on a body."

Induced abortion is the premature, willful, and violent penetration of a closed and safeguarded biological system. This unnatural medical procedure always exposes the mother to some risks. Unfortunately, the truth about these complications are often kept from the general public. The psychological aspects of abortion have devastated the lives of many women. Again, information about these potential damaging side-effects is normally kept from the general public.

MYTH 9:

Anti-abortionists do not really care what happens after the baby is born.

Former Clinton administration Surgeon General Joyceyln Elders admonished conservatives to "get over their love affair with the fetus." This accusation is simply designed to keep the real issues from being examined.

It is the Christian, conservative, and traditional movements that are building the programs that really help America's children:

- Schools that genuinely educate,
- Adoption services,
- Church children's programs, and
- Most importantly, strong homes.

These programs (most especially the home and family) are under attack from the new pagans. From homeschools to church camps, the best interests of America's children are being served by the same people who oppose abortion.

To many of the liberal crowd, the nation's children form the test subject for all kinds of social experiments. For Christian conservatives, proper care and training in child-rearing is one of mankind's highest callings.

MYTH 10:

Only pro-choice candidates can be elected to public office in America.

This myth has been around for 20 years in America and still continues to be repeated no matter how many times it is refuted.

Ronald Reagan was declared by many Democrats, most of the new media, and some liberal Republicans to be "unelectable" because of his pro-life stance. Yet he won in 1980 by a wide margin and was re-elected by a 49-state landslide in 1984. The charge was repeated against George Bush in 1988 and yet he was elected by a landslide. Only after the economy in America dipped into a recession did American voters reject his Presidency.

Pennsylvania Democratic Governor Robert Casey was declared unelectable because he was pro-life; yet, he was elected in 1986 and reelected in 1990.

Polling data after the 1992 Presidential election demonstrated that among the few voters who voted primarily on the abortion issue a slight majority voted pro-life.

Even more striking evidence from the 1994 election disproves this myth. In the Congressional elections of 1994, not one pro-life incumbent was defeated, and 43 new pro-life candidates were elected! Americans have elected far more pro-life governors in recent elections, as well.

The sad truth, however, is that the abortion issue rarely decides election outcomes in America. Economic issues, foreign policy, and law-and-order issues influence far more elections than abortion.

MYTH 11:

Pro-life people routinely use violence and
terrorism to promote their cause.

Ever since shootings have taken place outside several abortion clinics, tragically killing abortion clinic doctors and staff, this myth has been widely circulated and used as the basis for several laws restricting the free-speech rights of pro-life advocates.

The truth is just the opposite. For 20 years, thousands of pro-life demonstrators have been subjected to acts of violence and abuse for exercising their religious convictions and practicing free speech. The following are four examples of what pro-life Christians regularly experience (usually unreported by the media):

One Missouri pro-abortion group called "Church Ladies for Choice" conducted a demonstration outside the Calvary Temple in St. Louis, banging drums and shouting obscenities, eventually assaulting police.

A pro-abortion mob beset the Evangelical Free Church in Brooklyn Park, Minnesota, blocking access to the chapel, shouting obscenities, and vandalizing cars in the parking lot.

A Right To Life office in Gainesville, Florida, was fire-bombed by pro-abortion activists, with none of the publicity that attends assaults upon abortion clinics.

Alan Ross, co-owner of an abortion clinic in Gaithersburg, Maryland, was convicted of assault upon a pro-life activist. This was the second such conviction for Ross in less than three months.

MYTH 12:

Anti-abortion protestors are anti-women.

As anyone who has even been involved in promoting life over abortion can testify, the clear majority of protestors are women. In fact, groups like the National Right to Life and Concerned Women for America have far more female members than does the liberal pro-abortion National Organization for Women. Finally, half of the babies these concerned Christians are trying to save are females.

The liberals' overt attempts to spoil the American culture with their vain deceit—asserting as true that for which they can offer no evidence and shamelessly attacking anyone who demands evidence—have been largely successful. Many people accept these myths at face value without challenge.

This is why every Christian in fulfilling his or her duty to be salt and light must be informed and willing to stem the tide of false information.

VIOLENCE AND EUTHANASIA

"Their feet are swift to shed blood: Destruction and misery are in
their ways: And the way of peace have the not known: There is no
fear of God before their eyes." (Romans 3:15-18)

ABORTION AND VIOLENCE

In the book *Abortion and the Conscience of America*, President Ronald
Reagan is quoted as saying:

> *Regrettably, we live at a time when some persons do not value
> all human life. They want to pick and choose which individuals
> have value . . . We cannot diminish the value of one category of
> human life—the unborn—without diminishing the value of all
> human life.*

In February, 1994, (while standing between the United States' two
most important supporters of abortion, President Bill Clinton and Vice
President Al Gore), Mother Teresa, a Roman Catholic nun, made this
statement about abortion and the violence that follows it:

> *Nevertheless, I feel that the greatest destroyer of peace today
> is abortion, because it is a war against the child, a direct killing
> of the innocent child, a murder by the mother herself. And if we
> accept that a mother can kill even her own child, how can we
> tell other people not to kill one another? How do we persuade a
> woman not to have an abortion? As always, we must persuade her
> with love, and we remind ourselves that love means to be willing
> to give until it hurts. Jesus gave even His life to love us. So, the
> mother who is thinking of abortion should be helped to love, that
> is, to give until it hurts her plans, or her free time, to respect the
> life of her child. The father of that child, whoever he is, must also
> give until it hurts.*
> *By abortion, the mother does not learn to love, but kills even
> her own child to solve her problems. And, by abortion, the father*

is told that he does not have to take any responsibility at all for the child he has brought into the world. That father is likely to put other women into the same trouble. So, abortion just leads to more abortion. Any country that accepts abortion is not teaching its people to love, but to use any violence to get what they want. This is why the greatest destroyer of love and peace is abortion.

ETHICS OF VIOLENCE

Once a society has accepted the premise that unborn babies can be killed simply because they are inconvenient and they cannot protect themselves, that society is doomed to lose all respect for human life.

What is the ethical difference between killing a helpless baby and an inconvenient invalid?

What is the moral difference between exercising choice about killing the unborn and practicing euthanasia on the aged?

If taking the life of an unborn baby is not a moral dilemma, why should taking the life (and property) of a wealthy tourist be a moral dilemma?

This "Darth Vader" system of ethics (just kill anyone in your way) is leading to infanticide (killing of physically impaired infants), euthanasia (so-called "mercy killing" of the physically impaired and the elderly), and new American crime wave.

Far too many American young people are recognizing and understanding the ethical system of their political leaders' moral examples and are carrying this system out to its logical conclusion.

This acceptance of an "ethics of violence" is why we have so much violence (including random violence), why violent teen gangs have become so much more prominent, and why so many of our streets are unsafe.

EUTHANASIA

Ever since former Colorado Governor Richard Lamm referred to the elderly "having a duty to die," the proponents of euthanasia have been coming out in the open. The following quotes are shocking, but they accurately reflect the "ethics of violence" as it is being promoted in America.

Dr. Francis Schaeffer made this comment about an article which concerned this ethics of violence:

> *An example of this coming down naturally on the side of the nonreligious humanists is the article by Charles Hartshorne in the January 21, 1981, issue of The Christian Century, pages 42-45. Its title is, "Concerning Abortion, An Attempt at a   Rational View." He begins by equating the fact that the human fetus is alive with the fact that mosquitoes and bacteria are also alive. That is, he begins by assuming that human life is not unique. He then continues by saying that even after the baby is born it is not fully human until its social relations develop (though he says the infant does have some primitive social relations an unborn fetus does not have). His conclusion is, "Nevertheless, I have little sympathy with the idea that infanticide is just another form of murder. Persons who are already functionally persons in the full sense have more   important rights even than infants." He then logically takes the next step: "Does this distinction   apply   to the killing of a hopelessly senile person or one in a permanent coma? For me it does." No atheistic humanist could say it with greater clarity. It is significant at this point to note that many of the denominations controlled by liberal theology have come out, publicly and strongly, in favor of abortion (Christian Manifesto).*

Dr. William Gaylin told the American Association of University Women:

> *It used to be easy to know what we wanted for our children, and now, the best for our children might mean deciding which one to kill. We have always wanted the best for our grandparents, and now that might mean killing them. We have the awesomeness of knowledge to do these things, and inevitably we shall be forced to act on it.*

The Hemlock Society said, "We put dogs out of their misery, we should be at least as kind to human beings."

These ideas are not new, but they are just now spreading in America. This is the approach to human life taken by the Nazi regime of Hitler.

Hitler's director of national health care said:

> *The ill-conceived "love of neighbor" has to disappear, especially in relation to inferior or asocial creatures. It is the supreme duty of the national State to grant life and livelihood only to the healthy . . . in order to secure the maintenance of a hereditarily and racially pure folk for all eternity. The life of an individual has meaning only in the light of that ultimate aim, that is, in the light of his meaning to his family and his national state.*

DR. DEATH

In the 90's, the euthanasia debate in America focused on the activities of Michigan's Dr. Jack Kevorkian. In defiance of Michigan law, Dr. Kevorkian ("Dr. Death," as he is often called) has been helping patients commit suicide. He refers to those who disapprove as "silly religious nuts." In December of 1993, a Harris Poll reported that 58% of the American people approved of his activities while only 38% disapproved.

Referring to Dr. Death and the Dutch proponents of euthanasia (who have carried their proposals into national law), columnist Pat Buchanan writes:

> *Kevorkian and his Dutch allies have entered a post-Christian era that resembles the pre-Christian pagan era, when not all life was worth living, and suicide was an honorable way out. Their logic is inherent in Roe v. Wade. If a woman and her doctor can end the life of an unborn child, who are these "religious fanatics" to tell her she cannot end a life too painful to live? Whose life is it anyway?*

In the Old and New Testament, Augustine and Aquinas, natural law and Judeo-Christian tradition, God is the Author of Life; He has written the rules of human conduct in His words, His books, and on the human heart; no man is permitted to play God and take innocent life.

Nevertheless, in the New Age, that is the old dogma of a dead creed. God does not exist. If He does, He is not party to the debate. Each of us, individually, determines his own moral code. We will decide, democratically, of course, when life begins, and when it should end.

Because these conflicting beliefs are deeply held, compromise is impossible; one or the other will prevail in law and determine the character of the people and nation we shall become.

It should be noted that Dr. Kevorkian clearly understands the ethical relationship between abortion and euthanasia. He said, "The hypocrites permit abortion when there is no consent; how can they deny planned death when there is consent."

As an atheist, Dr. Kevorkian sees no purpose in a life that does not live up to his ideal. In a March 6, 1993, issue of World magazine, this report was given of a TV show on which Dr. Kevorkian appeared:

> [Dr. Kevorkian:] "Do you know what a person dying of Alzheimer's is like? I will tell you. They sit in their own feces, lie drenched in their own urine, they are not human any more, there is no person, no reason. They are a zero."
> Kevorkian was immediately followed by Woodrow Wirsid, whose wife Jane died 13 years after being afflicted with Alzheimer's. The host asked, "Woody, the day of Jane's death, was she still there? Or had she deteriorated that for all practical purposes she was a 'zero'?"
> Wirsid said, "I do not know how to answer that except to say that we had a little ritual that we continued to the end. She could see me coming from a distance. Her smile would grow as I approached. When I got close enough, she would lift her head to be kissed and I would say, "I love you, Jane." and she would say, "I love you, too." We did it to the end. I do not know. I do not think of her as a zero."

Dr. Kevorkian was eventually sentenced to prison for second degree murder.

LACK OF RESPECT FOR LIFE

The lack of respect for human life seen in the abortion and euthanasia debates is clearly spreading throughout American life. In January, 1994, a Gallup Poll showed that the nation's top concern was fear of violent crime. In America, your chances of being the victim of violent crime are greater than your chances of being injured in an auto accident. The odds of the average young male in an inner city being shot are greater than that of the average G.I. in World War II.

Romans 3:11-18 describes man as he develops without the work of God in his life. Notice especially the explicit references to the violence in the human nature:

11 *There is none that understandeth, there is none that seeketh after God.*

12 *They are all gone out of the way, they are together become unprofitable; there is none that doeth good, no, not one.*

13 *Their throat is an open sepulchre; with their tongues they have used deceit; the poison of asps is under their lips:*

14 *Whose mouth is full of cursing and bitterness:*

15 *Their feet are swift to shed blood:*

16 *Destruction and misery are in their ways:*

17 *And the way of peace have they not known:*

18 *There is no fear of God before their eyes.*

As the leaders of our society have justified violence against the innocent and helpless, it is clear that many in our society have gotten the message. Social scientist James Q. Wilson has warned that American young people have learned to value self-expression over self-control.

While our population has increased by 41% since 1960, violent crime has increased by 500%.

The number of teenagers arrested for violent crime has increased 300% since 1965.

The United States is living with the moral and social consequences of abortion!

2016:
OBAMACARE AND MODERN MEDICINE
Dr. Doug Levesque

Medicine affects the culture. Dr. Benjamin Rush was a man of medicine and a founding father. His medicine found its way into the Lewis and Clark Expedition by way of his own concoction of a purging agent called "thunderclappers". Modern archeologists have tracked the expeditions camping spots by locating the unique pills chemical agents in the soil. Rush's assistant revealed that the agent came from the Jalap plant and was from a region in Mexico. The drug was officially used in the U.S. until 1965 when it was proven that the agent caused a sort of mercury poisoning that made the body flush other bad materials. Different, safer purgatives have been used ever since. There are many stories of medicine involved in the life of American culture.

Today, medicine still remains on the forefront of cultural argument. Birth control pills, hormone replacement therapy, and suicide assisting chemicals or gases are hot button moral topics. The questionable morality of certain medical directives is another example of how America has slipped into darkness.

Modern medicine is tainted by big business and bad science. The broad acceptance of evolutionary theory in the last hundred years has twisted certain medical views. The wide scale practice of abortion and its acceptance as a right or "choice" is rooted in anti Biblical mindsets and procedures.

Though Christians have fought adamantly for a right to life legal ruling, abortion's acceptance has reconfigured the murder of a child in the womb into a "sacred" and meaningful "value" of a woman's right over her own body. Alongside skewed science and values lies unfortunate money making opportunities of the insurance and abortion industries along with vile body parts harvesting operations. The love of mammon truly takes every good thing and perverts it to the extreme. That medicine could become murder for money is devilish indeed, and we must never soften our hearts or countenances against the dark turns society is making.

Socialized medicine is a government monopoly on medicine. Marxist ideals are ungodly to the core and comprise the ethics of promoting governmental arbitration of the healthcare industry. No other sector of society has been bettered through government mandated services.

To allow the culture a view of their government as a god is to deify mankind. This is the original rebellion played out by the greedy hearts of selfish man. Cradle to grave government entitlements replace the hearty work ethic of "tending and keeping the garden" and faithful reliance upon God Himself as our provider. It is simply not fair to make everyone pay for the unhealthy and often sinful mistakes of others. Smokers, drinkers, perverts and gluttons are stealing from the pockets of disciplined and obedient people who simply live healthier lives. As other cultures have left God, they have also suffered the unsuccessful "communal" or "communist" system of economics. Remember President Obama said "Healthcare is the Economy."

Obamacare is controlling society through medicine. It is no wonder that President Obama has made this particular issue his claim to fame. He sold the system as a help to those who cannot afford insurance, but delivered a slave ship that forced the purchase of a product and then enforced it with IRS fines.

This is a first for American culture. Such totalitarianism was called evil when delivered by Nazi's, Stalinists, and Maoists. China's one child policy is clearly a tyranny over the family, but so is mandated insurance that ensures free abortions for everyone. That a whole generation would voluntarily put their own dossier in front of billions of facebook users is poor judgment by a collective culture, but that we would applaud the mandatory and medical dossier of every citizen to be turned over to a system that includes death panels is the sign of a very sick culture.

We have placed ourselves two steps from population control and eugenics through the horrible and failing promise of Obamacare. The next steps will be connecting Obamacare to employment and citizenship. Beware of any cultural swing, political or religious, that breaches that evil cohabitation of systems.

Abortion, euthanasia and psychological mayhem are the fruits of Pharaoh and Herod. Killing of innocent people instead of attempting to heal or comfort them is not medicine. It is sin. That greater numbers of medical societies are bowing to political philosophy for the practice and delivery of healthcare is a transformation in American culture of immense proportions. Only an ignorance or neglect of Biblical Christianity could allow such a descent into darkness. This particular culture war front has been neglected by pastors and churches mainly because of the self interested prospect of free healthcare. There is very little room for Christians in this area of nationalized healthcare. We cannot give ground to the darkness of enhanced and increased acceptance of heinous crimes like abortion.

TRANSFORMATION

4
THE WAR ON LAW

RESTORING LAW AND ORDER

"Let him that stole steal no more: but rather let him labour, working with his hands the thing which is good, that he may have to give to him that needeth." (Ephesians 4:28)

POVERTY, RACE, AND CRIME

Several political polls showed that the number one concern of Americans in 1994 was violent crime. It is important to see that our serious crime problems are not accidental; they stem from the rising rebellion against God.

Real answers to the crime problem are often obscured by the liberals' emphasis in the idea that poverty and victimization cause crime. If poverty causes crime, why do not all poor people become criminals? If poverty causes crime, why do some rich people become criminals?

Former President Richard Nixon wrote in *Beyond Peace* (his last book):

We cannot effectively address our nation's most pervasive social problems unless we face up to the fact that the urban interclass, where the breakdown of the family is worst, is primarily responsible for the plagues of violent crime and drug abuse on the streets of our great cities. Blacks are not the only members of this interclass, but they are the largest proportion of it. In 1992, half of all murder victims in the United States were black. Ninety percent were killed by other blacks. There can be no more dramatic evidence of a culture's deficiencies of values, discipline, and hope that when it turns against itself, as elements of urban America have in recent years.

The cop out of blaming crime on poverty is morally corrupt and intellectually vacuous. When I was growing up during the Depression, there was far more poverty but far less crime. The difference was that our families and communities enforced civilized standards. We now are reaping the whirlwind stirred up by an age in which the self-appointed cultural elites sneered at the standards that helped people overcome the problems diversity can bring, rather than wallow in them.

Arsonists, looters, muggers, and rioters burn, rob, and brutalize not because they are poor but because they are rotten. As Eric Hoffer has noted, "If poverty were indeed the fundamental cause of crime, history would be about nothing else, for the vast majority of people in world history have lived in poverty." Today's vicious young predators show only cold-blooded contempt for their victims. They kill not for food but for a pair of fancy sneakers. They have to be shown firmly, determinedly, and relentlessly that we will not compromise in our defense of civilized standards and values. These are not negotiable.

Successful police chief Reuben Greenberg of Charlestown, South Carolina, said in a June, 1994, interview with Rush Limbaugh:

You know, the root causes of crime were supposed to be poverty, unemployment, a poor education, this, that, and the other. Yet 90% of the people with those same characteristics, both blacks and whites, somehow never wound up in the criminal justice system. So I started orienting ourselves toward the protection of those who followed the rules and regulations of our society, rather than those who would victimize other people in the community. It is not an excuse to say, "Well I came from the wrong side of town, and I am black, and my great-grandfather was owned by this person." Yeah, that's true, but these other guys had great-grandfathers who were owned by this person as well, but they are not criminals. They are out working and paying taxes.

The first step in restoring law and order is to recognize that a lack of money and opportunity does not cause crime. A lack of values causes crime. Only by firmly focusing on the real cause can a solution be achieved.

The message of the last 40 years has been that there are no absolutes. The great question of the last 40 years has been, "Who is to say what is right and wrong?" When a young thug robs a stranger on the street, he is, in effect, saying that he does not respect any absolutes. He is saying that no one can say what is right and what is wrong. He has gotten the message.

The government's promotion of abortion must be stopped if we are going to restore respect for human life in America. A return to the moral values of our Christian culture is a prerequisite for turning our society around. Returning moral values to our educational process is crucial to any improvement in the new American crime wave. Dealing with the issue of values is central to improving the scene in America.

There are other steps that can be taken which will help to control the modern crime wave, also.

CRIME AND PUNISHMENT

The relationship between the amount of jail time served and the effectiveness of jail as a deterrent has been well established.

Whenever the time served is relatively minor compared to possible benefits of the crime, jail will not be a powerful deterrent.

Dr. Ernest Van Der Haag commented on this relationship between crime, punishment, and incentives in the May 30, 1994, issue of National Review:

Human actions are governed by incentives and disincentives. We are attracted by the hope of pleasure or gain, deterred by the fear of pain or loss. Expressive crimes (e.g. rape) are committed for the sake of expected pleasure; instrumental crimes (e.g. burglary) mainly for the sake of expected gain. Both can often be deterred by disincentives—the fear of pain . . . the threat of punishment. To be sure, people, including prospective criminals, seldom actually calculate the cost versus the benefit, the risk/reward ratio. Nor do rats. Yet rats, like people, respond as if they calculated. We can predict their behavior accordingly. Traffic lights would be useless if behavior were unpredictable.

Habits, based on often indirect experience, not on calculation, determine most behavior, law-abiding as well as criminal. When the cost of a good or service rises, less of it is used. If the cost of bananas, or of cars, goes up, fewer are bought. To the criminal, the cost of a crime is the risk of punishment. Not what is threatened by the law, but the punishment he risks, given his actual chances of being convicted and imprisoned.

Though the cost of keeping someone in prison is about $25, 000 a year, the cost of leaving dangerous criminals on the street is much greater.

Identifying career criminals would also be helpful to restoring law and order and putting them away for good. Seventy percent of all crimes are committed by seven percent of the criminal population. Protecting society from this relatively small number of people would make a big difference.

People are returning to the concept of community policing in many neighborhoods with some success. Letting the community and specific police officers develop working relationships with one another seems to have a positive effect.

Raising or eliminating bail for repeat violent offenders and regulating probation or parole (limiting these to non-violent offenses) help to protect the general public.

THE BIBLICAL CONCEPT OF RESTITUTION

Enforcing a strict concept of restitution for theft would greatly increase public respect for property. Under Old Testament Law, multiple restitution was required. "If a man steal an ox or a sheep and kill it, or sell it he shall restore five oxen for an ox and four sheep for a sheep." (Exodus 22:1)

The Old Testament is full of other examples of the concept of restitution. The following list will give several examples:

- **Restitution for assault:**
"And if men strive together, and one smite another with a stone, or with his fist, and he die not, but keepeth his bed: If he rise again, and walk abroad upon his staff, then shall he that smote him be quit: only he shall pay for the loss of his time, and shall cause him to be thoroughly healed." (Exodus 28:18-19)

- **Restitution for bodily injury:**
"And if a man smite the eye of his servant, or the eye of his maid, that it perish; he shall let him go free for his eye's sake. And if he smite out his manservant's tooth, or his maidservant's tooth; he shall let him go free for his tooth's sake." (Exodus 21:26-27)

- **Restitution where there is negligence**:
"And if a man shall open a pit, or if a man shall dig a pit, and not cover it, and an ox or an ass fall therein; The owner of the pit shall make it good, and give money unto the owner of them; and dead beast shall be his. And if one man's ox hurt another's, that he die; then they shall sell the live ox, and divide the money of it; and the dead ox also they shall divide. Or if it be known that the ox hath used to push in time past, and his owner hath not kept him in; he shall surely pay ox for ox; and the dead shall be his own." *(Exodus 21:33-36)*

- **Restitution for property damage**:
"If a man shall cause a field or vineyard to be eaten, and shall put in his beast, and shall feed in another man's field; of the best of his own field, and of the best of his own vineyard shall he make restitution. If fire break out, and catch in thorns, so that the stacks of corn, or the standing corn, or the field, be consumed therewith; he that kindled the fire shall surely make restitution." *(Exodus 22:5-6)*

- **Restitution for irresponsibility:**
"If a man shall deliver unto his neighbour money or stuff to keep, and it be stolen out of the man's house; if the thief be found, let him pay double. If the thief be not found, then the master of the house shall be brought unto the judges, to see whether he have put his hand unto his neighbour's goods. For all manner of trespass, whether it be for ox, for ass, for sheep, for raiment, or for any manner of lost thing, which another challengeth to be his, the cause of both parties shall come before the judges; and whom the judges shall condemn, he shall pay double unto his neighbor. If a man deliver unto his neighbour an ass, or an ox, or a sheep, or any beast, to keep; and it die, or be hurt, or driven away, no man seeing it: Then shall an oath of the LORD be between them both, that he hath not put his hand unto his neighbour's goods; and the owner of it shall accept thereof, and he shall not make it good. And if it be stolen from him, he shall make restitution unto the owner thereof. If it be torn in pieces, then let him bring

it for witness, and he shall not make good that which was torn."
(Exodus 22:14-15)

- **Restitution for losing borrowed things:**
"And if a man borrow ought of his neighbour, and it be hurt, or die,
the owner thereof being not with it, he shall surely make it good.
But if the owner thereof be with it, he shall not make it good: if it
be an hired thing, it came for his hire." *(Exodus 22:14-15)*

The Biblical concept of restitution focuses on the victim rather than on the government. It also creates a respect for property. It also makes the price-tag for crime a heavy one.

Until our historic Christian culture becomes the mainstream culture in our country again, Americans will have a regular reminder of the results of paganism. The amount of crime, the fear of crime, and the debate over crime are the heritage of our Culture War.

THE DEATH PENALTY

"Whoso sheddeth man's blood, by man shall his blood be shed: for in the image of God made he man." (Genesis 9:6)

THE NECESSITY OF CAPITAL PUNISHMENT

"You better vote for the death penalty, because, if you do not, I will get out and it may be one of you next or your family." This statement was made by convicted Indiana killer Steven Judy during the penalty phase of his murder trial.

The Biblical teaching concerning the death penalty for murder is simple: life for life. (Exodus 21:23) Consider these Scriptures which state so clearly:

"Whoso sheddeth man's blood, by man shall his blood be shed: for in the image of God made he man." (Genesis 9:6)

"And he that killeth any man shall surely be put to death." (Leviticus 24:17)

"Whoso killeth any person, the murderer shall be put to death by the mouth of witnesses: but one witness shall not testify against any person to cause him to die." (Numbers 35:30-31)

"But if any man hate his neighbor, and lie in wait for him, and rise up against him, and smite him mortally that he die, and fleeth into one of these cities: Then the elders of his city shall send and fetch him thence, and deliver him into the hand of the avenger of blood, that he may die. Thine eye shall not pity him, but thou shalt put away the guilt of innocent blood from Israel, that it may go well with thee." (Deuteronomy 19:11-13)

"For rulers are not a terror to good works, but to the evil. Wilt thou then not be afraid of the power? Do that which is good, and thou shalt have praise of the same: For he is the minister of God to thee for good. But if thou do that which is evil, be afraid: for he beareth not the sword in vain: for he is the minister of God, a revenger to execute wrath upon him that doeth evil."
(Romans 13:3-4)

There are many stories surrounding the activities of Patrick as he brought Christianity to the previously pagan tribes if Ireland. He insisted on many reforms in their violent way of life. It is said that he insisted on the death penalty for murder and rape. Only in this way could the seriousness of these crimes be kept before the people. Christian leaders have often been in the forefront of this issue, insisting on the need for the death penalty because of the very clear teaching of Scripture. However, the Biblical teaching about capital punishment puts this responsibility on the civil government.

Dr. Ernest Van Der Haag wrote:

I see no evidence for society somehow not having 'the right' to execute murderers. It has always done so. Traditional laws and Scriptures have always supported the death penalty. I know of no reasoning, even in a religious (theocratic) state, that denies the right of secular courts to impose it. We in America have a secular republic, of course, and, therefore, the suggestion that the right to punish belongs only to God, or that the right to impose capital punishment does, is clearly out of place. It is not a religious but a secular task to put murderers to death. Our Constitution does provide for it (Amendments V and XIV). However much we believe in divine justice, it is to occur after, not in, this life. As for justice here and now, it is done by the courts, which are authorized in certain cases to impose the death penalty. A secular state cannot leave it to God. And, incidentally, no theocratic state ever has. If they make mistakes, one can hope that God will correct the courts hereafter—but this is no ground for depriving courts of their duty to impose the penalties provided by law where required, nor is it the ground for depriving the law of the ability to prescribe the punishments felt to be just, including the death penalty.

In spite of overwhelming popular support for the death penalty (a 1993 Parade magazine poll showed 87% support for the death penalty), there is still a great deal of public debate over the subject. Every time an execution takes place there are protests, vigils, and public debates.

There are only two real questions to be answered in this debate:
- Does the government have the right to impose capital punishment?
- Is the death penalty effective in preserving law and order?

ARGUMENTS AGAINST THE DEATH PENALTY

There are many arguments offered by opponents of capital punishment: **Some say that the concept promotes violence and barbarism in our society.** It is interesting to note that many of those who make this argument see nothing wrong with mercilessly dissecting an unborn baby in the womb. What kind of national morality is it that condones the murder of an unborn baby (and offers to finance it), but agonizes over the execution of serial killers, torture-murderers, and those who stalk and murder little children? When it is carried out properly, the death penalty sends the message that there is a price tag for violence and barbarism. The seriousness of a crime to society is recognized by the price we demand from those who commit it. The ultimate crime demands the ultimate penalty.

A second objection that you hear is that it is not effective in preventing violent crime. It is pointed out that since the death penalty was re-instituted violent crime has increased. It is true that capital punishment –the way it is carried out today—is not very effective. There are more than 20,000 murders committed every year, and less than 40 executions are carried out. Most executions take place more than 15 years after arrest. As long as only two-tenths of one percent of murders result in an execution, capital punishment will not be very effective. Establishing capital punishment as routine in murder cases would result in an entirely different situation.

As long as potential murderers are convinced they will not be executed, capital punishment will be no deterrent. If society convinces them that they will be executed for committing murder, it will immediately become a major deterrent.

A third objection raised is that the government cannot be trusted with this option. It is true that some government officials cannot be trusted in this area. However, this is an argument for government and judicial reform, not an objection to the concept of the death penalty. Numbers 35:30-31 clearly indicates that two eye-witnesses are necessary for declaring capital punishment for the crime of murder. This simple judicial reform would greatly improve the discussion over capital punishment in America.

A fourth reason that capital punishment is opposed is the claim that it is unconstitutional—that it violates the cruel and unusual punishment prohibition in the Constitution. This is clearly inaccurate. The Constitution specifically allows civil government to take life if due process of law is followed. The prohibition against cruel and unusual punishment was clearly designed to be a prohibition against torture on the part of government agencies.

Another objection to the death penalty is that the Sixth Commandment teaches, "Thou shalt not kill." However, it is clear that this was an individual prohibition against murder. The civil government of Israel was authorized to use capital punishment for 11 different offenses. Theologian St. Thomas Aquinas spoke about this issue:

[T]he life of certain pestiferous men is an impediment to the common good which is the concord of human society of men . . .Therefore, the ruler of a state executes pestiferous men justly and sinlessly in order that the peace of the state may not be disrupted.

IN FAVOR OF THE DEATH PENALTY

There are a number of obviously good reasons for capital punishment.

It establishes a clear sense of justice. This is why the Bible commands it—a life for a life.

It communicates a clear sense of the value of the life that has been taken—again, the ultimate price for the ultimate crime. Capital punishment is 100% effective in preventing further murders by everyone who is executed. The consistent, effective use of the death penalty would deter violent crime. It certainly worked when the death penalty was regularly carried out in this country, and it is very effective in countries around the world which still use it.

It would discourage murder in kidnaping situations. When there is no capital punishment for murder, most kidnap victims are killed by their kidnappers to prevent the possibility of them ever being able to be identified. With capital punishment as a threat, many kidnappers are careful not to physically harm their victims.

Capital punishment removes the guilt of innocent blood from society. The law of innocent blood (an often overlooked Biblical principle) is that God demands that innocent blood be paid for with guilty blood (see Genesis 9:6-7, again). The following is a brief look at the Biblical law of innocent blood.

- God hates the shedding of innocent blood (Proverbs 6:17). No one has the right to arbitrarily take human life.
- Murder takes place because of the sinful condition of man. It is a natural act for the old sin nature. (Isaiah 59:7, Romans 3:15, Romans 1:28-32)
- The law of innocent blood requires the civil government to do its job in avenging the shedding of innocent blood, or the government and the people will bear the penalty of innocent blood.

The book of Deuteronomy explains how this was done in Old Testament Israel.

Deuteronomy 19:10-13:
10 That innocent blood be not shed in thy land, which the Lord thy God giveth thee for an inheritance, and so blood be upon thee.
11 But if any man hate his neighbour, and lie in wait for him, and rise up against him, and smite him mortally that he die, and fleeth into one of these cities:
12 Then the elders of his city shall send and fetch him thence, and deliver him into the hand of the avenger of blood, that he may die.
13 Thine eye shall not pity him, but thou shalt put away the guilt of innocent blood from Israel, that it may go well with thee.

Deuteronomy 21:1-9:
1 If one be found slain in the land which the LORD thy God giveth thee to possess it, lying in the field, and it be not known who hath slain him:

2 Then thy elders and thy judges shall come forth, and they shall measure unto the cities which are round about him that is slain:
3 And it shall be, that the city which is next unto the slain man, even the elders of that city shall take an heifer, which hath not been wrought with, and which hath not drawn in   the yoke;
4 And the elders of that city shall bring down the heifer unto a rough valley, which is neither eared nor sown, and shall strike off the heifer's neck there in the valley:
5 And the priests the sons of Levi shall come near; for them the LORD thy God hath chosen to minister unto him, and to bless in the name of the LORD; and by their word shall every controversy and every stroke be tried:
6 And all the elders of that city, that are next unto the slain man, shall wash their hands over the heifer that is beheaded in the valley:
7 And they shall answer and say, Our hands have not shed this blood, neither have our eyes seen it.
8 Be merciful, O LORD, unto thy people Israel, whom thou hast redeemed, and lay not innocent blood unto thy people of Israel's charge. And the blood shall be forgiven them.
9 So shalt thou put away the guilt of innocent blood from among you, when thou shalt do   that which is right in the sight of the Lord.

The Bible makes it clear that government leaders and civil government are held responsible for shedding innocent blood just as individuals are.

Saul had no right to try to kill David (I Samuel 19:5), and Manasseh was judged by God for filling the streets of Jerusalem with innocent blood by sacrificing the little children (I Kings 21:16).

The Bible makes it very clear how God feels about a society's tolerating the shedding of innocent blood. Psalm 106: 35-40:

35 But were mingled among the heathen, and learned their works.
36 And they served their idols: which were a snare unto them.
37 Yea, they sacrificed their sons and their daughters unto devils,
38 And shed innocent blood, even the blood of their sons and of their daughters, whom they sacrificed unto the idols of Canaan:

and the land was polluted with blood.

39 Thus were they defiled with their own works, and went a whoring with their own inventions.

40 Therefore was the wrath of the LORD kindled against his people, insomuch that he abhorred his own inheritance.

Think about how much innocent blood the United States is responsible for in the eyes of God. The innocent blood of 35 million abortions (tolerated by society), the innocent blood of all the unavenged murders, and the total lack of respect for God's system of justice are all included.

Judge Robert E. Crowe summed up the importance of the death penalty this way: "It is the finality of the death penalty which instills fear into the heart of every murderer, and is the fear of punishment which protects society."

PERSONAL RESPONSIBILITY

"Wash me thoroughly from mine iniquity,
and cleanse me from my sin." (Psalm 51:2)

Since the beginning of time, man has devoted his full intellectual capacity to finding ways to keep from taking responsibility for his actions. We see this illustrated by the very first man in Genesis 3:9-13:

9 And the LORD God called unto Adam, and said unto him, Where art thou?

10 And he said, I heard thy voice in the garden, and I was afraid, because I was naked; and I hid myself.

11 And he said, Who told thee that thou wast naked? Hast thou eaten of the tree, whereof I commanded thee that thou shouldest not eat?

12 And the man said, The woman whom thou gavest to be with me, she gave me of the tree, and I did eat.

13 And the LORD God said unto the woman, What is this that thou hast done? And the woman said, The serpent beguiled me, and I did eat.

Any explanation that does not involve sin, personal responsibility, or correction of bad behavior seems acceptable in today's culture. In America, it is fashionable to declare self-destructive behavior as a "disease" or "genetic." It is considered "enlightened" to blame antisocial and violent behavior on victimization by some segments of society against others. Do you remember the controversy when former Vice President Dan Quayle suggested that single motherhood was not as good a choice as the "traditional family?" The "media-elite" viciously attacked Quayle for "blaming the victims." Do you remember the aftermath of the Los Angeles riots in 1992? Republicans blamed former Presidents Reagan and Bush. Few public leaders blamed the rioters for their own actions.

Ignoring your responsibilities in a drunken stupor is no longer "sin" or even an unwise choice; it is the "disease" of alcoholism. An advertisement of KOALA reads, "Alcoholism is not a moral issue, nor is it a matter of will power. It is a disease." People are told that the first step to recovery is realizing that their behavior is not their fault. They simply have a disease! But, how many people who never decide to drink ever "catch" the "disease" of alcoholism?

A November 23, 1992, USA Today headline reads, "Half of All Divorces May be Due to Genes." That is right; divorce does not necessarily result from or both partners making selfish choices. It may simply be their genetic heritage.

"IT'S NOT MY FAULT"

When New York Judge Sol Wachtler was arrested for extortion and threatening to kidnap the teenage daughter of his ex-lover, he was immediately diagnosed by sexologist John Money as having Cleambault-Kandinsky syndrome (CKS). In other words, he was a "sex-addict" and was not responsible for his behavior.

When an FBI agent embezzled $2,000 dollars and lost it all in an afternoon of gambling in Atlantic City, he appealed for reinstatement as an FBI officer on the grounds that he was a "gambling addict" and not responsible for his behavior. He asked that his "gambling addiction" be declared a "handicap" and thus protected under federal law. A federal judge gave him his job back.

The Major League baseball player's union appealed for reinstatement for banned drug user Steve Howe by claiming he had "attention deficit hyper-activity disorder" (ADHD) and thus could not be held accountable for his drug use. The appeal worked, and he returned to professional baseball.

According to OPTIFAST (in a 1989 ad), obesity is "a complex and multi-faceted disease." According to Susie Orback, "Fat is not about food. To attribute compulsive eating to a simple inability to control one's appetite is to engage in the ineffective blame-the-victim approach." That is right: people are no longer overweight from overeating or underexercising; they just cannot help it!

The Indianapolis Star, October 19, 1989, carried the following headline: "Experts now view wife-battering as a disease that can be predicted and prevented." So now wife-beating is a disease, and you cannot help it! Perhaps a physically abused wife will invent "husband shooting disease."

In 1992, in Milwaukee, a teenage girl shot and killed another teenage girl for her leather coat. Her defense attorney claimed that she was the victim of "cultural psychosis." Society was responsible for her act of violence.

ALCOHOL, TWINKIES, JELLYBEANS?

Robert Alton Harris argued that he killed two teenage boys because he was the victim of "fetal alcohol syndrome." Dan White claimed he killed the San Francisco mayor and another supervisor because of his "junk-food" addiction in the now famous "Twinkie defense!" It is a wonder that no one from the Reagan administration blamed the Iran-Contra affair on President Reagan's well known "jellybean addiction."

In 1991, the Wisconsin Department of Industry, Labor, and Human Relations ruled that "offensive body odor" was "a physical handicap." No longer could the personal discipline to use soap, water, and deodorant be required of state employees.

Aaron Wildavasky claims that if you add up all the individuals and groups that have been claimed as "victims," it totals 374% of the American population. Therapy and related fields are now a $185 billion industry in America. America now has more therapists than librarians, fire fighters, or mail carriers, and twice as many therapists as dentists or pharmacists.

Writing about serial killers, author Ron Holmes says, "Serial killing is an addiction." Psychologist Robert Howe (University of British Columbia) disagrees, claiming that serial killing has a biological origin.

Former Senator William Cohen (R-Maine) released a report showing that $1.4 billion was paid in 1993 under the Social Security Disability Income program to drug addicts. They are eligible for these funds because their drug addiction was viewed as a disease.

According to the January, 1994, issue of the Archives of General Psychiatry, almost 50% of America's population suffers from mental illness. About nine percent of the population of Holland receives disability income as a result of suffering from "mental diseases." Concepts of disease and victimization have found their way into the judicial realm. Lorena Bobbit was found innocent of mutilating her husband because of claims that he had victimized her. The jury in the first Menendez brothers' trial ended up deadlocked in spite of the fact that the brothers admitted killing their parents. The jury was moved because the brothers claimed to be "victims" of childhood sexual abuse. Those who beat Reginald Denny (in the Los Angeles riots) within an inch of his life were found innocent of most charges because they had been caught up into a "mob mentality."

Virginia I. Postrel write in Reason magazine:

A government of laws cannot stand against a people who can see only victims, against juror who believe neither in criminals' responsibility nor in their own. Once, runaway juries driven by rage gave us legal lynching, a complement to the illegal kind. They would not reason, so they could find no reasonable doubt.

Today, their successors feel not rage but pity, not hatred but empathy. They, too, do not reason, but neither do they doubt. They can look at proof of guilt and still find innocence—innocence in the victimhood of the victimizer.

Many of the ordinary people who make up juries desire neither justice nor revenge. They desire absolution, the obliteration of all responsibility. We have created a culture of excuse, and it has conquered our courtrooms—not by judicial fiat but by the most democratic of means. Our juries have gone soft on crime.

An editorial in the March, 1994, Christian American (the magazine of the Christian Coalition) says:

What is lacking here is a sense of sin. The criminal justice system in America has historically been based on the Judeo-Christian concept of personal responsibility for individual actions. Man, created in the image of God, is a moral being with the free will to choose between good and evil, endowed with a God-given conscience that allows him to distinguish between right and wrong.

This concept of justice is now being lost in a New Age psychobabble of self-justification for the most heinous and unspeakable of crimes. We seem to have lost the concept of personal accountability and absolute standards of right and wrong. The result is the moral chaos these verdicts reflect.

But, the legal defense of victimization continues. In the fall of 1993, a 19-year-old girl claimed that she should not be held responsible for stabbing a young man to death because she had grown up surrounded by violence in her south Florida neighborhood. Her lawyer called this an "urban psychosis defense."

John Leo (writing in U.S. News and World Report) said, "Bonnie and Clyde came along too soon. Now days they could settle for a year at the Betty Ford Center as victims of compulsive bank-robbing addiction." This whole area of conflict is at the center of the modern Cultural Way and at the center of our political campaigns.

The "victim," "genetic predisposition," and "disease" excuses continue to pop up in the most amazing places. Rather than being the key to helping people, the "disease-genetic-victim" approach just reinforces destructive behavior.

Stanton Peele wrote in The Diseasing of America:

Describing behavior in terms of disease and addiction can legitimize, reinforce, and excuse the behaviors in question— concerning people, contrary to all evidence, that their behavior is not their own. Meanwhile, the number of addicts and those who believe they cannot control themselves grows steadily.

A blind faith in the myths of "personal therapy" just compounds problems. Therapists have totally destroyed the meaning of the word disease. Charles Sykes puts it this way in *A Nation of Victims*, "Almost by definition, disease is caused by agents of forces largely beyond the control of an individual—by viruses, microbes, genetic deficiencies or environmental factors." No one can identify the "disease factors" related to "behavior." People believe that "behavior" is caused by disease simply because the idea makes them feel good. No one can identify the "genetic causes" for homosexual perversion or child molesting; they simply "feel" that it is true.

In the Scriptures, God never refers to choices as being "value free." He did not excuse Adam and Eve as "culturally deprived," overlook Sodom and Gomorrah as "genetically different," or suggest that the Pharaoh who withstood Moses was simply the "victim" of Egyptian culture. God graciously forgives sin, but He never pretends that evil is good. God gives believers the grace to grow out of sinful behavior and the Scriptures to teach them right from wrong. If we are going to spare ourselves from the results of self-destructive behavior, we must identify that behavior as wrong and take the necessary steps to change.

Politicians race to make new promises to groups in rebellion against God. They promise to make them "feel" good and legislate away their problems. But, as Louis Sullivan, the former Secretary of Health and Human Services, said, "The very idea of a crime gene is misleading. Genes do not code for those kinds of things."

More and more people are beginning to protest this sort of thinking. In the February 18, 1993, Indianapolis Star, Abe Aamider says,

> *Some people seem to think that Education (with a capital "E") is a magic vitamin. Sometimes it is Counseling with a Capital "C."*
>
> *Either way, Education is seen not only as the cure for all sorts of ills, but Lack of Education is actually being diagnosed as the cause in just same way that a Vitamin C deficiency is seen as a cause of scurvy.*
>
> *Now, Education may be a good prescription at times such as when it works. But that is an empirical proposition.*
>
> *It is the assumption that Education is always the solution, and that Lack of Education is in and of itself pathological, that is troubling.Politically, of course, it is a great thing to support Education. Who, after all, could be against Education? It is like being for peace, or for national parks or something.*
>
> *And it is politically opportune to support education in another way. It says to all the overeaters, and the people who do not want to work, and people consumed by the   desire to have sex, that they are victims, and only victims, and that help is on the way.*

In the April 30, 1994, issue of World magazine, Frederica Mathews-Green writes:

> *Nevertheless, power victimhood has a terrible price: Because all your problems are someone else's fault, your only power is to go on being powerless. There is no place for hope, initiative, and self-control.*

Christians do not need to join the victim parade. We have a Leader who won eternal victory in the very act of submitting to an unjust victimization. We walk in a similar mastery, instructed to rejoice and leap for joy when we are persecuted—not instructed to go on Oprah and sniffle. It is a calling with a lot more dignity, and more potential for effective action. Absurd charges of victimization will continue to trudge by, but we do not have to fall in line.

We are following a different Way.

When God sent Nathan the prophet to confront David, Nathan did not tell David he had a sexual addiction that he could not help. He did not tell him that his culture was responsible for his act of violence against Uriah. And David knew how to respond. We read in Psalm 51:1-17:

To the chief Musician, A Psalm of David, when Nathan the prophet came unto him, after he had gone in to Bathsheba.

1 Have mercy upon me, O God, according to thy lovingkindness: according unto the multitude of thy tender mercies blot out my transgressions.

2 Wash me throughly from mine iniquity, and cleanse me from my sin.

3 For I acknowledge my transgressions: and my sin is ever before me.

4 Against thee, thee only, have I sinned, and done this evil in thy sight: that thou mightest be justified when thou speakest, and be clear when thou judgest.

5 Behold, I was shapen in iniquity; and in sin did my mother conceive me.

6 Behold, thou desirest truth in the inward parts: and in the hidden part thou shalt make me to know wisdom.

7 Purge me with hyssop, and I shall be clean: wash me, and I shall be whiter than snow.

8 Make me to hear joy and gladness; that the bones which thou hast broken may rejoice.

9 Hide thy face from my sins, and blot out all mine iniquities.

10 Create in me a clean heart, O God; and renew a right spirit within me.

11 Cast me not away from thy presence; and take not thy holy spirit from me.

12 Restore unto me the joy of thy salvation; and uphold me with thy free spirit.

13 Then will I teach transgressors thy ways; and sinners shall be converted unto thee.

14 Deliver me from bloodguiltiness, O God, thou God of my salvation: and my tongue shall sing aloud of thy righteousness.

15 O Lord, open thou my lips; and my mouth shall shew forth thy praise.

16 For thou desirest not sacrifice; else would I give it: thou delightest not in burnt offering.

17 The sacrifices of God are a broken spirit: a broken and a contrite heart, O God, thou wilt not despise.

2016
BLUE LIVES MATTER

Dr. Doug Levesque

Of course, all lives matter. All skin tones matter. All nationalities matter. All age groups matter. All lives matter, especially to God. He gave His Word and His Son so that all lives could be reconciled to Himself. If only all lives trusted God and His wonderful plan. Because of such a rebellious spirit within mankind, we are unable to unify properly. Even our attempts to unify against God are tumultuous affairs. The horrible face of racism is both a result of our sinful natures and our inability to fix such problems apart from the Scriptures. The fear we have of each other has led to many wars and cruelties such as slavery. When any group of people fail to see their own faults, they give way to imagining their particular supremacy. White supremacy is a lie and based in fear or an evil pride or both. Black lives matter is a cry for justice that has in some cases morphed into a black supremacy sentiment. It also is based in fear or an evil pride or both. To use such racial bias as an excuse to riot violently, kill police officers or even hate law and order shows the foolishness of our modern culture. We should continue to fight for justice, defend proper law enforcement, and respect police officers. Blue lives matter in a Christian culture.

To be sure, there are some instances of police corruption. People who have been on the receiving end of such injustices are left stinging and battle within themselves to trust officers of the law. This surely is also a result of the transformation in America of choosing darkness over light. Any person with power, a police officer with a badge and gun for example, is prone to a temptation to abuse their station. A virtuous America was a difficult place for such people to rise in authority, and they stood out when they did transgress. The courts quickly dispatched them with a proper ruling and better agents were then employed. But in a dark and corrupt culture where evil becomes tolerable and good vilified, would not cases of police going bad increase? It is not a police problem we have, but a culture problem. Most modern police agencies have to have internal investigation departments that keep a watch and handle on their officers. They are also now employed whenever a police officer shoots or kills a suspect. It is then up to departments and courts to determine whether such incidents were justified, accidental or nefarious. All too often a corrupt media and corrupt public languish in these sad stories, feeding a frenzy of angry rebels into further violence and discontent. The darkness of culture ensures such lawlessness.

Unfortunately, a new phenomenon is becoming a rampant disease in America today. Cop killing is surely a societal sin. It is a sure sign that the culture is on life support. It should be rejected as terrorism. Political leadership, educators and parents used to universally proclaim that police officers were to be respected and obeyed. Civilian authorities employed police with sure training and mandates that instructed their officers to protect and serve the citizenry. An insidious plan to blur the lines for all parties has been successful in creating a hazy cloud of confusion as to how to interact with police. This has led to officers being outfitted like paramilitary soldiers and issued with cameras on their cars and persons. It seems as though each stage of adjustment in policing leads to further distrust and violent action. Some university ought to do a study on the correlation between the historical percentage of the population attending Sunday school and police brutality. Think tanks should invest in studying the connection with societal growth in becoming religiously unaffiliated and the level of police being killed or targeted. Surely some news agency can make an effort to catalog the sales of violent cop killing video games with police deaths. Television and movies often portray police as bumbling, dishonest, corrupt and obsessed with control. The entire culture is being blinded to the necessity for law and order. The transformation into darkness will soon leave us either without a respect for police or needing a constant martial state where the merits of law are withdrawn altogether.

There is a real need for criminal justice reform in America. It is on the top of the list for black lives, white lives and blue lives alike. Early Americans all had the same concepts about the nature of law, individual rights, and punishment. They derived their legal understanding from the Bible, history, and *Black's dictionary of law*. Common law was a term mostly used because every citizen, no matter their status or personal interest, had a common understanding of law. The topics of police patrolling, court sentencing, and prison life should become commonly discussed again. When the cultural mores surrounding the topic of justice are mocked and belittled, a lawless society is birthed. Today we are reaping the whirlwind of decades of decay in the justice system. If we rot much further, we will have anarchy--a devilish form of disorder and a death knell for any nation.

TRANSFORMATION

5
THE WAR ON EDUCATION

TRANSFORMATION

OUTCOME-BASED EDUCATION

"Know ye that the LORD he is God: it is he that hath made us and not we ourselves; we are his people, and the sheep of his pasture."
(Psalm 100:3)

For over 190 years (over 300 if you count the colonial period), education in the United States had three primary purposes:

- To teach basic academic knowledge
  (reading, writing, arithmetic, and science),
- To teach our Christian heritage
  (history, Bible reading, and prayer),
- To teach citizenship
  (application of our Christian culture to daily life).

"Religion, morality, and knowledge" was how the Northwest Ordinance of 1789 phrased it. Roughly 40 years ago, the concept of "secular neutrality" was adopted in our schools, and, as a result, American history has been rewritten, and prayer and Bible study have been banned. There has been constant controversy over what principles of citizenship can still be taught.

The results of the last 40 years make it clear that there is a crisis of values in public life, and this is reflected in our schools. It is also clear that there is a decline in academic accomplishment in our schools.

Most of the professional education establishment wants to address these problems with two profound changes:

- Changing the basic method of education, and
- Changing the basic purpose of education.

The professional educational establishment has had the full support of the Clinton White House, the Department of Education, and many state Departments of Education. New curricula and a myriad of new programs have been developed to institute these changes. However, the educational establishment and the various government agencies involved have run into one major obstacle in implementing these programs: the ultimate special interest group, parents.

The best known and most widespread of these new programs is called Outcome Based Education (OBE). In fact, the term Outcome Based Education is often used to refer to this whole approach of changing the method and purpose of education. Other common programs with the same purpose include (among dozens of others):

- Mastery Learning
- Quest
- Performance-based Curriculum, and
- Competency-based Education.

The new educational method involves focusing not on what is taught, but what is learned. It is hard (if not impossible) to get any clear definition on how this is done. The concept seems to involve constantly reworking the same material until everyone master it, "dumbing down" academic standards, holding up bright students (Mastery Learning Reconsidered, Hopkins University, 1987), and revamping grading systems to remove competition and failure (which dampens self-esteem).

Minnesota teacher Cheri Yecke taught in one of the first OBE programs in Minnesota. She reported, "The prevailing attitude among students is 'Why study? They cannot fail me, so who cares?'"

Though OBE proponents cannot point to successful programs to demonstrate how these changes will help students, they are still willing to invest millions of dollars of taxpayers' money experimenting with young lives. This experimentation takes place during the formative years which cannot be recovered.

In 1902, the literacy rate was 98%. Nevertheless, rather than return to the successful methods of the past, the modern educational establishment demands drastic new programs.

But as much concern as there is about the academic weaknesses of OBE-style education, there is even more concern about the new purpose for education. Many OBE-type educators (Anthony Oettinger of Harvard and Thomas B. Sticht of the National Institute of Education, for example) have stated that producing the desired social objectives in the lives of children is more important than teaching them to read. Promoting these desired feelings is becoming more important than communicating academic information.

And by whom are these feelings desired? Are the social objectives of the professional establishment those of mainstream America? Do they return to the successes of the past? Do they promote the traditional values that prevent teen pregnancies, AIDS, and the violent of the present?

The National Education Association is in the hands of the most extreme liberal, anti-family, socialist leaning group of activists in the country. This is proven by looking at the resolutions passed during their annual conventions during any of the last 20 years.

Every totalitarian government that has existed in the last 200 years has controlled the education of the young. For totalitarianism to be implemented, the young must be taught to think "politically correct thoughts" and not to think for themselves. The Nazi regime of Hitler, the fascist government of Mussolini, and all Communist governments depended upon a professional educational establishment to serve as the "thought police" for the nation's children.

Today, kindergarten students are sometimes told that we must have big government to prevent "global warming" from destroying our planet. These same children are not taught the scientific facts which demonstrate that the average temperature has remained constant through our century (less than one-half degree variation over 93 years).

Under the guise of "cultural diversity," small children are taught that perversion is normal and are lied to about the consequences of perverted behavior.

Of course, the average teacher has no such agenda. Many try to do the best they can under adverse conditions. But, the more flawed the system becomes, the harder it is for good teachers to rise above the system. And OBE-style education is the most flawed American educational system yet.

How is OBE being received? The state legislatures of Oklahoma and Pennsylvania have both voted to remove OBE from their states, only to find that it is easier said than done.

Then-Governor Bill Clinton adopted an OBE-style program in Arkansas (with Hillary Clinton in charge of implementation). After four years, test achievement scores in Arkansas tumbled.

Six years into the Clinton administration, achievement test results for students from the United States lag far behind most of the industrialized world.

The city of Chicago was the first to adopt a city-wide OBE-type system in the 1970's. After ten years of decreased results, a group of parents sued the educational administrators for malpractice, and the program was dropped.

The National Education Association lauded the OBE program in Littleton, Colorado, as the national model for OBE. However, on November 3, 1993, the voters (by a two-to-one margin) voted out the pro-OBE candidates and replaced them with school board members who favored a traditional approach. OBE programs have also been tried and rejected in school systems in Montana, Tennessee, and New Mexico.

Anytime a school system has to hide what it is doing from parents, it is time to be alarmed. Anytime school administrators cannot give clear answers to simple questions, it is time to be suspicious. Anytime schools try to take over the role of parents, it is time to demand a change.

As Thomas Sowell has so well said, the only real question in the new debate about the method and purpose of education is this, "Whose children are these?"

Outcome Based Education seems designed to strip away the last influence of our historic Christian culture from the public school system.

CHRISTIAN EDUCATION

"Train up a child in the way he should go: and when he is old, he
will not depart from it." (Proverbs 22:6)

Martin Luther said, "I am much afraid that schools will prove to be the great gates of [H]ell unless they diligently labor in explaining the Holy Scriptures, engraving them in the hearts of youth. I advise no one to place his child where the Scriptures do not reign paramount."

David Feddes, a radio teacher on the Back to God Hour has been quoted as saying, "I don't believe in prayer in public schools. It's not that I don't believe in prayer; I just don't believe in public schools."

GOVERNMENT EDUCATION

Government control of education has become so accepted in the United States that most people take it for granted. Yet, there is no concept of civil government controlling education in the Bible, in the Constitution, or in the first 75 years of American history. The American people need to rethink the idea that the civil government should be responsible for educating children.

The problem is not just poor academic achievement, the wasteful spending of the public school system, of the loss of moral standards. The problem is that the government is the wrong agency to be involved in education.

Some would argue that education is too important to be left up to the public. But, such an argument could also be made about food, housing, clothes, shoes, and transportation. Such an argument is being made about health care. If the civil government were given charge of clothing, freedom would be lessened and special interest groups in the textile industry would soon have a stranglehold on American life. This is why the Founders of our country never considered putting the government in the education business.

Public education is unconstitutional and inefficient. But, most of all, it is unbiblical. All education is religious in nature, even when educators pretend that it is not. All forms of education are based upon a world view. All forms of education try to answer basic questions of life that are religious in nature. In fact, many of the current debates about separation of church and state involve the public schools. The Founders of our republic who authored the First Amendment never envisioned the day when American parents would surrender their educational freedom to the government. Our nation's original schools were home-based, church-based, or local community-based. The man who gave us the working of the First Amendment, Fisher Ames, said this about education: "We must keep the Bible the number one textbook in our education or we will fail without the only source of morality." Benjamin Rush, a signer of the Constitution, is sometimes called the Father of American Education. He wrote, "If we allow removal of the Bible from our education, we will see an explosion of rebellion and crime."

BIBLICAL PRINCIPLES OF EDUCATION

The Bible teaches a great deal about education.

First, it teaches that wisdom begins with the right attitude toward God. "The fear of the LORD is the beginning of wisdom: and the knowledge of the holy is understanding." (Proverbs 9:10) God is the Creator of reality. He is the infallible Explainer of reality. To leave God out of the education process is to totally surrender the education of our children to the imagination of man's heart. Explanations of science, history, and citizenship that leave God out distort and falsify the disciplines they supposedly represent.

A second Biblical principle of education is that al knowledge is related to Jesus Christ. Colossians 1:16-17 says, "For by him were all things created, that are in heaven, and that are in earth, visible and invisible, whether they be thrones, or dominions, or principalities, or powers; all things were created by him, and for him: And he is before all things, and by him all things consist." Colossians 2:3 says that in Christ are hid all treasures of wisdom and knowledge.

Christ is the unifying center of the universe. You can learn all kinds of facts but not see their importance. Truth is centered in Christ, and all facts have their meaning as they relate to Christ.

Disconnecting the education of our children from Christ has caused them to try to relegate Christ to a portion of their lives. Just as Christ should be the center of our lives, He should be the center of our education.

A third Biblical principle of education is that the foundational textbook is the Bible. The Bible should be the definitive Book in any curriculum. It should be the Book by which all other books are judged.

A fourth principle of Biblical education is that parents are responsible for the education of their own children. Deuteronomy 6:6-7 says, "And these words, which I command thee this day, shall be in thine heart: And thou shalt teach them diligently unto thy children, and shalt talk of them when thou sittest in thine house, and when thou walkest by the way, and when thou liest down, and when thou risest up." The oft-quoted Proverbs 22:6, "Train up a child in the way he should go: and when he is old, he will not depart from it," is directed at parents. No place in the Scriptures are parents ever allowed to pass their responsibilities for training their children over to anyone else.

Parents may choose to use a formal school setting as a tool to educate their children, but they are still responsible for the training.

Parents should remember that neutrality in education is impossible. Is it neutral to pray? Is it neutral to ban prayer? Is it neutral to study history and ignore Jesus Christ? Is it neutral to study biology and geology without mentioning the Creator?

SCHOOL CHOICE

Many Americans are beginning to challenge the concept of public education and are demanding school choice in some form. Michigan Governor John Engler said, "Public education is a monopoly and monopolies do not work. Why? Because in a monopoly customers do not come first."

Many parents are already exercising school choice. Thirteen percent of America's school-age children are in private schools. Homeschooling is the fastest growing movement in American education.

It is no wonder that a worried Keith Geiger, president of the National Education Association [NEA], said on a radio program, "We've got to quit talking about letting the kids escape."

The NEA spends millions of dollars yearly to defeat school choice initiatives, yet 22% of its membership with school-age children send their own children to private schools. Prominent leaders in the Democratic party like Bill Clinton, Al Gore, Jesse Jackson, and Ted Kennedy work against any programs to empower all parents to be able to choose schools for their children, yet they all choose to enroll their own children in private schools.

There are four possible approaches to solving the school choice debate.

You could, of course, maintain the status quo and reject any changes in favor of parental choice. This is the goal of the professional educational establishment and a number of politicians (especially in the Democratic party). But this seems to fly in the face of the growing public demand for change. Several national surveys have demonstrated that over 80% of black parents favor school choice. A poll conducted for Parent Power in the summer of 1993 indicates that 61% of Indiana parents wanted full school choice and 79% wanted inter-district public school choice. These reports are similar to reports in other states (76% support full choice in Minnesota, for example). If these numbers hold up, it will become harder and harder for politicians to resist the demand for change.

A second option would be to allow school choice, but only among public schools. This would eliminate the concept of mandatory school districts and create competition among the public schools. This, however, would do nothing to empower parents to be able to choose and afford private education. President Clinton expressed openness to this type of education reform. Thirty-six states are experimenting with choice among public schools now. This may (at least temporarily) satisfy some of the public demand for change. But, this approach will not help parents concerned about new curricula, new educational methods, or the need for religious or moral instruction in the educational process. And it certainly will not satisfy taxpayers concerned about the amount of control that the professional educational establishment appears to have over our schools.

A third approach would be the "voucher system" which is being tried in Milwaukee. Under this system, all parents with school-age children are given a cash voucher by the state, which could be spent at the school of their choice—public or private. Ballot initiatives to establish voucher systems have been defeated in California and Colorado. Many of the strongest proponents for private education oppose the voucher system for fear that the acceptance of government funds by private schools will eventually lead to government control of private schools.

A fourth approach would be to grant tax deductions and/or tax credits to parents for the amount of money they spend on their

children's education. This would recognize the role of parents as "choice-makers" and keep the government out of any direct entanglement with the private schools. Businesses and individuals who provide educational scholarships could also receive tax deductions for their expense. The government would simply reduce the tax burden on those who provide for education, while saving itself the expense of educating those in private schools or at home.

The American free-market economy is built on the premise that consumer choice will ultimately lead to the best quality product at the lowest cost. We assume that parents will generally make the best choices about shoes, clothing, food, and medicine for their children. Why should we assume that a government bureaucrat can make better choices about the education of these children?

After experiencing 75 years of total government control over education, the Russians are reforming their failed educational system with parental choice programs. In fact, many Russian parents have more "educational freedom" than American parents.

As William H. Meller III, president of the Institute for Justice, said, "After all, what we're talking about here is a fundamental freedom. It's the notion that parents should have the freedom to select the education that best meets the needs of their children."

Noah Webster, the great educator who worked on the wording of the United States Constitution, wrote, "All evils are fostered from not knowing and practicing the moral principles and precepts of the Bible."

Private Christian education, whether at home or in a Christian day school, is one of the best investments of time and money that parents can make in the lives of their children. Christian education is one of the most important weapons in the Culture War.

2016:
DEFINING PUBLIC EDUCATION

Dr. Doug Levesque

In every arena of American culture war, a vocabulary of terms has been fought in order to reframe arguments, re-postulate institutional missions, and confuse the populace. Nowhere has this been more evident that in the realm of public education. Even the term 'public education' has been re-defined. A distinct form of government has been created in the last 40 years through federal and state legislative mandates upon local schools. Strong mayors have given way to city managers, and hired school superintendents have given way to appointed school board presidents. Through the change in vocabulary, a different educational system has been put in place that has out of control budgets and seemingly impenetrable command structures. Fortresses of humanism have been therefore entrenched in every town in America. We need to re-examine the very definition of public education.

What does the word 'public' in public education really mean? If it means free access for children of American citizens, that's great. If it means free daytime childcare for illegal aliens, then let's redefine the word. Or better yet, let's get back to the original definition all together.

'Public' does not mean government interference into parental affairs. It does not mean endless funding for poor production through federal, state and local taxes. It does not mean tax funded unions can virtually dictate what is taught or not taught. Lastly, it does not mean 'secular' or without relation to faith and religion.

There is nothing wrong with the term 'public' education if that education is funded locally, determined locally, reflects local values, and is free to pursue local will. Federal and state mandates have gone wild, removing all local distinctions and thereby creating a Washington D.C. inspired, institutionally secular, anti-religious machine. Students success is based upon establishing a utopian social standard rather than academic achievement. 'Public' should not be equated to a government mandated or administered superstructure.

'Public' can mean parental. Imagine a parent initiated, parent inspired, parent involved education. King Solomon wisely charged, "My son, hear the instruction of thy father, and forsake not the law of thy mother: For they shall be an ornament of grace unto thy head, and chains about thy neck." -Proverbs 1:8-9. This 'parental' distinction is one that makes 'private' education perform better and produce a better product. The attack on the family and the capitulation of lazy parents to a cheap system is to blame. There are so many better models of education than the one now being universally touted by the National Education Association.

'Public' can mean performance. Extra funding should be based on performance, and so should opportunity. Schools that perform well should be funded well. This would motivate others to copy or compete for more funding based upon successful models and hard work rather than be funded by artificial mandates. Students that perform well should get additional schooling. Who says we should have twenty years of available daycare for every student, especially poorly performing students? Eight years of acceptable performance can open the door to two more then two more. Of course, special needs children are always the exception. "Study to shew thyself approved unto God, a workman that needeth not to be ashamed, rightly dividing the word of truth." -II Timothy 2:15.

Distribution of equal funds per student is the fairest model. When state capitols withhold funding to poor performing areas a sort of apartheid takes place. Each city or district should receive its funds directly. They then become fully responsible through locally elected leaders for the achievement within their local schools. The only "withheld" funds would be those based on achievement and rewards. This will create an improvement through competition and reward. If poor performance gets constantly rewarded by increased funding then high achieving schools will lose incentive for working hard. District competition in this funding could function to spread the wealth and increase innovation around a state.

'Public' should include 'choice'. Local peculiarities should be allowed to be included in public offerings. Farming classes, particular ethnic histories, even Bible surveys should be reflected in that localities 'public' education. Most communities (80%) would choose to allow academic instruction regarding the Bible. 'Public' education could then be defined by wisdom and knowledge rather than by pride or Washington D.C.'s so called false measurements of equality in the classroom standards.

Unfortunately, the United Nations educational arm, UNESCO, is the chief purveyor of bad ideas into American educational systems. They spread Marxist ideals and lower American standards by usurping regional organizations like the National School Board Association, turning them and every state board into United Nation franchises. This may be the darkest part of the transformation of our society.

TRANSFORMATION

6
THE WAR ON MARRIAGE

TRANSFORMATION

THE BIBLE AND HOMOSEXUALITY

"But as he which hath called you is holy, so be ye holy in all manner of conversation; Because it is written, Be ye holy: for I am holy."
(I Peter 1:15-16)

Until the Culture War began in earnest in the 1960's, homosexuality was clearly seen as contrary to America's Christian culture. Homosexual acts were illegal in all 50 states. Churches were virtually unanimous in their condemnation of homosexuality as sin. The medical and psychiatric communities debated whether homosexuality was a "mental" or "emotional" illness, but no one was openly promoting homosexuality as positive. The following definition is from *The Modern Medical Encyclopedia*, Vol. 10, 1965:

SEXUAL DEVIATION: An emotional illness that is expressed in a form of sexual behavior of an abnormal sort; also known as sexual perversion. The sexual deviate is compelled by his inner drives to seek satisfaction through specific forms of abnormal behavior— sadism, homosexuality, masochism, exhibitionism, nymphomania, and many other variations. Sexual deviation is considered an illness with roots in deep emotional conflicts.

There are many complex factors which can lead to a sexual attitude not acceptable to society as a whole; not all of these are fully understood. In general, however, children who have a full and happy family life and whose parents are an example of a normal and healthy relationship are far less likely to develop emotional conflicts of the sort that can lead to sexual deviation.

Sexual deviation may cause legal as well as personal difficulties. Most types of deviant activity are illegal and punishable by imprisonment. However, an increasing number of judges recognize that deviation is more an illness than a crime and they refer offenders to psychiatrists for treatment of the condition. Pronounced sexual deviation is treated by psychotherapy, which attempts to uncover and resolve the unconscious sources of the deviation.

There are some today who claim that the Bible has nothing to say about homosexuality. When President Bill Clinton was asked to reconcile his professed belief that the Bible is the Word of God with his pro-homosexual position, he replied, "The Ten Commandments don't mention homosexuality." The Ten Commandments do not, but the subject is often mentioned in the Scriptures.

The most famous passage is Romans 1: 18-32. Other passages include:

- Leviticus 18:22, "Thou shalt not lie with mankind, as with womankind: it is abomination."
- Leviticus 20:13, "If a man also lie with mankind, as he lieth with a woman, both of them have committed an abomination: they shall surely be put to death; their blood shall be upon them."
- Deuteronomy 23:17, "There shall be no whore of the daughters of Israel, nor a sodomite of the sons of Israel."

Since some homosexual advocates claim that the Old Testament prohibitions against homosexuality were done away with in the New Testament, it is good to look there as well. Besides Romans 1, some other New Testament passages include:

- I Corinthians 6:9-11, "Know ye not that the unrighteous shall not inherit the kingdom of God? Be not deceived: neither fornicators, not idolaters, nor adulterers, nor effeminate, nor abusers of themselves with mankind. Nor thieves, nor covetous, nor drunkards, nor revilers, nor extortioners, shall inherit the kingdom of God. And such were some of you: but ye are washed, but ye are sanctified, but ye are justified in the name of the Lord Jesus, and by the Spirit of our God."
- I Timothy 1:9-10, "Knowing this, that the law is not made for a righteous man, but for the lawless and disobedient, for the ungodly and for sinners, for unholy and profane, for murderers of fathers and murderers of mothers, for manslayers, For whoremongers, for them that defile themselves with mankind, for menstealers, for liars, for perjured persons and if there be any other thing that is contrary to sound doctrine."
- Jude 7, "Even as Sodom and Gomorrah, and the cities about

them in like manner, giving themselves over to fornication, and going after strange flesh, are set forth an example, suffering the vengeance of eternal fire."

There are several other passages throughout the Bible.

The Lord records two particular stories to indicate his attitude toward homosexuality. The first is the famous story of Sodom and Gomorrah found in Genesis 19:1-15:

1 And there came two angels to Sodom at even; and Lot sat in the gate of Sodom: and Lot seeing them rose up to meet them; and he bowed himself with his face toward the ground;

2 And he said, Behold now, my lords, turn in, I pray you, into your servant's house, and tarry all night, and wash your feet, and ye shall rise up early, and go on your ways. And they said, Nay; but we will abide in the street all night.

3 And he pressed upon them greatly; and they turned in unto him, and entered into his house; and he made them a feast, and did bake unleavened bread, and they did eat.

4 But before they lay down, the men of the city, even the men of Sodom, compassed the house round, both old and young, all the people from every quarter:

5 And they called unto Lot, and said unto him, Where are the men which came in to thee this night? bring them out unto us, that we may know them.

6 And Lot went out at the door unto them, and shut the door after him,

7 And said, I pray you, brethren, do not so wickedly.

8 Behold now, I have two daughters which have not known man; let me, I pray you, bring them out unto you, and do ye to them as is good in your eyes: only unto these men   do nothing; for therefore came they under the shadow of my roof.

9 And they said, Stand back. And they said again, This one fellow came in to sojourn, and he will needs be a judge: now will we deal worse with thee, than with them. And they pressed sore upon the man, even Lot, and came near to break the door.

10 But the men put forth their hand, and pulled Lot into the house to them, and shut to the door.

11 And they smote the men that were at the door of the house with blindness, both small and great: so that they wearied themselves to find the door.

12 And the men said unto Lot, Hast thou here any besides? son in law, and thy sons, and thy daughters, and whatsoever thou hast in the city, bring them out of this place:

13 For we will destroy this place, because the cry of them is waxen great before the face of the LORD; and the LORD hath sent us to destroy it.

14 And Lot went out, and spake unto his sons in law, which married his daughters, and said, Up, get you out of this place; for the LORD will destroy this city. But he seemed as one that mocked unto his sons in law.

15 And when the morning arose, then the angels hastened Lot, saying, Arise, take thy wife, and thy two daughters, which are here; lest thou be consumed in the iniquity of the city.

A less famous but equally important story is found in Judges, chapters 19 and 20. Gibeah was a little Benjaminite town in the days of the Judges. A Levite and his concubine stopped there to stay the night. They were taken in by residents of Gibeah. A group of angry homosexuals demanded that the Levite surrender himself to them. When he refused, they took his concubine and abused her all night resulting in her death. They were angry because they could not have the Levite himself.

When the Levite awoke he found the dead body of his concubine dumped on the doorstep. The Levite cut the woman's ravaged body into 12 pieces and sent a piece to each of the 12 tribes of Israel. The message was, "Nothing like this has ever happened in Israel before." The men of Israel gathered to punish the wicked men of Gibeah, but their kinsmen, the Bejaminites decided to defend them. Forty thousand Israelites died in the resulting civil war, and Benjamin was almost destroyed. Even though the vast majority of the Benjaminites were not homosexuals, they were willing to overlook the violence of the homosexual movement and fight a civil war for "gay rights."

Centuries later God rebuked Ephraim for the same mistake—tolerating homosexuality. Hosea 9:9-10:

They have deeply corrupted themselves, as in the days of Gibeah: therefore he will remember their iniquity, he will visit their sins. I found Israel like grapes in the wilderness; I saw your fathers as the firstripe in the fig tree at her first time: but they went to Baalpeor, and separated themselves unto that shame; and their abominations were   according as they loved.

Several truths are clear in the Scripture:

- God considers homosexuality an abomination.
- Homosexuality is an act of rebellion against God.
- Homosexuality is an act of rebellion against nature.
- Homosexuality involves a whole different set of values. It is more than just a different sexual orientation. These values often involve recruitment, violence, and pressure on society.
- God judges homosexuality.
- God judges the society that tolerates homosexuality.

When America's culture was distinctively Christian, there was no public debate about homosexuality. Occasionally an individual adopted homosexuality behavior but never with the approval of society. Local communities very carefully protected children from homosexual influence. All states had laws against homosexual acts, recognizing them as both health and moral hazards.

The Culture War has changed all that. Powerful forces in politics, education, and the media promote homosexuality as good, normal, and natural. America is reaping the whirlwind.

MYTHS OF HOMOSEXUALITY

"But as he which hath called you is holy, so be ye holy in all manner of conversation; Because it is written, Be ye holy: for I am holy."
(I Peter 1:15-16)

MYTH 1:

Homosexuality is genetic.

This is the most common myth regarding homosexuality. Homosexual activists work tirelessly at spreading this myth. It is interesting to note that the very people who want to proclaim homosexuality as "good" do not want to admit that they chose the homosexual lifestyle.

Large numbers of scientific studies have been undertaken to discover the cause of homosexuality. No reliable study has concluded that there is any genetic cause for homosexuality. Dr. Charles Waugh, a researcher in this area, said, "The vast preponderance of evidence clearly indicates that homosexuality is a learned disorder and is not genetically inherited."

Homosexual activists are fond of quoting a few "scientific studies" conducted by homosexual activists which are said to indicate the possibility of genetic factors relating to homosexuality. Despite the fact that these studies were conducted by activists without academic qualifications, without normal guidelines and control groups, and without observation or verification of results, activists are quick to accept them and promote their purported results.

The news media and some politicians are also quick to accept these studies and quote them as if they are proven scientific facts. The truth is, these studies are based more upon wishful thinking than any scientific results.

In fact, homosexuals are heterosexuals who have twisted God's purpose for them. Homosexuality is a behavior, not a genetic condition.

The Bible declares that rebellion against God and His moral code is the basis for homosexuality. The vast majority of homosexuals are the victims of homosexual abuse or homosexual manipulation in their childhood or teenage years. How a person responds to such a perversion determines how they will develop. Some respond in such a way as to free themselves from these bonds. Others give in to them completely.

The influence of this myth is so great that many professing Christians are starting to believe it. Rather than simply asking what the Bible says, or questioning the purported evidence, they respond to the subtle pressure of having heard this myth repeated so often. However, the testimony of the Scripture refutes this myth.

MYTH 2:

Ten percent of the American population are homosexual.

This oft-repeated myth is based upon a statement in Alfred Kinsey's 1948 book Sexual Behavior in the American Male. One reference in the book has resulted in in this widespread myth. Actually, even the statement is misquoted from this work. Kinsey actually stated that four percent of the male population is homosexual. He goes on to suggest than an additional six percent may try homosexuality and eventually reject it. Furthermore, Kinsey's study was based upon his interviews with people who had volunteered to participate in a "sexuality study." This was hardly a representative group of society as a whole.

A 1989 National Opinion Research Center study concluded that less than one percent of America's population was homosexual (with perhaps another one percent being described as bisexual). A 1993 study by the Alan Guttmacher Institute (funded by $1.8 million tax dollars) also concluded that about one percent of American males were homosexual with an additional one percent having experimented with homosexuality. Similar studies in Britain, Canada, Denmark, France, and Norway have also come up with the one-percent figure.

MYTH 3:

Homosexuality is just another sexual orientation and does not affect other areas of life.

Homosexuals regularly engage in parades and demonstrations. Routinely these parades include public nudity, sex acts committed in public, and the promotion of abusive sexual behaviors and sexual abuse of children. The participants are not just promoting a "different sexual orientation" or crusading for their civil rights; they are seeking approval of their acts and even encouraging expanded participation. They are, in fact, demanding an "anything goes" society.

The behavior of these homosexual demonstrators is reminiscent of the homosexual demonstrators of Sodom, Gomorrah, and Gibeah in the Old Testament. Isaiah 3:8-9 speaks to such public displays of wickedness:

8 For Jerusalem is ruined, and Judah is fallen: because their tongue and their doings are against the LORD, to provoke the eyes of his glory.
9 The show of their countenance doth witness against them; and they declare their sin as Sodom, they hide it not. Woe unto their soul! for they have rewarded evil unto   themselves.

While homosexual leaders want to convince the general public that they are as normal as this myth would suggest, their methods communicate the opposite.

MYTH 4:

Homosexuals do not recruit.

This myth is based upon myth one—the idea that homosexuality is genetic. The truth is that homosexuality is chosen. No one is born homosexual, and so either all homosexuals must volunteer or be recruited (either directly or indirectly). There are only two ways to recruit someone into homosexuality: either force them or persuade them. Since children are easier to both force and-or persuade, they are most often the prime targets of homosexual recruitment.

Although homosexuals account for only one to two percent of the population, they are responsible for 50% of the acts of child molestation (Dr. Brad Hoyton, The Homosexual Agenda). One survey by two homosexual authors found that 73% of homosexuals had at least one experience with a teenager or child.

The Boy Scouts of America have wisely refused to allow homosexuals to be scout leaders, understanding that men in such positions would be with boys on campouts, etc. Homosexual activists attack the organization, accuse them of hate crimes, and otherwise try to destroy them legally. Sensible, concerned parents applaud them for not caving in to political pressure and the "politically correct" myths of the day.

MYTH 5:

Homosexuals are a persecuted minority.

No homosexual publication, speech, demonstration, interview, or protest is complete without the customary complaint that homosexuals are victims of a discriminatory society. Vague references to violent hate crimes always follow this comment. This myth is told by activists to hide the truth: that the homosexual movement is an aggressive, militant movement designed to gain power and influence (by intimidation if necessary). The militant homosexual movement demands special rights, tax-payer funding to spread their messages, and the force of big government to make everyone approve of them.

Deep down inside, under all their bravado and public bluster, homosexuals still feel wicked, different, and bizarre. They think that if they can just get the government to declare them "normal," then they will feel better; then they want the government to force people to accept them as normal. They want government-imposed acceptance of homosexuality forced upon employers, schools, churches, and society in general. But, normal people do not need the full force of government power to make people accept them as normal. Deep down inside, "gays" know that government force is their only hope of being treated as the normal human beings that they know they really are not.

The real question here is simple: is there any room left in American society for individuals to decide for themselves? Can we make judgments based upon our religious convictions or personal opinions, or must we blindly accept a moral code handed to us by the government?

Public decency laws are not waived every time a "victimized" minority wants to have a parade. Law enforcement officials do not look the other way when a "victimized minority" firebombs a parsonage (*When the Wicked Seize a City* by Charles McIlheny) or when churches are attacked while having services (several examples in 1993 and 1994). "Victimized minorities" are not promoted by all the major television networks.

The truth is that the militant homosexual movement receives more cooperation from the cultural forces shaping our society than any other group, but in their consciences, they still do not feel normal, and most of society still does not accept them as normal.

MYTH 6:

Homosexuals cannot change.

Despite all the liberal propaganda to the contrary, many organizations are successfully helping homosexuals abandon that lifestyle. Groups like Harvest and Exodus International are having a major impact. There are many others. These groups have to deal with hate campaigns from the homosexual activists and negative publicity from the mainstream media.

John Freeman, Executive Director of Harvest, describes his ministry to homosexuals in this excerpt from World magazine, March 6, 1993:

Many homosexuals are essentially saying, "I didn't choose this and it is unfair of you to ask me to change," Freeman notes. Homosexuality is symptomatic of deeper things, he says, and Harvest tries to go to the roots. In Bible studies, participants examine anger, bitterness, rejection, fear, and envy. Unless something shakes a person out, someone who starts into the homosexual lifestyle is there for life, and will often accept "gay theology." According to Freeman, gay theology says: "God loves you and accepts you just the way you are, so there is no need to change."

Gay theology usually has three appeals, Freeman notes: to feeling instead of Scripture, to fatalism, and to individual rights. Those appeals are backed up with the following arguments: I fell this way. I'm gay now; I'll always be gay; or, I have the right to express my sexuality any way I want to, no matter what God said. People who follow the "once gay always gay" belief do not look at the choices in life, Freeman said. People are rarely consciously aware of when they started feeling same-sex attractions, but when actions are traced through the years, small choices began to accumulate.

Freeman struggled with homosexuality himself and lived a gay lifestyle until he became a Christian in his 20's through the help of some Christian men "who modeled to me what a Christian man is all about." Freeman later married; he and his wife now have three children.

Homosexuals who come to Harvest are asked, "Why are you here?" One of the most frequent answers is: "I want to be like everybody else." That usually means being married and having a family.

MYTH 7:

The health dangers to homosexuals are the fault of the administrations of Presidents Ronald Reagan and George H.W. Bush.

- The average age of men dying with AIDS is 39.
- The average age of death for all homosexual males is 41.
- Only one percent of homosexuals live to age 65.
- Homosexual women are 19 more times likely to get venereal disease than non- homosexual women.
- Seventy-eight percent of homosexuals report having had at least one sexually transmitted disease.
- Male homosexuals are 5,000 times more likely to contract AIDS than heterosexuals.

Homosexual literature and speeches are replete with statements placing the blame for all of these health dangers on Ronald Reagan and George H.W. Bush. "If they had only cared," we are told, "this would not have happened. They could have prevented all this."

The facts are quite different. The Reagan and Bush administrations spent more money on research and treatment of AIDS (per patient afflicted) than on any other disease. The sex education information that the activists wanted them to spread simply is not true—it reflects a fantasy world view with no medical or scientific basis.

While the recognition of AIDS is new, the recognition of the health hazards of homosexuality is not. The state laws (which did exist in all 50 states) were based upon the threat of homosexuality to the public health. When the body is used in a fashion for which it was never designed by its Designer, it is wrecked and ruined. Objective observers have long realized that homosexuality is a health hazard.

Homosexuals themselves are responsible for the health dangers to the homosexual community. The attempt to blame all of this on the Presidents

Reagan and Bush is only the most irresponsible of fantasies. The health risks that homosexuals face have not been reduced any under the two administrations of Bill Clinton.

MYTH 8:

Homosexuals are very careful and selective about their partners.

Those who have been concerned about forcing military personnel to share barracks, close living quarters, and showers with homosexuals are always assured that homosexuals are very selective about choosing partners. This idea, however, exists only in the liberal fantasy world. Studies show that homosexuals average between 20 and 100 partners each year, 300 to 500 partners in a lifetime. It is no wonder that disease is transmitted at an incredible rate. Homosexual practices are as unsanitary as they are disgusting, and they communicate diseases among a large number of partners.

CONCLUSION

Homosexuality has been one of the most hotly contested battlegrounds of the Culture War. In order to promote homosexuality, homosexual activists have had to resort to vain deceit, myths, and intimidation.

As stated in the chapter on "Myths of Abortion," the liberals' attempts to spoil the American culture with their vain deceit have been largely successful. In fact, the battle for public understanding of the real issues surrounding homosexuality has, for all practical purposes, been lost. The next real battleground involves man's lust at its worst: preying after children in the scourge of pedophilia which often has its roots in pornography.

ABSTINENCE: TRUE LOVE WAITS

"But fornication, and all uncleanness, or covetousness, let it not be
once named among you, as becometh saints."
(Ephesians 5:3)

THE PROBLEM OF TEEN PREGNANCY

Teen sexual behavior has become the subject of a great deal of public debate in America. Everyone agrees that there are a number of major problems facing our society as a result of teen sexual activity.

In the early 1990's, over one million teenage girls became pregnant each year. These pregnancies resulted in about 400,000 abortions, 134,000 miscarriages, and 490,000 births. About 65% of these births were among unmarried teens.

Over two million teenagers a year are treated for sexually transmitted diseases (STD's). Twenty-six percent of all abortions are performed on teenage girls.

The two sides in the Culture War have entirely different solutions to the problem of teen sexuality.

Those opposed to America's historic Christian tradition believe that America's teenagers just need more education, encouragement, and help in practicing "safe" methods of moral impurity. Bible-believing Christians believe that teens need more education, encouragement, and help in developing moral values.

SEX-ED AND THE SCHOOL BOARDS

In 1992 and 1993, the attention of the country was focused on a battle over sex education and school board authority in New York City. Joe Fernandez, Chancellor of New York City schools, had stripped the Queens School Board of authority to determine curriculum. The dispute was over the use of a curriculum promoted by Fernandez called "Children of the Rainbow," a pro-homosexual curriculum. Fernandez was opposed by the school board president Mary A. Cummins. Mrs. Cummins described her position this way: "We will continue to teach our children to respect social, religious, and ethnic differences. However, we are not going to teach our children to treat all types of human behavior as equally safe, wholesome, or acceptable." Parents overwhelmingly sided with Mrs. Cummins. The controversy finally ended with Mr. Fernandez's contract not being renewed and the "Children of the Rainbow" curriculum being removed.

ABSTINENCE—A RELIGION?

A second area of controversy has been the legal battles over whether or not abstinence can be taught in public schools. Fred Ray summed up the legal conflict this way in the September, 1993, Defender newsletter (published by the author and edited for use in this material):

> What is this sexual education curriculum that has the American Civil Liberties Union and Planned Parenthood in such an uproar? It is Sexual Abstinence Education. And the new curricula such as "Sex Respect," "Facing Reality," and "Postponing Sexual Involvement" not only tells teens the dangers they face by becoming sexually active before marriage, but also teaches teens how to resist peer pressure with assertiveness training. Why would anyone fault that, you ask?
>
> To get a better understanding, you have to go to Louisiana and the case of Bettye Coleman v. Caddo Parish School Board. Bettye Coleman sued the Caddo Parish School Board to prevent the two abstinence-based sex education curricula from being taught. It was her contention that they taught moral beliefs that were religiously based and therefore unconstitutional.
>
> However, from the Louisiana Revised Statute 17:281, "The major emphasis of any sex education instruction offered in the public schools of the state (of Louisiana) shall be to encourage sexual abstinence between two unmarried persons." This is exactly what the Caddo Parish School Board had in mind when they adopted the curricula "Sex Respect" and "Facing Reality."
>
> But, the revised statutes also go on to say that, "It is the intent of the legislature   that 'sex education' shall not include religious beliefs, values, customs, practices in   human sexuality, nor the subjective moral and ethical judgments of the instructor or other persons."

160

Since the "Facing Reality" curriculum is very open about wanting to change the moral framework that teenagers currently have about premarital sex, it contradicts the Louisiana code. In fact, as stated in the "Facing Reality" material, any curriculum that goes beyond bare, anatomical facts will be teaching a moral/ ethical system because the "authors of most human sexuality materials will present the moral themes that personally engage them." Thus, this statute is so vague that it is doubtful any curriculum could meet the intent of Louisiana's sexual education legislation and still be taught. However, as the Facing Reality" curriculum says, "We can encourage moral/ethical behavior without advocating sectarian doctrines." So with minor changes to this poorly written statute, it is possible to have an abstinence-based program, even in Louisiana.

In Rush Limbaugh's The Way Things Ought To Be, *he tells of another battle over abstinence-based education in Jacksonville, Florida. The Jacksonville School Board "decided to teach real safe sex, which is abstinence. However, six families, along with Planned Parenthood and the ACLU, are suing the schools over this program. This bunch of curious citizens says that teaching abstinence puts the children at a greater risk of catching AIDS or other sexually transmitted diseases . . .The suit alleges that the schools are provided a 'fear-based program that gives children incomplete, inaccurate, biased, and sectarian information.'" Says Linda Lanier of Planned Parenthood, "It's not right to try and trick our students."*

No development so clearly illustrates the Culture War as this. Basic moral teaching, taken for granted in our schools 40 years ago, is considered controversial today. This same moral information is the subject of lawsuits and is outlawed or restricted in some communities.

NEW PAGANISM & SEX

Clinton administration officials illustrated the "new pagan" thinking about teen sex. Kristine Gebbie (former AIDS "czar" in the Clinton Administration) said, "Unless Americans embrace sex as an essentially important and pleasurable thing, we will continue to be a repressed,

Victorian society that misrepresents information, denies homosexuality, particularly in teens, and leaves people abandoned with no place to go."

Former Clinton Administration Surgeon General Joycelyn Elders offered her advice as to how to help American teenagers deal with their sexuality: "We have to be more open about sex. We need to speak out to tell people that sex is good, sex is wonderful." She also said, "I think the religious community could be very, very powerful and very, very influential. They have the prestige and the acceptance and I feel that if they would stop trying to moralize these issues and educate our children, then we could eradicate many of these problems." She has also insisted that her ideas about sexuality and health education should be taught in all the public schools as early as kindergarten. As hard as it is to believe, these leaders believe the problem is a lack of emphasis on sexuality for teens. They clearly believe that any emphasis on moral teaching makes teens think that sex is bad.

However, many parents, religious leaders, religious groups, and many teenagers have taken exception to this emphasis. A 1986 Harris Poll (commissioned by Planned Parenthood) found that teens who had been through a supposed "safe-sex" education course were 53% more likely to participate in sexual relationships. The message that "everybody's doing it" is very powerful, especially when it is presented by school administrators, teachers, and political leaders.

POSITIVE ALTERNATIVES; ENCOURAGING RESULTS

A number of programs like "True Love Waits" have provided a totally different answer for teenagers. These programs encourage teens to take a public vow to wait for sex until marriage. Using slogans like, "Wait for the ring," these programs are designed to provide positive peer pressure and accurate information for today's teens. One teenager described these as being for "teens who are tired of being talked to like they were animals in heat."

Because of our Culture War, even programs such as these are controversial. Liberal critics have described this approach as naïve, outdated, and misleading. When America had a common moral code and a common culture, most churches, government agencies, schools, and parents encouraged American young people to morality. Now a Culture

War is being fought over what moral code to teach America's young people.

The ultimate debate over teaching moral values was the Dan Quayle-"Murphy Brown" controversy. In a speech, then-Vice President Dan Quayle suggested that the "Murphy Brown" television show was providing a poor example by having the main character have a baby out of wedlock. He was immediately subjected to an unending stream of abuse accusing him of attacking single parents, claiming that single-parent homes were not really families, and accusing him of trying to impose his moral beliefs on everyone. The actual quote from his speech is as follows:

Ultimately, however, marriage is a moral issue that requires cultural consensus, and the use of social sanctions. Bearing babies irresponsibly is, simply, wrong. Failing to support children one has fathered is wrong. We must be unequivocal about this.

It doesn't help matters when prime TV has "Murphy Brown"—a character who supposedly epitomizes today's intelligent, highly-paid, professional woman—mocking the importance of fathers, by bearing a child alone, and calling it just another "lifestyle choice." I know it is not fashionable to talk about moral values, but we need to do it. Even though our cultural leaders in Hollywood, network TV, the national newspapers routinely jeer at them, I think that most of us in this room know that some things are good, and other things are wrong. Now it's time to make the discussion public.

It is a clear indication of how heated the Culture War is that such a statement has become controversial in America.

What are the results of teaching abstinence? A five-year study on the pro-abstinence curriculum "Sex Respect" in California showed that the pregnancy rate for girls who had taken the course was five percent, compared to 49% (in the same schools) for girls who had not taken the course. When Marion Howard, a professor of obstetrics and gynecology, asked 1,000 teenage girls what subject they wanted to learn about most in sex education, 82% answered, "How to say 'no!'" After this, Howard developed an abstinence curriculum which was tried out in the Atlanta, Georgia, schools in the eighth grade. Results showed that students who took the course were four times less likely to become sexually active in high school than those who did not.

GOD'S METHOD WORKS BEST!

Hebrews 13:4, "Marriage is honourable in all, and the bed undefiled: but whoremongers and adulterers God will judge.

Colossians 3:5, "Mortify therefore your members which are upon the earth; fornication, uncleanness, inordinate affection, evil concupiscence, and covetousness, which is idolatry."

Ephesians 5:3, "But fornication, and all uncleanness, or covetousness, let it not be once named among you, as becometh saints."

DIVORCE AND AMERICAN LIFE
"Therefore shall a man leave his father and his mother, and shall
cleave unto his wife: and they shall be one flesh."
(Genesis 2:24)

In the first generation after World War II, more than 80% of all children grew up in a family with two biological parents married to each other. By 1980, that number had dropped to 50%. By 1990, the same figure had dropped to 40%.

Two main trends account for the change:
- Births out of wedlock
- Divorce.

The impact American society has been overwhelming. More than 70% of juveniles in reform schools come from homes where the biological father does not reside. Single-parent families are six times more likely to live in poverty. A 1988 survey by the National Center for Health Statistics found that children in single-parent family to have emotional and behavioral problems. Also in 1988, it was determined that 12 million children under the age of 18 were living with a divorced parent.

DAN QUAYLE WAS RIGHT

In a now famous article entitled "Dan Quayle Was Right" (April, 1993, issue of Atlantic Monthly), Barbara Dafoe Whitehead wrote:

Across time and across cultures, family disruption has been regarded as an event that threatens a child's well-being and even survival. This view is rooted in a fundamental biological fact: unlike the young of almost any other species, the human child is born in an abjectly helpless and immature state. Years of nurture and protection are needed before the child can achieve physical independence. Similarly, it takes years of interaction with at least one but ideally two or more adults for a child to develop into a socially competent adult. Children raised in virtual isolation from human beings, though physically intact, display few recognizably

165

human behaviors. The social arrangement that has proved most successful in ensuring the physical survival and promoting the social development of the child is the family unit of the biological mother and father. Consequently, any event that permanently denies a child the presence and protection of a parent jeopardizes the life of the child.

Because of this, the American culture originally discouraged all forms of family disruption. Separation, divorce, out-of-wedlock births, homosexual marriages, and open marriages were vigorously discouraged by religious, social, and legal sanctions. Divorce was considered a failure and was discouraged. Only 11% of the children born in the 1950's and the early 1960's could expect to see their parents divorce by the time they were 18. Divorce happened, but it was not normal! However, family disruption through divorce (and other factors) has become common. This creates a number of challenges for families.

EFFECTS OF DIVORCE ON CHILDREN

One of the major concepts that has to be evaluated is the concept of step-parents. Over 25% of America's young people will deal with a step-parent sometime before they are 18,

Those who wish to destroy America's historic Christian culture have sought to make divorce acceptable (just as they have done concerning single parenthood). A book on divorce from the 1940's said, "Children are entitled to the affection and association of two parents—not one." This reflects the Biblical ideal. A 1970's book on divorce reads, "A two-parent home is not the only emotional structure within which a child can be happy and healthy . . . The parents who take care of themselves will best be able to take care of their children." While God promises special help to Godly widows and orphans, the two-parent home is always presented as the ideal. Those who resent Christianity want to promote single-parenthood as equally ideal.

All over America selfish parents are divorcing their mates and quoting the politically correct myth, "Children always bounce back after divorce." This myth is just another example of the vain deceit of the Culture War. Where does this idea come from? There is no polling data to suggest this. In fact, one survey indicates that only 33% of young people from broken homes felt that they were not significantly impacted by their parents' divorce. Even the most casual observation of children from divorced homes will note that, often (though not always), they suffer from serious emotional problems. While this myth may provide a convenient excuse for thoughtless parents, it has no foundation in reality.

Increasingly, the media attacks the concept of the historic family. Pop therapist John Bradshaw insists that 96% of all families are dysfunctional. Author Stephanie Coontz wrote in *The Way We Were: American Families and the Nostalgia Trip* that life for married mothers in the 1950's was "booze, bridge, bowling, and boredom." The Hallmark greeting cards company sells cards congratulating individuals on becoming divorced.

Children suffer from the social structure of divorce. Not only do they lose time and contact with the absent parent, but often the custodial parent is forced into situations which allow less time with the child.

DIVORCE AND ECONOMICS

Economically, divorce creates many poverty situations for both children and parents. Half the single mothers in the United States live below the poverty line. Only ten percent of the married mothers find themselves in the same situation. Most families simply do not have enough income to maintain two separate homes and lifestyles. Not only does this create immediate poverty situations, if often creates cycles of poverty. Whitehead writes:

Single-mother families are vulnerable not just to poverty but to a particularly debilitating form of poverty: welfare dependency. The dependency takes two forms: First, single mothers, particularly unwed mothers, stay on welfare longer than any other welfare recipients. Of those never-married mothers who receive welfare benefits, almost 40 percent remain on the rolls for ten years or longer. Second, welfare dependency tends to be passed on from one generation to the next. McLanahan says, "Evidence of intergenerational poverty indicates that, indeed, offspring from [single-mother] families are far more likely to be poor and to form mother-only families than are offspring who live with two parents most of their pre-adult life." Nor is the intergenerational impact of single motherhood limited to African-Americans, as many people seem to believe. Among white families, daughters of single parents are 53% more likely to marry as teenagers, 111 percent more likely to have children as teenagers, 164 percent more likely to have a premarital birth, and 92 percent more likely to dissolve their own marriages. All these intergenerational consequences of single motherhood increase the likelihood of chronic welfare dependency.

In fact, over one-half of the increase in child poverty in America is related to the increase of divorce in America (study by David Eggebeen and Daniel Lichter of Pennsylvania State University). According to sociologist Lenore Weitzman:

Even if single mothers escape poverty, economic uncertainty remains a condition of life. Divorce brings a reduction in income and standard of living for the vast majority of single mothers. One study, for example, found that income for mothers and children declines on average about 30 percent, while fathers experience a 10 to 15 percent increase in income in the year following a separation. Things get even more difficult when fathers fail to meet their child support obligations. As a result, many divorced mothers experience a wearing uncertainty about the family budget: whether the check will come in or not; whether new sneakers can be bought this month or not; whether the electric bill will be paid on time or not. Uncertainty about money triggers other kinds of uncertainty. Mothers and children often have to move to cheaper housing after a divorce. Even several years later the rate of moves for single mothers is about a third higher than the rate for two-parent families. It is also common for a mother to change her job or increase her working hours or both following a divorce. Even the composition of the household is likely to change, with other adults, such as boyfriends or babysitters, moving in and out.

Judith Wallerstein began researching the long-term effects of divorce on children in 1971. At that time most experts were promoting the "Children always bounce back" myth. Her conclusions demonstrated otherwise. She wrote, "Divorce is deceptive. Legally it is a single event, but psychologically it is a chain—sometimes a never-ending chain—of events, relocations, and radically shifting relationships strung through time, a process that forever changes the lives of the people involved." Wallerstein's study and others conclude that children often react to divorce with guilt, insecurity, anger, and depression. Novelist Pat Conroy has written, "each divorce is the death of a small civilization."

Christians should not allow themselves to be influenced by the Culture War's attack on marriage or the growing cultural acceptance of divorce. God's ideal is for marriage to be a permanent union involving one man and one woman for life. Careful loyalty to Bible teaching about marriage (by both partners) will prevent divorce. Christians should not seek to add to the pressures faced by those who have gone through divorce. Those who have been divorced should dedicate themselves to living the rest of their lives in God's will.

Children of divorce should not despair because they face special challenges. They should face the fact that there are issues they must address in their own lives. They must protect themselves from bitterness by forgiving their parents who have been divorced. They should examine the influence of the divorce on their lives and be careful to respond to each challenge Biblically.

Those who have attacked the Christian concept of marriage have not done anyone a favor: not the husbands and fathers who have been freed from responsibility, not the wives and mothers who have gained responsibility, and certainly not the children who have been deprived of the traditional Christian family.

2016:
LGBTQ: THE MODERN SODOM
Dr. Doug Levesque

As already well defined, the slide into homosexuality as normal in American life has disastrous repercussions. Confusing, gay with happy, homosexual with perverse, or gender confused with sodomite recruitment is a curse of insanity. Christians should have no confusion whatsoever. They need not hide from the rhetorical or cultural fight in fear. In fact, warning society is the kindest thing a Bible believer can do. A reminder of the evolution of our sodomite society is in order.

1. **The pride of Sodom**...Ezekiel 16:49 reminds us of where the dark transformation starts, "Behold, this was the iniquity of thy sister Sodom, **pride**, fullness of bread, and abundance of idleness was in her and in her daughters, neither did she strengthen the hand of the poor and needy." American excess and callousness were additional slides into the perversion.

2. **A place of perversion**...Genesis 19:4-7 introduces us to their pandemic perverseness, "But before they lay down, the men of the city, even the men of Sodom, compassed the house round, both old and young, all the people from every quarter:

   *And they called unto Lot, and said unto him, Where are the men which came in to thee this night? **bring them out unto us, that we may know them**. And Lot went out at the door unto them, and shut the door after him, And said, **I pray you, brethren, do not so wickedly.**"*

   We must beg our fellow citizens to cease from such wickedness.

3. **An example of judgement**...Genesis 19:24-25 clearly reports that The LORD Himself did utterly destroy the whole place,

"Then the LORD rained upon Sodom and upon Gomorrah **brimstone and fire from the LORD** *out of heaven; And he overthrew those cities, and all the plain, and all the inhabitants of the cities, and that which grew upon the ground."*

Society knows of this account, but rejects to remember it.

4. **Encoded in the law**... Leviticus 20:13 signals a death penalty within the nation of Israel for such nastiness, "If a man also lie with mankind, as he lieth with a woman, both of them have committed an abomination: **they shall surely be put to death**; their blood shall be upon them." Yes, it is in there folks. In company with incest, bestiality, rape... Leviticus 20:15-17 goes on to list the other grievous sexual sins,

"And if a man lie with a beast, he shall surely be put to death: and ye shall slay the beast. And if a woman approach unto any beast, and lie down thereto, thou shalt kill the woman, and the beast: they shall surely be put to death; their blood shall be upon them. And if a man shall take his sister, his father's daughter, or his mother's daughter, and see her nakedness, and she see his nakedness; it is a wicked thing; and they shall be cut off in the sight of their people: he hath uncovered his sister's nakedness; he shall bear his iniquity." Lord help the the culture that defends for a sodomite national character.

5. **Assigned as Abomination**... And Leviticus 20:13 again, "If a man also lie with mankind, as he lieth with a woman, **both of them have committed an abomination**: they shall surely be put to death; their blood shall be upon them." The argument that it is just another sin is not accurate. It is extreme sin, has extreme consequences, and as we will see, seeks to pull one away from the possibility of exercising a saving faith.

6. **Example of government removal**... 1 Kings 15:12 reports, "And **he took away the sodomites out of the land**, and removed all

the idols that his fathers had made." And again, in 1 Kings 22:46, "And the **remnant of the sodomites**, which remained in the days of his father Asa, **he took out of the land**." And again, in 2 Kings 23:7, "**And he brake down the houses of the sodomites**, that were by the house of the LORD, where the women wove hangings for the grove." Notice that sodomites were even adjacent to the very house of the LORD.

7. **Jesus mentions it as a measure of wrath**... Matthew 11:23-24 warns, "And thou, Capernaum, which art exalted unto heaven, shalt be brought down to hell: for if the mighty works, which have been done in thee, had been done in Sodom, it would have remained until this day. But I say unto you, That it shall be **more tolerable for the land of Sodom in the day of judgment, than for thee**." What must be in store for America?

8. **Remembrance of as motivation to righteousness**... Luke 17:32 came out of Jesus own mouth, "**Remember Lot's wife**." Just a reminder, she did not escape, but turned into a pillar of salt, simply for looking back!

9. **A sign of the end times** . . . Luke 17:28-30 is clearly a sign,

*"Likewise also as it was in the days of Lot; they did eat, they drank, they bought, they sold, they planted, they builded; But the same day that Lot went out of Sodom it rained fire and brimstone from heaven, and destroyed them all. **Even thus shall it be in the day when the Son of man is revealed.**"*

10. **An end of the line with God's patience**... Romans 1:26-28 likens God giving up on certain within the sodomite culture,

*"For this cause **God gave them up unto vile affections:** for even their women did change the natural use into that which is against nature: And likewise also the men, leaving the natural use of the woman, burned in their lust one toward another; men with men working that which is unseemly, and receiving in themselves*

that recompence of their error which was meet. And even as they did not like to retain God in their knowledge, God gave them over to a reprobate mind, to do those things which are not convenient;"

Our forefathers could never have imagined America in its perverseness today.

11. **A final and ultimate form of wickedness**… 2 Peter 2:4-6 gives an ultimatum, We are at the threshold of national life.

*"For if God spared not the angels that sinned, but cast them down to hell, and delivered them into chains of darkness, to be reserved unto judgment; And spared not the old world, but saved Noah the eighth person, a preacher of righteousness, bringing in the flood upon the world of the ungodly; And turning the cities of Sodom and Gomorrha into ashes condemned them with an overthrow, **making them an ensample unto those that after should live ungodly;"***

12. **Bringing about their own destruction**… 2 Peter 2:7-9 contrasts Lot's deliverance with the sodomites reserve ticket to destruction,

*"And delivered just Lot, vexed with the filthy conversation of the wicked: (For that righteous man dwelling among them, in seeing and hearing, vexed his righteous soul from day to day with their unlawful deeds;) The Lord knoweth how to deliver the godly out of temptations, and **to reserve the unjust unto the day of judgment to be punished:"***

13. **Personal and national path of suicidal madness**… Jude 1:7 is a national example,

"Even as Sodom and Gomorrha, and the cities about them in like manner, giving themselves over to fornication, and going after strange flesh, are set forth for an example, suffering the vengeance of eternal fire."

Should we not take that as an example for our own transformation? Therefore we should,

- Be on God's side in this issue.
- Hate the evil of this great sin.
- Warn society of sodomite perils.
- Not compromise with modern sodomites pleadings one bit
- Teach our current generations truth surrounding this issue.
- Gladly be counted as enemy of this wickedness.
- Never allow sympathy with this deception.
- Totally reject modern laws and cultural arguments.
- Suffer associated persecution willingly, knowing God will avenge His own.
- Fight to remove this terrible evil from our culture as long as we are able.

Who is the real bully? With Christian small businesses being sued, State political well-being threatened with boycott, and school policies that practically support recruitment into the horrors of the LGBTQ madness, can Christian dissent really be labeled as threatening?

LGBTQ is modern Sodom.

THE WAR ON MARRIAGE

TRANSFORMATION

7
THE WAR ON FAMILY

TRANSFORMATION

THE CHRISTIAN FAMILY

"And these words, which I command thee this day, shall be in thine heart: And thou shalt teach them diligently unto thy children, and shalt talk of them when thou sittest in thine house, and when thou walkest by the way, an when thou liest down, and when thou risest up." (Deuteronomy 6:6-7)

THE CONCEPT OF FAMILY IN AMERICAN HISTORY

Much of America's historic Christian culture stems from the fact that the Biblical model for the home was the standard for American families. Husbands and fathers has specific spiritual, social, and financial obligations and responsibilities. They also had the necessary authority and respect Biblically, culturally and legally to carry out those responsibilities. The earliest situation comedies (sit-coms) showed—in the 1950's and early 1960's (the first TV generation)—a different role for husbands and fathers than is seen today on TV (or in real life) in many homes. Wives and mothers had specific spheres on which to focus. Mothers of young children were specifically thought of as "stay-at-home" mothers. This ideal was reflected in early TV shows such as "I Love Lucy," "The Dick Van Dyke Show," "Leave It To Beaver," and "Ozzie and Harriet." These all reflected the common family structure of the 1950's.

Children were not considered little adults. They were recognized as immature in their thought processes as well as physically. They were clearly the responsibility of their parents. Their parents were just as responsible for the development of their character as they were for their physical development. Parents had rights, and the government was not even in the picture (except for public education). This scenario was on television as well as in real life.

Many have taken for granted both the significance and the origin of this approach to family. In most cultures, men are dominant, and women and children have the status of property. In the historic Christian culture of America, men and women have equal worth though they play different roles. When this image of father is neglected or absent, social development is challenged, and there is a tendency to ignore the concepts of justice and right and wrong. Both images together help to form the moral conscience of the child and provide goals, self-government, and moral standards.

Simply put, God made men and women different for good reasons. His ideal assigns one man and one woman to each other and gives each child a unique man and woman for the development of that child.

When society tries to take the role of the parent, it does not provide more and better resources for the child; it robs the child of the roles of mother and father in his or her life.

THE BIBLE MODEL FOR THE HOME

The Biblical perspective on the home is simple and often repeated. A husband is expected to provide his wife and children spiritual leadership, physical sustenance, and protection. A wife is expected to follow her husband's leadership and provide him with emotional support. Ephesians 5:22-33 reads:

22 Wives, submit yourselves unto your own husbands, as unto the Lord.

23 For the husband is the head of the wife, even as Christ is the head of the church: and he is the saviour of the body.

24 Therefore as the church is subject unto Christ, so let the wives be to their own husbands in every thing.

25 Husbands, love your wives, even as Christ also loved the church, and gave himself for it;

26 That he might sanctify and cleanse it with the washing of water by the word,

27 That he might present it to himself a glorious church, not having spot, or wrinkle, or any such thing; but that it should be holy and without blemish.

28 So ought men to love their wives as their own bodies. He that loveth his wife loveth himself.

29 For no man ever yet hated his own flesh; but nourisheth and cherisheth it, even as the Lord the church:

30 For we are members of his body, of his flesh, and of his bones.

31 For this cause shall a man leave his father and mother, and shall be joined unto his wife, and they two shall be one flesh.

32 This is a great mystery: but I speak concerning Christ and the church.

33 Nevertheless let every one of you in particular so love his wife even as himself; and the wife see that she reverence her husband.

The basic roles of the husband and wife are also described in I Peter 3:1-7:

1 Likewise, ye wives, be in subjection to your own husbands; that, if any obey not the word, they also may without the word be won by the conversation of the wives;
2 While they behold your chaste conversation coupled with fear.
3 Whose adorning let it not be that outward adorning of plaiting the hair, and of wearing   of gold, or of putting on of apparel;
4 But let it be the hidden man of the heart, in that which is not corruptible, even the ornament of a meek and quiet spirit, which is in the sight of God of great price.
5 For after this manner in the old time the holy women also, who trusted in God, adorned themselves, being in subjection unto their own husbands:
6 Even as Sara obeyed Abraham, calling him lord: whose daughters ye are, as long as ye do well, and are not afraid with any amazement.
7 Likewise, ye husbands, dwell with them according to knowledge, giving honour unto the wife, as unto the weaker vessel, and as being heirs together of the grace of life; that   your prayers be not hindered.

The Bible also communicates to parents that their care for their children is the key to their future happiness. The Book of Proverbs in particular gives much counsel regarding the family:

- Proverbs 10:1 says, "The proverbs of Solomon. A wise son maketh a glad father, but a foolish son is the heaviness of his mother."
- Proverbs 10:5, "He that gathereth in summer is a wise son: but he that sleepeth in harvest is a son that causeth shame."
- Proverbs 15:20, "A wise son maketh a glad father: but a foolish man despiseth his mother."

- Proverbs 19:13, "A foolish son is the calamity of his father: and the contentions of a wife are a continual dropping."
- Proverbs 23:24-25, "The father of the righteous shall greatly rejoice: and he that begetteth a wise child shall have joy of him. Thy father and thy mother shall be glad, and she that bare thee shall rejoice."
- Proverbs 28:7, "Whoso keepeth the law is a wise son: but he that is a companion of riotous men shameth his father."

The greatest investment that parents can make in their own future is the investment they make in developing the character of their children.

PARENTAL RESPONSIBILITIES

These four statements summarize the Biblical principles for parents in the character development of their children:

- Parents must properly teach and train their children.
- Parents must correct their children when they are wrong.
- Parents must discipline their children (with a rod) when correction does not work.
- Parent need to treat their children with love and respect (not provoking them to wrath).

The following passages teach one or more of these principles:

- *Deuteronomy 6:6-7, "And these words, which I shall command thee this day, shall be in thine heart: And thou shalt teach them diligently unto thy children, and shalt talk of them when thou sittest in thine house, and when thou walkest by the way, and when thou liest down, and when thou risest up."*
- *Proverbs 3:12, "For whom the LORD loveth he correcteth; even as a father the son in whom he delighteth."*
- *Proverbs 13:24, "He that spareth his rod hateth his son: but he that loveth him chasteneth him betimes."*
- *Proverbs 19:18, "Chasten thy son while there is hope, and let not thy soul spare for his crying."*
- *Proverbs 22:6, "Train up a child in the way he should go: and*

when he is old, he will not depart from it."
- *Proverbs 22:15, "Foolishness is bound in the heart of a child; but the rod of correction shall drive it far from him."*
- *Proverbs 23:13-14, "Withhold not correction from the child: for if thou beatest him with the rod, he shall not die. Thou shalt beat him with the rod, and shalt deliver his soul from hell."*
- *Proverbs 29:15, "The rod and reproof give wisdom: but a child left to himself bringeth his mother to shame."*
- *Ephesians 5:4, "Neither filthiness, nor foolish talking, nor jesting, which are not convenient: but rather giving of thanks."*
- *Colossians 3:21, "Fathers, provoke not your children to anger, lest they be discouraged."*

RESPONSIBILITIES OF CHILDREN

Bible principles about the responsibilities of children to their parents can be summed up this way:

- Children should listen to their parents.
- Children (while still dependent upon their parents) should obey their parents.
- Children should honor their parents.

One or more of these principles is in each of the following passages:
- *Exodus 20:12, "Honor thy father and thy mother: that thy days may be long upon the land which the LORD thy God giveth thee.*
- *Proverbs 1:8-9, "My son, hear the instruction of thy father, and forsake not the law of thy mother: For they shall be an ornament of grace unto thy head, and chains about thy neck."*
- *Proverbs 4:1, "Hear, ye children, the instruction of a father, and attend to know understanding."*
- *Proverbs 4:10, "Hear, O my son, and receive my sayings; and the years of thy life shall be many."*
- *Proverbs 6:20, "My son, keep thy father's commandment, and forsake not the law of thy mother."*
- *Proverbs 13:1, "A wise son heareth his father's instruction:*

but a scorner heareth not rebuke."
- *Proverbs 23:22, "Hearken unto thy father that begat thee, and despise not thy mother when she is old."*
- *Ephesians 6:1-3, "Children, obey your parents in the Lord: for this is right. Honour thy father and mother; which is the first commandment with promise. That is may be well with thee, and thou mayest live long on the earth."*
- *Colossians 3:20, "Children, obey your parents in all things, for this is well pleasing unto the Lord."*

During the 40-year Culture War against historic Christianity, nothing has been under more furious attack than the Christian concept of the family. The new paganism despises the Biblical roles of husband, wife, father, and mother. They want to redefine the nature of children and teens. They want to replace Christian families with nurturing communities (collectivism and big government).

Nothing can change the fact that God's pattern for the home is effective. The anti-Christian concept of the family just does not work. Children grow up without the proper social development. Homes become a never-ending competition for control. The ability to manipulate replaces precise Biblical standards. Confusion exists instead of focus.

God's ways work!

ATTACKS AGAINST THE FAMILY

"But as he which hath called you is holy, so be ye holy in all manner of conversation; Because it is written, Be ye holy; for I am holy."
(I Peter 1:15-16)

NEW PAGANS' ATTITUDE TOWARD THE HOME

The new pagans take particular offense to the concept of the traditional Christian home. Redefining the family is a major priority in the Culture War as is destroying the traditional Christian concept of the home.

Homosexual activist Roberta Achtenberg has been a leading spokesperson for the attempt to redefine the family. (She also was a high-ranking official is the Clinton administration Department of Housing and Urban Development.) In a 1985 speech she said:

We are building our own tradition of family for which we demand recognition and respect. We are entitled to love and protect our partners, to keep the children we have, to have the children we want, to teach and counsel of the children of others, and to stand against anyone who tries to take these cherished rights away from us.

When Achtenberg was on the San Francisco Task Force for Family Diversity, she suggested this legal definition for the term family:

"A unit of interdependent and interacting persons, related together over time by strong and emotional bonds and/or by ties of marriage, birth, and adoption, whose central purpose is to create, maintain, and promote the social, mental, physical, and emotional development and well being of each of its members."

If this definition of "social and emotional" bonds is given the same status as natural birth, or the legal contracts of marriage and adoption, the entire meaning of family changes. This philosophy is behind the "domestic partner" legislation in San Francisco and other cities. One simply registers as a "partner" and qualifies for all the benefits (legal and financial) of a traditional marriage relationship.

Activists are serious about using the force of government to redefine the family and society and overwhelm anyone who objects.

As a member of the San Francisco Board of Supervisors, Achtenberg sought to have the Boy Scouts of America expelled from the public schools. She asked, "Do we want children learning the values of an organizations that provides character-building exclusively for straight, God-fearing children?"

Most of the supporters of domestic partnership legislation, however are not satisfied with legislation like that in San Francisco. They want to be able to register "multiple domestic partnerships" (three or more people joined together) and they want to remove all age restrcitions, allowing "minors" to be listed in the partnerships.

The Federal Tax Code is another example of the war against the family. For over two decades, the tax code has had a "marriage penalty." Couples who "play by the rules" and help to create a sound family base for society are taxed at a higher rate than those who do not marry.

The prevalence of divorce also provides a major attack on the stability of the American family. Over 40% of all first marriages and over 60% of all second marriages end in divorce. The social stigma against divorce has been virtually lost and most state laws concerning divorce have been liberalized to the point that divorces are now usually easy to obtain.

"Open marriages," "contract marriages," "wife-swapping," and "living together" have all become part of American culture. All have weakened the role of the traditional American family in our culture. As George Santayana observed, "The chief aim of liberalism seems to be to liberate men from their marriage vows."

The "women's liberation" or militant feminist movement is also an attack on the traditional family. In the name of freedom, women are being set free to function outside the traditional family structure. More emphasis is being placed on the idea of being a "career woman" than on being a mother. However, many "modern" women report that even cultural pressure cannot undo the God-given maternal instinct. After two decades of career preparation many women realize that their "biological clocks" are ticking and opt for "focusing on the family."

For the most part, the women's liberation movement has only set women free from the kind of security (emotional and financial) found in the traditional home.

CHILDREN'S RIGHTS

The concept of "children's rights" is another attack on the traditional family. Though the public spokespeople for "children's rights" usually talk about child abuse (physical and sexual)—an issue that is legitimate—their agenda involves much more than that. They want to empower children against the authority and guidance of their parents. Hillary Rodham Clinton wrote in the Yale Law Review in 1979:

Decisions about motherhood and abortion, schooling, cosmetic surgery, treatment of venereal disease, or employment, and others where the decision or lack of one will significantly affect the child's future should not be made unilaterally by parents. Children should have a right to be permitted to decide their own future if they are competent.

GOVERNMENT CONTROL OF CHILDREN

There is a difference between saying that parents have responsibilities (seeing that their children are secure from physical and sexual abuse) and saying that children have rights. Liberals want the government to have the final say over children and see biological parents as only "caretakers" for "government-owned" children.

The assertion of government control over education is another attack on the authority of the home. This was the first (and the most widely successful) transfer of parental power over to the government. As more and more parents are reclaiming control over the education of their children through private schools and homeschools, a growing open tension exists between government agencies and parents. As Thomas Sowell so well puts it, the question is "Whose children are these?" Too often, the state is willing to claim the children as its own.

The assertion of welfare agency control and authority over families has become another source of attack on the family. What began as the government helping in emergency cases (neglect, abuse, etc.) has often become an exertion of control. Local governments (or even individual welfare agents and case workers) have been known to classify Biblical discipline as child abuse or to label basic Christian teaching as "mental abuse." Christians can expect many legal battles over these issues.

The glorification of single life and even single parenthood is also an attack on the traditional family. The Dan Quayle/"Murphy Brown"/family values debate is an illustration of the controversy. Situation comedies (sit-coms) that once illustrated traditional values are now used to promote anti-traditional family ideas. Even unmarried teen mothers are sometimes told by social workers that single motherhood is no problem and that it is better than adoption.

Adoption laws have been changed to make adoption harder and to limit the rights and security of adoptive parents. This happens because so many government agencies are pro-abortion instead of being pro-adoption. Only recently has there been any government support of adoptive parents.

Massive government pro-abortion and pro-homosexuality campaigns are, of course, attacks on the traditional family. Exalting choice above responsibility is the opposite of the attitude that builds strong families.

George Gilder summed up the importance of this attack on the family in his book Sexual Suicide:

Marriage attaches males to families, the source of community, individuality, and order in a free society. As we are increasingly discovering in our schools, prisons, mental hospitals, and psychiatric offices, the family is the only agency that can be depended upon to induce truly profound and enduring changes in its members. The family is the only institution that works on the deeper interior formations of human character and commitment. Thus it is the only uncoercive way to transform individuals, loose in social time and space . . . into voluntary participants in the nurture of society.

God's way works best.
It always has and always will!

MILITANT FEMINISM

"The aged women likewise, that they be in behaviour as becometh holiness, not false accusers, not given to much wine, teachers of good thinks; That they may reach the young women to be sober, to love their husbands, to love their children, To be discreet, chaste, keepers at home, good, obedient to their own husbands, that the word of God be not blasphemed." (Titus 2:3-5)

"Freedom for women cannot be without the abolition of marriage," wrote Sheila Craven, feminist author.

This incredible statement was made by the National Organization for Women in 1988: "The simple fact is, every woman must be willing to be recognized as a lesbian to be fully feminine."

The following is a quote from The Document: *A Declaration of Feminism*:

All of history must be rewritten in terms of the oppression of women. We must go back to ancient female religions (like witchcraft) . . . Marriage has existed for the benefit of men and has been a legally sanctioned method of control over women . . . The end of the institution of marriage is a necessary condition for the liberation of women. Therefore, it is important for us to encourage women to leave their husbands and not live individually with men . . . Now we know it is the institution that has failed us and we must work to destroy it . . . With the destruction of the nuclear family must come a new way of looking at children. They must be seen as the responsibility of an entire society rather than individual parents.

The militant feminist movement is at war with the Christian concept of family and the distinction in roles between men and women. The modern militant feminist movement of the last century (which focused on the right of women to vote) or even the women's rights movement of the 1970's (which focused on equal pay for equal work and changes in inheritance laws). The militant feminist movement demands the right to remake society. Encyclopaedia Britannica defines the women's liberation movement this way:

> *One aim of the movement's activities has been to demonstrate to women that they need not be satisfied with their traditional maternal and housekeeping functions and that they can participate equally with men in every sphere of life.*

In his book *The Way Things Ought to Be,* radio talk show host Rush Limbaugh describes feminism this way:

> *Unfortunately, feminism is another of those vehicles which attempt [sic] to transport unpopular liberalism into mainstream society. Leftist extremists have finally recognized the fact that they are unable to sell their inimical ideas to society as a whole. Cleverly, they have decided to repackage those ideas in more politically palatable gift wrapping, and feminism is one of those packages. After all, who can be opposed to equality for women, which is the way to feminist leadership chooses to phrase the question. Admittedly, the phenomenon of the feminist movement is far too complex to describe it simply as a group of liberal women who have donned a disguise for the purpose of attacking American values, capitalism, and our form of government—although that is certainly part of it. The movement is also driven by women who are angry—very angry, for a number of reasons—with their particular lot in life. Many of the women who have risen to leadership ranks in the movement are man-haters. They are not seeking equal pay for equal work on behalf of their so-called women constituency. They are at war with traditional American values and fundamental institutions such as marriage and the American family.*

In order to portray women as victims, some feminists have resorted to myths. In *Revolution from Within*, the famous feminist leader, Gloria Steinem, reported that 150,000 females were dying in America each year from anorexia. (This was the fault of men; they were to be blamed for preferring slimmer females.) In reality, the National Center for Health Statistics reported 101 deaths from anorexia in 1983 and 67 in 1988.

Many feminists try to portray violence against women as the norm in traditional homes. Gloria Steinem wrote:

Patriarchy requires violence or the subliminal threat of violence in order to maintain itself . . . The most dangerous situation for a woman is not an unknown man in the street, or even the enemy in wartime, but a husband or lover in the isolation of their own home.

Throughout 1991, -92, and -93, numerous references were made to a March of Dimes report showing that domestic violence was responsible for more birth defects than all other causes. But the March of Dimes says there is no such report. Other feminists have reported that "Super Bowl Sunday" is the worst day for domestic violence. Supposedly, football brings out the beast in men! However, there are absolutely no increases reported anywhere to back up this claim. Much of the militant feminist movement depends upon "vain deceit."

In 1987, the "Danvers Statement," a report developed by a group of evangelical leaders, was designed to summarize the Bible's teaching on the roles of men and women and to provide a Biblical perspective on the militant feminist movement. It reads as follows:

1. *Both Adam and Eve were created in God's image, equal before God as persons and distinct in their manhood and womanhood.*
2. *Distinctions in masculine and feminine roles are ordained by God as part of the created order, and should find an echo in every human heart.*
3. *Adam's headship in marriage was established by God before the Fall, and was not a result of sin.*
4. *The Fall introduced distortions into the relationships between men and women. —In the home, the husband's loving, humble headship tends to be replaced by domination or passivity; the wife's intelligent, willing submission tends to be replaced*

by usurpation or servility. —In the church, sin inclines men toward a worldly love of power or an abdication of spiritual responsibility, and inclines women to resist limitations on their roles or to   neglect the use of their gifts in appropriate ministries.

5.   *The Old Testament, as well as the New Testament, manifests the equally high value and dignity which God attached to the roles of both men and women. Both Old and New Testaments also affirm the principle of male headship in the family and in the covenant community.*

6. *Redemption in Christ aims at removing the distortions introduced by the curse.—In the family, husbands should forsake harsh or selfish leadership and grow in love and care for their wives; wives should forsake resistance to their husbands' authority and grow in willing, joyful submission to their husbands' leadership. —In the church, redemption in Christ gives men and women an equal share in the   blessings of salvation; nevertheless, some governing and teaching roles within the church are restricted to men.*

7.   *In all of life, Christ is the supreme authority and guide for men and women, so that no earthly submission—domestic, religious, or civil—ever implies a mandate to follow a human authority into sin.*

8. *In both men and women, a heartfelt sense of call to ministry should never be used to set aside Biblical criteria for particular ministries.   Rather, Biblical teaching should remain the authority for testing our subjective discernment of God's will.*

9.   *With half the World's population outside the reach of indigenous evangelism; with countless other lost people in those societies that have never heard the gospel; with the stresses and miseries of sickness, malnutrition, homelessness, illiteracy, ignorance, aging, addiction, crime, incarceration, neuroses, and loneliness, no man or woman who feels a passion from God to make His grace known in word and deed need ever live without a fulfilling ministry for the glory of Christ and the good of this fallen world.*

10. *We are convinced that a denial or neglect of these principles*

will lead to increasingly destructive consequences in our families, our churches, and the culture at large.

Titus 2:3-6 demonstrates the special role that God has designed for women to play:

3 The aged women likewise, that they be in behaviour as becometh holiness, not false accusers, not given to much wine, teachers of good things;
4 That they may teach the young women to be sober, to love their husbands, to love their children,
5 To be discreet, chaste, keepers at home, good, obedient to their own husbands, that the word of God be not blasphemed.
6 Young men likewise exhort to be sober minded.

It is amazing that some who claim to speak for women feel that femininity is inferior and that they must be masculine to be equal to men. Historic Christianity exalts the God-given role for women!

In the 1830's, during the height of America's Christian culture, Alexis de Tocqueville wrote in *Democracy in America*:

In no country has such constant care been taken as in America to trace two clearly distinct lines of action for the two sexes and to make them keep pace one with the other, but in two pathways which are always different. American women never manage the outward concerns of the family, or conduct a business, or take a part in political life; nor are they, on the other hand, ever compelled to perform the rough labor of the fields, or to make any of those laborious exertions which demand the exertion of physical strength. No families are so poor as to form an exception to this rule. If, on the one hand, an American woman cannot escape from the quiet circle of domestic employments, she is never forced, on the other, to go beyond it. Hence it is, that the women of America, who often exhibit a masculine strength of understanding and a manly energy, generally preserve great delicacy of personal appearance, and always retain the manners of women, although they sometimes show that they have the hearts and minds of men.

Nor have the Americans ever supposed that one consequence of democratic principles is the subversion of marital power, or the confusion of the natural authorities in families. They hold that every association must have a head in order to accomplish its object, and that the natural head of the conjugal association is man. They do not therefore deny him the right of directing his partner; and they maintain that, in the smaller association of husband and wife, as well as in the great social community, the object of democracy is to regulate and legalize the powers that are necessary, and not to subvert all power.

This opinion is not peculiar to one sex, and contested by the other; I never observed that the women of America consider conjugal authority as a fortunate usurpation of their rights, nor that they thought themselves degraded by submitting to it. It appeared to me, on the contrary, that they attach a sort of pride to the voluntary surrender of their own will, and make it their boast to bend themselves to the yoke—not to shake it off.

2016
MODERN FAMILY MISNOMER

Dr. Doug Levesque

Father Knows Best has somehow been replaced by *Modern Family*. The Biblical and natural nuclear family comprised of father, mother, and children has been undermined by wholesale divorce, remarriage, step families, and multicultural acceptance. While great sympathies can be had for broken families, and there are positive examples of "second" family experiences, the normal definition of a family has been transformed into any combination of people living together under the auspice of family. Sometimes very tragic circumstances lead to very little choice in living arrangements, but the circumstantial family must be delineated from the Biblical family for principle's sake. The culture depends upon it. Indeed the greatest catalyst to America's dark transformation has been this assault upon the family. It started in the garden of Eden when Adam somehow failed to protect Eve from the devil's lie, and Eve succumbed to pretense of superiority over God, and Adam. When divine order was usurped it resulted in the catastrophe called the fall of mankind. It is indeed a grace that Jesus saves us from this state of guilt. He can also reconcile broken families and heal nations, but we must revere again, the holy Word and will of God, especially concerning the ideal notion of what a family is.

The American Broadcasting Corporation is not the first company to peddle the wares of an alternative family. Whether sold as a comedy or drama, the proper family has been mocked for decades. Sometimes the jest would be a portrayal of naughty children as funny, or the role of bumbling dad as cute. The emotion of a single mother, or good wife gone bad added fodder to the national conversation through the media of television. Divorcee's and step parents were normalized through Hollywood charms and New York values. As America laughed at these portrayals we displayed a soft acceptance of our cultural slide. When we shed a tear for the adulterer or sympathized with the teen rebel lines were crossed in our national psyche. Was America following the lead of movie characters or was the silver screen just magnifying an underlying fact of society's ills? Blaming media moguls sounds right, but churches and Christians must take their fair share of the blame. When pulpits quit preaching the absolute definition of marriage and family, when the pews filled up with divorced persons who were almost championed, when re-marriages were being celebrated by excuse laden sermons, defenders of traditional marriage began to partner with cultural villains

Consider the premise of ABC's show Modern Family as defined on Wikipedia:

"Modern Family revolves around three different types of families (nuclear, step- and same-sex) living in the Los Angeles area who are interrelated through Jay Pritchett and his children, Claire Dunphy (née Pritchett) and Mitchell Pritchett. Patriarch Jay is remarried to a much younger woman, Gloria Delgado Pritchett (née Ramirez), a passionate Colombian with whom he has a baby son, Fulgencio (Joe) Pritchett; and a son from Gloria's previous marriage, Manny Delgado. Jay's daughter Claire was a homemaker, but has returned to the business world; she is married to Phil Dunphy, a real-estate agent and self-professed "cool Dad". They have three children- Haley Dunphy, a stereotypical ditzy teenage girl; Alex Dunphy, a nerdy, smart middle child; and Luke Dunphy, the off-beat only son. Jay's lawyer son Mitchell and his husband Cameron Tucker have an adopted Vietnamese daughter, Lily Tucker-Pritchett. As the name suggests, this family represents a modern-day family and episodes are comically based on situations which many families encounter in real life."

This multicultural and often vulgar TV sitcom does not hide the fact that it indeed mocks the wholesome rendition of a family in order to celebrate the broken, confused and sodomite renditions. The personal pains of such living are hidden, the national side effects are not discussed, and the resultant damages are not even existent in ABC's world. Add to this strange doctrine of family, twisted slants on news coverage, bizarre children's cartoons, violent and pornographic dramas with the result being a modern family that is doomed and surrounded with no hope. The Bible offers a better picture, a more realistic hope, and a society that can abound. Indeed America has always been exceptional compared with European and Asiatic family ideals. We did not start this way. We backslid into it.

The final downward turn into familial darkness will be the UN proposal of the universal "it". This is a Satanic delusion where the whole world is a global family comprised of selfish beings experiencing life however they want to with the consequences being absorbed by the international society. Of course, such a promise is not able to be kept by society. Society, by then, will be given over to the strongman, and no person will then have a real family to stand behind them.

Cling to your family. Embrace the true definition of marriage. Enlist yourself in the defense of proper parenting. Practice enduring love toward your spouse, children and parents. The happiest people in life are Biblically married with children. The most successful culture is one that is filled with such examples.

TRANSFORMATION

8
THE WAR ON MORALITY

TRANSFORMATION

ALCOHOL AND AMERICAN LIFE

"Wine is a mocker, strong drink is raging: and whosoever is
deceived thereby is not wise." (Proverbs 20:1)

It is almost impossible to over-estimate the influence of alcohol in American life. The alcohol industry is a $30 billion-a-year industry in the United States. There is one outlet serving beverage alcohol for every 80 homes in America. Thirty-three percent of Americans are regular drinkers, ten million Americans are labeled as problem drinkers, and another ten million are labeled as alcoholics.

Five percent of our teenagers are daily drinkers, and 37% drink in the course of the average month.

Every year in the United States there are 200,000 deaths directly related to alcohol abuse. Alcohol abuse is involved in:

- 66% of fatal accidents,
- 70% of all murders,
- 41% of assaults,
- 53% of fire deaths,
- 50% of rapes,
- 60% of sex crimes against children,
- 60% of child abuse,
- 56% of fights and assaults in homes,
- 37% of suicides,
- 55% of all arrests,
- 36% of pedestrian accidents,
- 22% of home accidents,
- 45% of drownings,
- 50% of skiing accidents, and
- More admissions to mental hospitals than any other cause.

There are more than 16,000 deaths in alcohol-related traffic accidents every year. This is more deaths yearly than those caused by AIDS or homicide. A fully loaded 747 jet would have to crash every week to create a similar figure for air disasters. Mothers Against Drunk Drivers (MADD) calls drunk driving the nation's most frequently committed violent crime.

Thirty billion dollars is lost to American economic production every year because of the influence of alcohol upon employees. Over $20 billion worth of medical payments every year are generated by alcohol abuse. Fetal alcohol syndrome, cirrhosis of the liver, and other alcohol-generated diseases have become major American medical problems.

WHAT IS ALCOHOL?

Alcohol, the major active ingredient in wine, beer, and distilled liquor, is a natural substance formed by the reaction of fermenting sugar with yeast spores. There are many kinds of alcohol, but the kind in alcoholic beverages is ethyl alcohol—a colorless, inflammable liquid with an intoxicating effect.

Ethyl alcohol is a drug which can produce feelings of well-being, sedation, intoxication, or unconsciousness—depending on the amount and the manner in which it is drunk. Technically, it can also be classified as food since it contains calories; however, it has no nutritional value.

Various alcoholic beverages are produced by using different sources of sugar for fermentation. For instance, beer is made from germinated or malted barley, wine from grapes or berries, whiskey from malted grains, and rum from molasses. Hard liquors—such as whiskey, gin, and vodka—are produced by distillation, which further concentrates the alcohol resulting from fermentation.

The typical alcohol content of common alcoholic beverages is:

- Beer: 4%,
- Wine: 20%, and
- Distilled liquor: 40-50%.

HOW ALCOHOL WORKS IN THE BODY

Unlike other "foods," alcohol does not have to be digested. When an alcoholic beverage is consumed, 20% of the alcohol in it is normally absorbed immediately into the bloodstream through the stomach walls. The other 80% of the alcohol enters the bloodstream almost as fast after being quickly processed through the gastrointestinal tract. After it is consumed, alcohol eventually can be found in all tissues, organs, and secretions of the body. The alcohol immediately acts on the brain's central control areas to slow down or depress brain activity.

A low level of alcohol in the blood, such as would result from sipping one drink—for example, a 12-ounce can of beer—has a mild tranquilizing effect on most people. Although basically a sedative, for many people alcohol seems to act temporarily as a stimulant after the first drink or two. This is due to the fact that alcohol's initial effects are on those parts of the brain affecting learned behavior patterns such as self-control. After a drink or two, this learned behavior may be altered, making one lose learned inhibitions, talk more freely, or feel like the "life of the party." Others may feel aggressive or depressed.

Higher blood alcohol levels depress brain activity to the point that memory, as well as muscle coordination and balance, may be temporarily impaired. Even greater alcohol intake within a relatively short period of time depresses deeper parts of the brain, severely affecting judgment and dulling the senses.

If steady, heavy drinking continues, the alcohol anesthetizes the deepest levels of the brain and can cause coma or death by depressing heart functions and breathing.

HOW DOES ALCOHOL AFFECT THE BRAIN?

The following is quoted from the June, 1970, Reader's Digest article, "Alcohol and Your Brain":

Physiologists have long recognized that many of the familiar effects of drinking are really manifestations of alcohol's effects on our brains. In fact, they have established a direct relationship between the quantity of alcohol we put into our bloodstreams and the area of our brain the alcohol affects. If, for example, a 150-pound man consumes two bottles of beer on an empty stomach, the level of alcohol dissolved in his blood will reach about five hundredths of one percent [.05%]. At this level, the normal activity of the cortex, or outer layer of the brain—particularly in the centers concerned with worry or anxiety—will be affected. The drinker will feel falsely "lifted up," because the inhibitions that usually hold him steady have, in effect, been paralyzed.

If he drinks enough to raise his blood alcohol level to about ten hundredths of one percent [.10%], activity in the motor centers at the back of his brain will be depressed and he'll begin to lose the ability to control his muscles. If his blood alcohol level rises to 20 hundredths of one percent [.20%], the deeper portions of his midbrain will become affected and he'll become increasingly sleepy. Should the level pass one-half of one percent [.50%], the respiratory centers in the lowest part of his brain may become paralyzed and the drinker will quietly pass from stupor to death.

"Sludging" Phenomenon. *Just how alcohol exerts these successive effects on the brain has long mystified physiologists. Over the last three decades, however, increasing numbers of them have come to believe that alcohol acts indirectly upon the brain's various layers by depriving them of the oxygen essential for the functioning of their cells. This theory derives its strong support from the fact that a direct deprivation of oxygen—such as that experienced by mountain climbers or aviators—produces exactly the same sequence of effects as does alcohol. (Numerous studies have shown that as a flier climbs over 9,000 feet, he begins to experience a sense of exhilaration that closely parallels that of a drinker after a cocktail or two. Should he rise above 18,000 feet—without an oxygen mask—his respiratory centers will stop functioning and he will die.)*

Yet only recently has the mystery of how alcohol deprives the brain of oxygen been solved—by a brilliantly simple series of experiments conducted by Prof. Melvin H. Knisely and two young associates, Drs. Herbert A. Moskow and Raymond C. Pennington, at the Medical University of South Carolina. Dr. Knisely's work has long centered upon studies of the blood, and he is recognized throughout the scientific world as one of the outstanding experts on the strange phenomenon known as "blood sludging."

In a normal, healthy individual the heart pumps the blood through a series of ever-smaller arteries until it reaches the network of minute capillaries that spread through every tissue of the body. It is in these tiny, narrow blood vessels that the red cells surround the capillary walls. For reasons not yet completely clear, a large number of disease conditions—from malaria to typhoid fever—bring about the production of a substance that coats the red cells and makes them stick together in   clumps. As these bits of "sludge" reach the capillaries, they pile up into a wad that may entirely plug the capillary. When sludging is extensive and many capillaries become plugged, cells in entire areas of an organ will starve for oxygen.

Highballs and Eyeballs. In most of the body's tissues, of course, it is impossible to observe this sludging directly. But as far back as the early 1940s, Dr. Knisely was illuminating the eyeball, where numerous capillaries lie just below the transparent surface. He thus observed through a microscope all the variations of sludging and capillary-blocking that occur in more than 50 human diseases. For his investigations, he needed a sludge-causing substance that might by administered to a healthy person in precisely controlled amounts; one that would permit him to create, and observe, any desired degree of sludging.

Alcohol proved to be the perfect substance for his purpose. He could give it in controlled quantities to laboratory animals or student volunteers, determine precisely the percentage of alcohol that appeared in the blood and observe by microscope exactly its effect on the eye's capillaries.

One key question remained: Were the capillaries in other organs affected in the same way as the eye's by alcohol-induced sludging? Dr. Pennington gave alcohol to rabbits and then examined a wide range of internal organ tissues. In each test animal he found sludged blood plugging capillaries in every organ and tissue that could be properly illuminated for microscopic study.

The experimenters quickly discovered that they could detect sludging of the blood in the eye capillaries of students who had consumed as little as one large glass of beer. They went on to study every intoxicated person admitted to one private sanitarium over a 17-month period. At the time of each admission, a member of the team would draw a blood sample from which he would later— to avoid prejudicing their observations—determine the patient's blood alcohol concentration. Two of the team would then carefully examine the patient's eye capillaries and record what they saw in detail. They found that with every increase in alcohol in the blood, the number of wads of red cells also increased and the rate of blood flow slowed. In patients with higher blood alcohol levels, they observed an increasing number of fully plugged capillaries. At the highest concentrations, a substantial number of the capillaries had been ruptured, producing microscopic hemorrhages into the neighboring tissues of the eye.

WHY AMERICANS DRINK ALCOHOL

Human nature has a desire to escape from reality and live in a surreal world (where actions have no consequences). Alcohol temporarily provides an escape from reality.

Alcohol is heavily promoted and advertised in our country. It is connected with fun, recreation, being athletic, sexy, successful, and wealthy. Former athletes are never shown being killed in car wrecks on the way home from the bar, living in the gutter, in the hospital dying from cirrhosis of the liver, or unable to remember their own name. The alcohol industry spends billions of dollars a year in "false advertising."

Human weakness, encouraged by false images of liquor created in our society, has made alcohol abuse a major factor in our society.

The Bible is full of warnings about alcohol:

- **Solomon gave a blanket command, setting forth the Biblical principle that all fermented wine is to be avoided.**
  Proverbs 31:4-5: "It is not for kings, O Lemuel, it is not for kings to drink wine; nor for princes strong drink: Lest they drink, and forget the law, and pervert the judgment of any of the afflicted."

- **Solomon says not even to "look" upon wine.** The word look as Solomon used it means "to lust for" or "to desire." He is simply saying that we are to have nothing to do with wine after it has fermented.
  Proverbs 23:31, "Look not thou upon the wine when it is red,

when it giveth his colour in the cup, when it moveth itself aright."

- **Wine is a mocker.**
  Proverbs 20:1, "Wine is a mocker, strong drink is raging: and whosoever is deceived thereby is not wise."

- **Heavy drinking brings poverty.**
  Proverbs 23:21, "For the drunkard and the glutton shall come to poverty: and drowsiness   shall clothe a man with rags."

- **The use of intoxicating wine brings trouble physically and socially.**
  Proverbs 23:29-30, "Who hath woe? who hath sorrow? who hath contentions? who hath   babbling? who   hath   wounds without cause? who hath redness of eyes? They that tarry long at the wine; they that go to seek mixed wine."

- **Intoxicating wine ultimately harms the user.**
  Proverbs 23:32, "At the last it biteth like a serpent, and stingeth like an adder."

- **Beverage alcohol is the companion of immorality and untruthfulness.**
  Proverbs 23:33, "Thine eyes shall behold strange women, and thine heart shall utter perverse things."

- **The urge to drink can be so strong that it overcomes good judgment, making one forget the misery of his last binge.**
  Proverbs 23:35, "They have stricken me, shalt thou say, and I was not sick; they have beaten me, and I felt it not: when shall I awake? I will seek it yet again."

- **When religious leaders indulge in strong drink, they deceive their followers as to the realities of life and the importance of getting right with God while there is time.**
  Isaiah 56:12, "Come ye, say they, I will fetch wine, and we will

fill ourselves with strong drink; and to morrow shall be as this day, and much more abundant."

- **Drinking makes a proud and selfish person.**
  Habakkuk 2:5, "Yea also, because he transgresseth by wine, he is a proud man, neither keepeth at home, who enlargeth his desire as hell, and is as death, and cannot be satisfied, but gathereth unto him all nations, and heapeth unto him all people."

There are dozens of other Biblical warnings about alcohol.

- Genesis 9:20-26; 19:30-38; 27:25
- Leviticus 10:9
- Numbers 6:3
- Deuteronomy 21:30; 29:2-6
- Judges 13
- I Samuel 1; 25
- II Samuel 11:3; 13:28-29
- Esther 1
- Amos 6:6
- Proverbs 4:17; 21:17
- Ecclesiastes 2:3
- Isaiah 5:11-12; 22:13; 24:9; 28:1, 3, 7
- Jeremiah 35
- Habakkuk 2
- Romans 13; 14
- Galatians 5:1

Someone has presented the following version of Psalm 23 for the drunkard:

King Liquor is my shepherd, I shall always want. He maketh me to lie down in the gutters. He leadeth me beside the troubled waters. He destroyeth my soul. He leadeth me in the paths of wickedness for the effort's sake. Yea, I shall walk through the valley of poverty and will fear all evil, for thou, alcohol, art with me. Thy bottle can try to comfort me. Thou strippest the table of groceries in the presence of my family. Thou robbest my head of reason. My cup of sorrow runneth over. Surely alcoholism shall stalk me all the days of my life and I will dwell in the house of the damned forever.

ALCOHOLISM: A SIN OR A DISEASE?

It has become common to refer to alcoholism as a disease unrelated to will-power or morality. In fact, this view of alcoholism as a disease is often contrasted with the concept of drinking and drunkenness as a sin. A promotion by KOALA dated October 4, 1989, says, "Everyone should remember that alcoholism and drug abuse are diseases, not a matter of will power or good or bad."

The following is from a United States Department of Health and Human Services pamphlet from 1981:

Nevertheless, it is often difficult to make the decision to seek help. Most of us have grown up with the notion that an alcoholic person is somehow "weak" or "immoral," and although these false stereotypes are gradually fading, many people still think there is something shameful about acknowledging a drinking problem. In dealing with these feelings, it is important to recognize that you are suffering from an illness, as defined by the American Medical Association, the World Health Organization, and other m a j o r health organizations. Alcoholism is no more sign of weakness than is diabetes or heart disease.

In fact, it is sometimes asserted that a religious concept of alcoholism somehow contributes to the problem of alcoholism and hinders effective treatment. George Wendel, M.D., wrote in the prologue to *Alcoholism: The Genetic Inheritance:*

To the degree that we call a disease by the name of a sin or social problem and to the degree myth, misconception, and misunderstanding surround an illness, recovery is blocked. The myth of alcoholism is that its victims are weak-willed, sinful, and selfish. As if they sought and reveled in their illness. As if they felt no pain. As if they ought to   control themselves.   It is easier to control diarrhea than to assert one's will over alcoholism.

Others, however, question how alcoholism can fit any realistic definition of disease. Helen Calvin, M.D., challenges the "disease concept" of alcoholism with these statements:

Alcoholism is a disease? If so:
- It is the only disease contracted by an act of will.
- It is the only disease that is habit-forming.
- It is the only disease that comes in a bottle
- It is the only disease causing hundreds of thousands of family disruptions.
- It is the only disease promoting crime and brutality.
- It is the only disease contributing to hundreds of thousands of automobile accidents.
- It is the only disease playing a major part in over 50% of the more than 50,000 annual highway deaths.
- It is the only disease which is sold by license.
- It is the only disease that is bought in grocery stores, drug stores, and well-marked retail outlets.
- It is the only disease that is taxed by the government.
- It is the only disease that is necessary for medical doctors to fellowship with one another.
- It is the only disease in which medical support for the disease outweighs any effort to prevent it.
- It is the only disease advocated by almost all the advertising media.
- It is the only disease given as Christmas gifts.
- It is the only disease that has been "legalized" for [sale on] Sunday by our legislators.

THE CASE FOR ABSTINENCE

Avoiding alcohol abuse is simple: practice total abstinence from alcohol. There are several reasons this is such very wise advice:

- The abstainer will never develop emotional dependence on alcohol.

210

- The abstainer does not have to worry about whether or not he has a genetic pre-disposition to alcohol.
- Abstinence is healthier.
- The abstainer never has to worry that his example will lead someone else into a pattern of alcohol abuse.
- Abstinence is the clearest Christian witness and the best encouragement to recovering drunkards.

THE DRUG MENACE

"For God hath not given us the spirit of fear; but of power, and of love, and of a sound mind." (2 Timothy 1:7)

THE SCOURGE OF DRUG USE

During the 40 years that the Culture War has raged, drug use in the United States has increased 3,000%, according to Dr. William Pollin, former director of the National Institute on Drug Abuse.

Americans now spend over $100 billion on illicit drugs yearly. It is estimated that another $100 billion is spent yearly on prevention and treatment costs, drug-related crime, property destruction, and lost productivity. After a drop in drug use in the mid- and late-1980's, American drug use began to rise again in the 1990's. Drug sales are increasing yearly. Drug-related crime is on the increase, costing over $25 billion yearly. Drug use among teens is increasing. Drug production is increasing in many countries with these drugs primarily being aimed at the United States and Western Europe. New drugs are becoming common, while LSD is making a comeback. Cocaine and marijuana are becoming increasingly accepted in American life, and some political leaders have suggested legalization.

Many of the drugs popular now had not even been invented 30 years ago. The most famous and popular illegal drugs in America are marijuana and cocaine. Eight other popular illegal drugs are described in the pamphlet, "Eight More Dangerous Drugs You Should Know About:"

PCP (Phencyclidine)

Commonly known as "killer weed," "green," or "angel dust," PCP can have devastating effects on young people. Usually smoked in tobacco, marijuana cigarettes, or sprinkled on parsley, PCP is sometimes sold on the street as "Super Pot." It is a drug that can distort reality so drastically for users that symptoms can closely resemble mental illness. Users can become violent and destructive towards themselves and others. Death can ultimately result from overdose or accidents that occur while the user is under the influence of the drug. Some abusers have drowned in shallow ponds or burned to death in fires because PCP actually blocked their ability to feel pain.

LSD (lysergic acid diethylamide)

Also a hallucinogen that distorts reality, LSD is most commonly known as "acid." It is a liquid that is usually swallowed, often after having been placed in a sugar cube or on blotter paper. Users can suffer from wide mood swings, and can feel fear, nausea, and other forms of extreme discomfort. Results can be so severe that complete emotional breakdown can occur.

Mescaline

Derived from peyote, a cactus that grows in the southwestern part of the United States, mescaline is a mind-altering hallucinogen. Sometimes called "mesc" or "cactus," mescaline is usually swallowed directly in thin slices or boiled in water, which is then drunk. Users go into a dreamlike state, with heightened sensations and a feeling of unreality. They run the risk of suffering emotional breakdowns.

Barbiturates

Pentobarbital, secobarbital, and amobarbital—all classed as barbiturates—are drugs which have a general depressant effect of the central nervous system of the user. They go under a wide variety of names such as "barbs," "downers," "yellow jackets," "red devils," and "blue devils." Usually swallowed in pill or capsule form, barbiturates calm tensions and relieve anxiety, so they can quickly lead to dependency. Heavy doses can impair judgment, cause drowsiness and confusion, and noticeably slur speech. People with barbiturate dependency should only attempt withdrawal under a doctor's care. Withdrawal from barbiturates can be even more dangerous than withdrawal from heroin. Overdoses can result in death, and the risk is greatly increased when barbiturates are taken with alcohol.

Quaaludes (Methaqualone)

"Ludes," as they are commonly called, produce similar results in the body as barbiturates. Quaaludes produce drowsiness and interfere with mental processes and coordination. Overdoses can lead to unconsciousness, lung and heart failure, and death.

Heroin

Also called "smack," "junk," or "horse," heroin is an extremely addictive drug that usually comes in the form of a white powder that is either injected after dissolving, or sniffed into the nostrils. The drug affects the central nervous system, reduces the ability to feel pain, depresses the respiratory system, and causes drowsiness. Once the user is addicted, withdrawal is terribly difficult. Heroin overdose can lead to coma or death.

Amphetamines

This is the general term used for amphetamine, dextroamphetamine, and methamphetamine—stimulants which affect the central nervous system. They are also called "speed," "uppers," "pep pills," and several other names. Amphetamines are swallowed in pill or capsule form, or injected. Their general effect is exaggerated activity, irritability, and nervousness. An excessive amount may even produce symptoms of paranoia. Hallucinations are common. Some abusers can remain awake continuously for as long as six days . . . but the "crash" that occurs when the drug wears off can be devastating. The danger of suicide exists. Overdoses can result in death.

Inhalants

Substances that are abused by sniffing fall under the category of inhalants. These include gasoline, glue, paint thinner, dry cleaner solution, and others. The central nervous system is affected by the chemical fumes from inhalants. A euphoric high can be produced seconds after sniffing. Abusers can suffer impaired judgment and poor motor coordination. They can become abusive and violently dangerous to themselves and others. Since inhalants are so easy to acquire, they are particularly hard to control. Brain damage and damage to the liver, kidneys, and bone marrow are often the result of prolonged abuse of inhalants. Inhalants may produce irregular heartbeat and death by arrhythmia. Sometimes death by anoxia, or loss of oxygen, can occur.

MARIJUANA

Marijuana is the most widely accepted and used illegal drug in America. It has a long history and has been widely used in the Mideast since at least the fifth century A.D. It is the easiest to produce as it grows in almost every climate. It is also the easiest to produce as it does not require any special equipment. Unfortunately, a lot of inaccurate mythology contributes to the popularity of marijuana. It is widely believed that there are no physical side-effects to marijuana, but this is not true.

Marijuana is a $10 billion dollar industry in the United States. Over 18 million people in America smoke marijuana at least once a month, almost six million use it weekly, according to *The Facts About Drugs* and Alcohol by Mark S. Gold, M.D. According to Dr. Gold, more marijuana is grown for consumption in the United States than soybeans, grapes, lettuce, or tomatoes.

Marijuana is an innocent-looking plant containing a potent active ingredient called Cannabis sativa. This substance is found in a resin taken from the dried, flowering tops and leaves of the female Indian hemp plant. Common names for marijuana include "ganja," "hashish," "Mary Jane," and "pot."

MARIJUANA IS DANGEROUS!

Contrary to the widespread mythology about marijuana, it does involve many harmful side effects. Studies among military personnel in Europe showed that soldiers who used pot had considerable lung damage as well as more frequent cases of acute bronchitis, sinus trouble, and coughs.

There is considerable evidence that marijuana damages the body's basic cellular structure. According to Dr. Gabriel Dahas of Columbia University, pot interferes with the body's production of genetic material which weakens the body's immunity to disease. Dr. Forrest S. Tennant, Jr., director of the University of California Los Angeles drug treatment center, believes that there is a definite relationship between the disruption of the immune system and the development of cancer. Dr. Louis Sonya of St. Dimas Hospital warns that after the first few experiences with pot the DNA in the genes is damaged.

Dr. Walter Lehmann of the Vitamin Youth Foundation warns that breakdown products of marijuana accumulate in the brain tissues and produce a kind of short circuit in the brain. This kind of damage to the brain has been confirmed by Dr. Constandinos J. Miras of the University of Athens in Greece. Bob Greene, national newspaper columnist, made a related observation when commenting on former Beatle [singer] Paul McCartney's arrest for trying to smuggle marijuana into Japan: "He has lost all of his talent and judgment, and his mind has turned to mush. His record albums are Exhibit 'A' in the argument that marijuana will evaporate your soul."

Robert L. DuPont, former director of the National Institute on Drug Abuse said, "I get a very sick feeling in the pit of my stomach when I hear talk about marijuana being safe. Marijuana is a very powerful agent which is affecting the body in very many ways." In July, 1978, in Rheims, France, 41 scientists from three nations testified that one of marijuana's harmful physical side effects is genetic damage to unborn children, damage which is often fatal.

Studies of the University of Texas indicate that marijuana usage reduces the body's ability to enter slow wave sleep (the deepest stages). This greatly reduces a person's ability to rest and refresh his body physically even though he spends hours asleep every night.

COCAINE—THE RICH MAN'S DRUG

Cocaine is also a popular and widely accepted drug in America. It is often the drug of choice among wealthy people in America.

Cocaine-related emergencies rose 167% from 1983 to 1986. Cocaine-related deaths soared 124% during the same period. An estimated 25 million Americans have tried cocaine.

Cocaine comes from the coca plant (not the plant that produces chocolate and not from the coconut tree, as is sometimes alleged.) It is an alkaloid produced in the leaves of the coca plant. Cocaine was originally thought to be a harmless drug; and traces of it were even used in the original version of the soft drink Coca-Cola, but it was removed by 1906.

As medical evidence became more available, it became clear that cocaine was associated with serious medical problems.

Cocaine use interferes with three chemicals found in the brain. These chemicals are called "neurotransmitters," and they act as messengers or bridges between individual nerve cells. They have a natural stimulant effect on the brain. They are normally released only in rare circumstances. Cocaine use causes the brain to be flooded with these chemicals creating the "rush" the drug user feels. Eventually, the brain adjusts to the process and begins to "crave" this stimulation.

HARMFUL SIDE EFFECTS OF COCAINE

This unnatural process can create many harmful side effects. An extreme heart rate, high blood pressure, an increased breathing rate, raised body temperature, nausea, and abdominal pain have all been associated with cocaine use, as have loss of appetite and digestion problems. However, the most serious problems affects the circulatory and respiratory systems causing both serious (and possibly fatal) lung and heart problems.

Since cocaine is often injected by needle, cocaine use is connected with all the common problems associated with using unsanitary needles. In fact, unsanitary needle use (for drugs like cocaine, heroin, and opium) is the second leading cause of the spread of the AIDS virus.

COMMON SYMPTOMS OF DRUG USE

There are several common symptoms of drug use:

- Inflammation of the eyelids and nose is common. The pupils of the eyes are either very wide or very small, depending on the kind of drugs internalized.
- The extremes of energy may be represented. Either the individual is sluggish, gloomy, and withdrawn, or he may be loud, hysterical, and jumpy.
- The appetite is extreme—either very great or very poor. Weight loss may occur.
- The personality suddenly changes; the individual may become irritable, inattentive, and confused, or aggressive, suspicious, and explosive.

- Body and breath odor is often bad. Cleanliness is generally ignored.
- The digestive system may be upset—diarrhea, nausea, and vomiting may occur. Headaches and double vision are also common. Other signs of physical deterioration may include change in skin tone and body stance.
- Needle marks on the body, usually appearing on the arms, are an important symptom. These punctures sometimes get infected and appear as sores and boils.
- Moral values often crumble and are replaced by new, way-out ideas and values.
  (It should be noted that these can be symptoms of other disorders, as well.)

Unfortunately, in the "anything-goes" attitude of the Culture War, some have recommended legalizing drug use. Some have used the argument that since drug use is so wide-spread it might as well be legalized. Others use the argument that no one can say what is right and wrong. But any sense of approval from society in general will send an already epidemic problem to new heights.

If nothing is declared wrong, why are there laws against murder, robbery, speeding, etc.? As great a menace as drugs already are, the menace would greatly expand if society granted full approval.

Despite overwhelming evidence, the mythology surrounding marijuana is being accepted. Voters in several states have approved measures to legalize so-called "medical marijuana."

Because of drug-related crime and public-financed welfare and treatment programs, everyone pays for the drug menace.

It is interesting to note that the need to hide from reality in chemical blindness has increased as the Culture War has increased. The farther man gets from God, the more his inner needs are left unsatisfied.

THE PORNOGRAPHY PLAGUE

"Let thine eyes look right on, and let thine eyelids look straight
before thee." (Proverbs 4:25)

Matthew 6:22-23 says:

*The light of the body is the eye: if therefore thine eye be single, thy
whole body shall be full of light. But if thine eye be evil, thy whole
body shall be full of darkness. If therefore the light that is in thee
be darkness, how great is that darkness!*

The point of this passage is that much of our lifestyle is determined by
how we use our eyes—what we choose to look at. This is why Proverbs
4:25 (a passage about keeping your heart right with the Lord) says, "Let
thine eyes look right on, and let thine eyelids look straight before thee." II
Peter 2:14 warns about people in rebellion towards the Lord having "eyes
full of adultery."

- The United States has become the pornography capital of the
  world.
- Over 400 different pornographic magazines are sold through
  20,000 adult bookstores.
- X-rated cable channels are offered on over 400 cable networks.
- There are more outlets selling and renting pornographic videos
  than there are McDonald's restaurants.
- X-rated videos account for over 14% of the video rental market
  and 25% of video sales. The pornography industry has become an
  $8 billion a year industry in the United States.

The main argument given in favor of pornography is that it is a
"victimless crime"—that it does not hurt anyone. However, research
done by professors from Indiana University, the University of Kentucky,
and the University of Houston was summarized by psychotherapist David
A. Scott to give these nine warnings:

1. Pornography leads to a devaluation and depreciation of the importance of monogamy, and a lack of confidence in marriage as a viable institution.
2. Porn leads to an increased acceptance of premarital and extramarital sexuality, and increased distrust among sexually intimate partners, both married and single.
3. Pornography makes people twice as likely to believe that children are a liability and a handicap, especially female children.
4. Porn leads to diminished satisfaction with the physical appearance and sexual performance of intimate partners.
5. Porn leads to an enhanced sense of importance of sex without emotional involvement.
6. Porn creates an appetite for more unusual and bizarre materials such as those depicting sadomasochism and sexual violence.
7. Initial repulsion and boredom toward porn is over-ridden by engaging in increasingly bizarre sex acts with a greater variety of sexual partners. Such behavior is soon perceived as normal.
8. Porn leads to insensitivity towards victims of sexual violence. Exposure to porn leads to a belief that such materials do not harm even children.
9. Porn is used by pedophiles [child molesters] to lower children's inhibitions to initiate them into specific sexual practices. Adolescents who were sexually molested as children often begin sexually molesting children as young as two or three years of age.

Dr. James Dobson gives these eight warnings about the dangers of pornography:

- Depictions of violence against women are related to violence against women everywhere. The most cursory examination of the material being marketed today makes it clear why that is true. I could not describe the offensiveness of these publications without being pornographic even in this context.
- The use of pornography seems to be addictive and progressive in nature. That is, those who get hooked on sexually explicit material tend to become obsessed by their need. It also interferes with the normal sexual relationship between husbands and wives.

- The river of obscenity which floods our homes has reached the eyes and ears of children! Boys and girls are finding and viewing their parents' X-rated videos and magazines. They are also being bombarded by vile lyrics in rock music on radio, television, and videos. Their morals are being corrupted by R-rated movies which dangerously link sex and violence. They are being shocked and titillated by obscenity on dial-a-porn phone lines. And on and on it goes. As a direct consequence, psychotherapists are seeing increasing numbers of disturbed young patients who may never enjoy healthy attitudes about sex.
- Pornography is degrading and humiliating to women [who are] deprived of dignity and modesty. Men and boys are purchasers of this material. The entire female gender has reason to feel used and abused by this industry.
- Pornography is often used by pedophiles to soften children's defenses against sexual exploitation. They are stripped of innocence and subjected to brutalities that will be remembered for a lifetime.
- Outlets for obscenity are magnets for sex-related crimes. When an adult bookstore moves into a neighborhood, an array of "support services" typically develops around it. Prostitution, narcotics, and street crime proliferate. Ask anyone who lives near a sex shop. You will hear an immediate protest.
- So-called adult bookstores often become cesspools of disease and homosexual activity. In this day of concern over AIDS and other STD's, it is difficult to understand why local health departments have refused to close down these foul businesses.
- Finally, pornography is damaging to the family in countless ways. We are sexual creatures, and the physical attraction between males and females provides the basis for every dimension of marriage and parenthood. Thus, anything that interjects itself into that relationship must be embraced with great caution.

According to an F.B.I. study, 81% of sex murderers said their biggest sexual interest was pornography (1986 Attorney General's Commission on Pornography). According to the March, 1995, Psychology of Living, 82% of all child molesters admit to trying out or imitating behavior that they saw depicted in pornography.

The 1986 Attorney General's Commission of Pornography warned that:

> *A certain percentage of adolescents whose first sexual experiences are triggered by pornography of violent sex, will develop a fetish, a conditioning, that will associate violence with sex. We are training rapists and murderers with pornography.*

This concern is further explained in the Commission report:

> *The commission heard testimony in Houston for Dr. Victor Cline, Professor of Psychology at the University of Utah, who also cites the work of Dr. James McGaugh at the University of California, Irvine, on memory. The "research suggests that experiences at times of emotional (or sexual) arousal get locked in the brain by the chemical epinephrine and become virtually impossible to erase. These memories, very vivid and graphic in nature, keep intruding themselves back onto the mind's memory screen serving to stimulate and arouse the viewer," he said. "This may help explain pornography's addicting effect. These powerfully sexually arousing experiences become vivid memories which the mind 'replays' stimulating the child again and again suggesting the need for further stimulation . . . Most evidence suggests that all sexual deviations and their variations are learned behavior. I know of no good evidence anywhere suggesting genetic transmission of sexual pathology."*

Medical doctor Elizabeth Holland warns about the relationship between pornography and child molestation:

> *There exist in our nation . . . those men and women who have been abused, who have been damaged for life by those who feed on pornography . . . who have a sickness, who need to feed on dirty pictures and pornography. And when touching pictures and fantasizing and looking no longer satisfies these people's insatiable appetites, then they move. And they move to love children. I know because I treat these children.*

In his book *Exploding the Myths That Could Destroy America*, Dr. Irwin Lutzer makes this statement about the influence of pornography on marriage:

Those who are addicted to pornography soon find that the normal relationship between a man and a woman in marriage loses its appeal. The only way the marriage can be sustained, if at all, is through bizarre forms of sexuality, often against the objection of one of the partners. Even then one must move on to multiple sexual partners to continue the wild goose chase that inevitably ends in the wilderness of guilt, frustration, and emptiness. As John Drakeford wrote in an article entitled "The Sexual Mirage," pornography has "strained the traditional relationship between husband and wife. Pornography presents an unreal view of human sexuality. It is an exaggerated, fantasized view. If a husband or wife see this perspective as the norm, it is going to do a great deal of damage to the sexual relationship." One-half of all divorces take place because of adultery; often the adultery was encouraged by pornography.

God is very careful to warn His children about moral purity. Matthew 5:27-28 says, "Ye have heard that it was said by them of old time, Thou shalt not commit adultery: But I say unto you, That whosoever looketh on a woman to lust after her hath committed adultery with her already in his heart." I Thessalonians 4:3-7 reads:

3 For this is the will of God, even your sanctification, that ye should abstain from fornication:
4 That every one of you should know how to possess his vessel in sanctification and honour;
5 Not in the lust of concupiscence, even as the Gentiles which know not God:
6 That no man go beyond and defraud his brother in any matter: because that the Lord is the avenger of all such, as we also have forewarned you and testified.
7 For God hath not called us unto uncleanness, but unto holiness.

Finally, II Timothy 2:22 instructs, "Flee also youthful lusts: but follow righteousness, faith, charity, peace, with them that call on the Lord out of a pure heart."

The importance of moral purity is why the patriarch Job said, "I made a covenant with mine eyes; why then should I think upon a maid?" (Job 31:1)

In addition to God's instructions, His judgments are also very evident. It is interesting to note how the 1993 California earthquake hit the pornography industry. The epicenter of the earthquake was in the northern San Fernando Valley. In this valley are the communities of Chatsworth, Northridge, and Canoga Park. There were more than 70 pornography-producing companies in this area. They produce more than 95% of the pornographic videos made in the United States every year. Every one of them was damaged.

GAMBLING AND THE PROTESTANT WORK ETHIC

"Wealth gotten by vanity shall be diminished: but he that gathereth by labour shall increase." (Proverbs 13:11)

"He that tilleth his land shall have plenty of bread: but he that followeth after vain persons shall have poverty enough. A faithful man shall abound with blessings: but he that maketh haste to be rich shall not be innocent." (Proverbs 28:19-20)

THE SOMETHING-FOR-NOTHING URGE

Best-selling author Robert Ringer comments on how governments exploit human weakness by legalizing gambling in his book *Million Dollar Habits:*

The something-for-nothing urge is part of the human psyche and based on sheer self-delusion. To one degree or another, we all possess the something-for-nothing urge. It is the urge that has made gambling a national pastime in most countries throughout history. State governments understand this all too well. They have increasingly appealed to the gambling urge to appropriate more dollars from citizens by enticing them into state-sponsored lotteries. Of course, this is in addition to the take that most states skim off the top from wagering at horse and dog tracks, jaialai frontons, and gambling casinos. With such an explicit stamp of approval, it's little wonder that a recent survey estimated that as many as 4.2 million Americans may be addicted to gambling.

In reality, compulsive gambling is a serious mental illness that endangers both the compulsive gambler and those around him. It involves the ultimate self-delusion—the b e l i e f that something for nothing is possible, which, of course, is a totally false perception of reality and brings about negative results.

The "Protestant Work Ethic" is summed up in II Thessalonians 3:10,

"For even when we were with you, this we commanded you, that if any would not work, neither should he eat." For a long time in America, every government program was expected to support this principle. This became known as the Protestant Work Ethic. As long as this was government policy, reinforced by most of our culture, the American economy was always booming.

However, under our new approach to culture, the Protestant work ethic has come under attack from the government in two basic ways:

- The welfare system and
- Government-sponsored gambling.

Government agencies (usually state governments) spend hundreds of millions of dollars every year to convince citizens that gambling is the way to prosperity.

The only defense ever given for legalized, government-owned or licensed gambling establishments is that they are a supposed financial boon for local communities and county and state governments. But there are other considerations. The late Senator Estes Kefauver said:

Gambling produces nothing and adds nothing to the economy or society of our nation. Americans will be in a bad way if we ever have to resort to taxing crime and immorality for the purpose of raising revenue to operate our institutions.

Gambling does not create any wealth; it only redistributes it. And, it usually redistributes it in a way that harms society in general. One study reported that gambling institutions brought in an average income of $4.35 per adult in the community. But a Maryland study indicated that increased crime, increased welfare costs, and dealing with gambling addicts was costing the average adult between $13 and $23 in taxes every year!

The government entity that erodes the Protestant Work Ethic erodes its own income base. People can debate whether or not Christianity is a good idea, but it is those who practice the Christian work ethic that earn taxable income.

One Maryland study showed that one-third of the families with annual incomes of less than $10,000 spend one-fifth of their incomes on lotteries. And, it was their government who spent millions of dollars convincing them that the lottery was their ticket to the "Lifestyles of the Rich and Famous."

Government should reward self-reliance, hard work, and initiative. Government should not put its stamp of approval on the plans of millionaire developers to take advantage of human weakness. And, it should not directly exploit the weakness of its citizens.

Columnist William Safire said:

Gambling promotion has become a key to state budget-balancing. Card-carrying right-wingers are not supposed to mind taxing the poor, but really soaking the poor—as this excessively regressive taxation does—sticks in my craw.

Why? Because it is wrong for the state to exploit the weakness of its citizens. It is the most unfair and painful form of "painless" taxation. The money isn't coming from a few big bookies and coupiers, but from the pockets of millions.

And gambling taxation feeds on itself. We cannot give up the state income from betting, say legislators who feel guilty about pretending that gambling is good, because the states have become dependent on the money, or because other states will use casinos to lure their tourism. They have become as hooked on gambling as a source of revenue as any compulsive gambler betting the milk money.

2016:
MODERN TECHNOLOGICAL
SEXUAL PERVERSIONS

Dr. Doug Levesque

The topic is dreadful. The title is distasteful. The reality is worst of all. America is in a deep dark tunnel of wicked sexual gratification. "Lovers of pleasures, more than lovers of God" is a true description of modern American culture. Aberrant sexual practices used to be universally rejected and even outlawed. As society turned to darkness, these sensual wants were marketed, legalized and proclaimed profitable. Today, the Internet, wireless technology and smart phones can promote and deliver the very worst smut 24 hours a day, 7 days a week. Perverted souls a generation ago had to make great efforts and take great risks to satisfy their lusts. Modernity has delivered it to any desiring person with ease. Even the great availability of sensuality and its' products is not the end game. Today, the tech sector, entertainment industry, marketing and manufacturing communities are evil coalitions of perversion. New frontiers never before even considered by Americans are being explored with passionate fervor.

Gender neutrality is a sad excuse for the LGBTQ adherents. These perverts have gone from the lie of "I am born gay" to a new jurisprudence and vocabulary of "gender identity". Public education is now spreading this evil teaching that the gender assigned at birth is based on mistaken ideas that reproductive parts and DNA determine male or femaleness. Hence, children are now told that their "gender identity" does not have to be in agreement with their "gender assignment" on their birth certificate. Some pre-birth psychology is given credit for each person's idea of their own sexuality. Furthermore, and to their shame, the new sex educators are adding the notion that one's' "gender attraction" can be unique from all other factors. "Gender neutrality" is the goal for such teachers. So apparently, the transformation into darkness includes an existence where your DNA produces a male, your birth certificate is potentially oppressive and wrong, your identity is confused, and your attraction is your own.

Such confusion is ridiculously being touted as education policy, when in reality it is public recruitment into the homosexual lifestyle.

3D and virtual reality technologies are collaborating with the porn industry to sell fantastic lies. Who needs a husband or wife when you can experience the intimacies of marriage with . . . someone else's imposed dreams and imaginations? Sadly, the youth of America are being sold a manufactured idea that is quite opposite of God's ideal for the marriage bed. Such practices can become addictive, and certainly ruin the real expression of Biblical sexuality for a lifetime. This is a dangerous development indeed. The Bible speaks of women leaving natural affections and even forsaking motherhood. That day is certainly upon us and is defining America's cultural future. It can be sadly forecast that the next stop on this virtual reality experience will be something like a collaborative video game of sex where the character is immersed in unrealistic fantasies. This will quickly turn to dissatisfaction, evolve into real sexual violence and make people mad or even suicidal. The prospects make one want to flee to the wilderness in order to escape.

New robotic breakthroughs are being exploited for sensual markets. These new markets will try to assuage guilt by removing the need for pornography, rape, and prostitution. Of course, such reasoning is foolish. In addition to the perverseness of robotic sex, a godlike demeanor is being built up in mankind. The culture of "ye shall be as gods" is not new, but the ability for every man and woman to experience the euphoria of a Nimrod like power over their own creations will certainly bring a society ready for the Antichrist. Swapping robotic slaves is the new Babel and our culture is racing toward it unaware of the towers' sure fall. Such confusion! Clear voices of Biblical truth must proclaim the love of Christ and at the same time the justice of God against sin. The price for faithfulness will not just be a perceived "missing out" on futuristic sensuality, but perhaps a backlash of national hatred not experienced since the grand persecutions of Rome.

Psa 119:9, "Wherewithal shall a young man cleanse his way? by taking heed thereto according to thy word."

TRANSFORMATION

9
THE WAR ON FREEDOM

TRANSFORMATION

GUN CONTROL AND FREEDOM

"But know this, that if the goodman of the house had known in what watch the thief would come, he would have watched and would not have suffered his house to be broken up." (Matthew 24:43)

Thomas Jefferson said, "When governments fear the people there is liberty. When people fear the government there is tyranny."

The issue of gun control has become a battleground in the Culture War for several reasons.

Liberals believe	Conservatives believe
That the availability of guns causes violent crime.	That violent crime is a result of a lack of values.
That society is responsible for protecting people	That a man is responsible for protecting his own family.
That government should be more powerful than the citizens	That the citizens should be more powerful than the government.

THE SECOND AMENDMENT

Much of the debate has to do with the purpose of the Second Amendment which reads:

A well-regulated militia being necessary to the security of a free State, the right of the people to keep and bear arms shall not be infringed.

The much discussed "right to hunt" was only of secondary importance to our Founding Fathers. Even the right to self-defense was not the primary reason for the Second Amendment. The primary reason was to serve as a check on big government. American educator and journalist Noah Webster, commenting on the Second Amendment, said, "The supreme power in America cannot enforce unjust laws by the sword because the whole body of the people is armed and constitutes a force superior to any band of regular troops that can be on a pretense raised in the United States."

American patriot and Virginia Governor Patrick Henry said of the Second Amendment:

> *Guard with jealous attention the public liberty, suspect everyone who approaches that jewel, unfortunately nothing will preserve it but downright force; whenever you give up that force, you are ruined. The great object is that every man be armed.*

In a U. S. Supreme Court decision in 1833, Justice Joseph Story stated:

> *The right of the citizens to keep and bear arms has justly been considered the palladium of the liberties of a republic, since it offers a strong moral check against usurpation and arbitrary power of rulers and will generally, even if these (rulers) are successful in the first instance, enable the people to resist and triumph over them.*

Alexander Hamilton said of the Second Amendment:

> *If the representatives of the people betray their constituents, there is then no recourse left but in the exertion of that original right of self-defense, which is paramount to all positive forms of government.*

Many Americans are wondering if it is a coincidence that those who want to see the government impose a new culture on America are the same people who want gun control.

The Founding Fathers had just ended several years of bloody warfare to replace a tyrannical government with one which protected the rights of the people. During the early days of the War for Independence, the citizens had fought with privately owned guns (the battles of Lexington and Concord, for example). These battles bought the new government time it needed to develop the armed forces necessary to achieve military victory. They were very conscious of the dangers of tyranny and the importance of an armed populace.

Throughout history, tyrants and potential tyrants have feared private ownership of guns. Gun control was one of Adolph Hitler's first programs after being elected in Germany—but before establishing a dictatorship. In 1935, on the day he signed gun control legislation into law in Germany, Adolph Hitler said, "This year will go down in history. For the first time, a civilized nation has full gun registration. Our streets will be safer, our police more efficient, and the world will follow our lead into the future." Of course, Hitler did not admit his real motive for gun control.

In most countries where Communist tyrannies were established, gun control laws preceded the Communist government. When the Communists tried to establish a dictatorship in Afghanistan, they ran into problems. Private gun ownership was widespread there. The Afghanistani people resisted, and the pro-Communists were forced to call for a Russian invasion force. The people fought the Russians with privately owned arms until military equipment arrived from other countries. They fought the Russian armies to a standstill. Eventually the Russians withdrew.

Gun ownership also serves a self-defense purpose. About 75% of all uses of guns in crime-related incidents are defensive uses by crime victims (about 2.4 million incidents annually). Without private gun ownership these citizens would be at the mercy of the most lawless element of society. Actress Kathy Najimy wrote to actor Charlton Heston and asked him, "Dear Charlton, You are a fine, fine actor, but when are you going to put down the guns and join us liberals?" His reply was clear: "When the bad guys put down their guns."

MYTHS OF GUN CONTROL

"But know this, that if the goodman of the house had known in what watch the thief would come, he would have watched and would not have suffered his house to be broken up." (Matthew 24:43)

In order to promote gun control, many myths are promoted.

MYTH 1:

Gun control is the only way that violent crime can be reduced.

No one has yet explained how gun control will take one gun out of the hands of one single criminal who plans a violent crime. There are over 200 million guns available in America, and a violent criminal will simply break the law and obtain and use one anyway.

Actually, guns are used in 400,000 potentially life-saving situations yearly. Thirty-seven thousand lives are taken by guns yearly. Restricting the right to self-defense would only increase the number of deaths yearly. As the famous bumper sticker says, "If guns are outlawed, only outlaws will have guns."

MYTH 2:

More lives are lost in gun accidents than in violent crime activity.

This is an argument without any foundation. In 1991, homicides accounted for 47% of all gun deaths, suicides 48%, and accidents only four percent. Almost all of these accidents could be prevented with greater gun education and, in fact, the number of accidental gun deaths has been dropping consistently since 1980.

MYTH 3:

The Second Amendment was only designed for organized
state militias, not individuals.

In 1788, George Mason, who was primarily responsible for the wording of the Bill of Rights, wrote that the militia should be defined as,

"The whole people except a few public officials." The phrase, "right of the people," in the First Amendment and Fourth Amendment is universally taken to refer to all of the people—as was obviously intended. It should be taken the same way in the Second Amendment.

MYTH 4:

Nations with strict gun control laws have substantially less violent crime than the United States.

In low crime countries like Switzerland, Israel, and New Zealand, guns are more readily available than they are in the United States. Taiwan and South Africa have the strictest gun control laws in the world (imposing capital punishment on those who illegally own guns), but have murder rates almost as high as the United States. Britain has had strict gun control laws since 1920, but violent crime is on the increase. It is true that there is less violent crime in Britain and Japan than there is in the United States, but there was less violent crime in these cultures before they had gun control, as well.

MYTH 5:

Private gun ownership is to blame for the high teen suicide rate in the United States.

In Great Britain and Japan, where there is more gun control and little private gun ownership, teen suicide has risen by 25% in recent years. The teen suicide rate in the United States has remained constant during the same period.

MYTH 6:

Gun control would make our streets safer.

Twenty percent of our homicides occur in just four cities (with just six percent of our population). These cities—New York, Chicago, Detroit, and Washington D.C.—all have strict gun control laws.

In 1982, the Chicago suburb of Evanston, Illinois, adopted the strictest gun control laws in the United States. Also in 1982, the Atlanta suburb of Kennesaw, Georgia, passed a city ordinance that requires heads of households (with a few exceptions) to keep at least one firearm in the house! Since 1982, murder, armed robbery, and aggravated assault have all increased in Evanston. In Kennesaw, incidents of murder, rape, and armed robbery are almost non-existent.

MYTH 7:

Gun registration provides no danger to gun ownership.

In 1967, the New York City Council enacted an ordinance requiring owners of shotguns and rifles to register their guns by make, model, and serial number. They were also required to obtain a permit to possess such weapons. In 1991, the Council outlawed semi-automatic rifles and shotguns. Since the New York police already had records of the owners of such guns, the police were in a position to confiscate these weapons from the private, law-abiding citizens who owned them.

Before World War II, Poland, France, Denmark, Norway, and Czechoslovakia all had gun registration laws. When the Nazis invaded, they simply seized these lists and used them to confiscate privately owned weapons. During the same way, Russia invaded Finland. (Russia had a population of 170 million versus Finland's four million citizens.) Finland had no gun control laws and private ownership of weapons was common. The Finns were able to resist and humiliate the mammoth Russian army.

GOD AND SAM COLT

More than two centuries ago (1764), criminologist Cesare Becaria wrote:

> *[Gun control laws] disarm those only who are neither inclined not determined to commit crimes . . . Such laws make things worse for the assaulted and better for the assailants. They serve rather to encourage than to prevent homicides, for an unarmed man may be attacked with greater confidence than an armed man.*

Some have questioned whether or not the Bible allows the use of physical force for self-defense. Exodus 20:13 clearly says, "Thou shalt not kill." But the Old Testament clearly indicates that this refers to murder. Self-defense was allowed, and an individual could serve as the "avenger of blood" (Numbers 35 and Deuteronomy 19). Civil government carried out capital punishment for at least 11 offenses.

Under Old Testament law, defending your home from intruders and thieves was expected. Exodus 22:2-3 says:

"If a thief be found breaking up, and be smitten that he die, there shall no blood be shed for him. If the sun be risen upon him, there shall be blood shed for him; for he should make full restitution; if he have nothing, then he shall be sold for his theft."

In the New Testament, Matthew 24:43 says, "But know this, that if the goodman of the house had known in what watch the thief would have come, he would have watched, and would not have suffered his house to be broken up."

There should be no question that the radical gun control lobby wants to remove all guns from private citizens. Consider these quotes:

- A December 21, 1993, editorial in the New York Times said: *"Gun violence won't be cured by one set of laws. It will require years of partial measures that will gradually tighten the requirements for gun ownership, and incrementally change expectations about the firepower that should be available to ordinary citizens."*
- A deputy commissioner of the Florida State Health Department was quoted in the Chicago Tribune, November 7, 1993: *"The goal is an ultimate ban on all guns, but we also have to take one step at a time and go for limited access first."*
- Michael K. Beard of the Coalition to Stop Gun Violence was quoted in the December 9, 1993, *issue of the Washington Times: "Our goal is not to allow anybody to buy a handgun. In the meantime, we think there ought to be strict licensing and regulation."*

The cultural and political conflict in the American colonies broke out into a full scale "hot" war after British Governor Thomas Gage tried to confiscate the weapons of the Massachusetts militia. The people would not tolerate this, and they came from all over as individuals and as community militias to fire upon the military column charged with the confiscation of their weapons.

In the "Old West," a common statement was, "God and Sam Colt make all men equal." God created all men equal; the Colt revolver had made it possible for the average man to defend himself against the lawless element of society.

The concepts of self defense, a limited government, and the Second Amendment to the Constitution all go together in a free society.

2016:
HATE CRIME AND
FREEDOM OF THOUGHT

Dr. Doug Levesque

Hate is an emotion. Emotions are internal feelings that sometimes have external expressions. Hate as an internal feeling must answer to God. Hate as an external expression sometimes has to answer to man. Hate as a motive to crime like murder is hard to measure. Even if a person admits he hates someone, the confession may or may not be a clear reflection of what is inside. The current hate crimes legislation now being discussed in society assumes that all internal hate is bad, and that it can be quantified, and that it can be punished. It is proposed that hate as a motive to crime now adds time to any judicial prison sentence. This is a dangerous precedent. It puts emotions under the arbitration of judges. It opens the door for the emotion itself to be criminalized. This is a breach of the freedom of thought or conscience so sacred to American existence. Crime as an act is measurable, quantifiable and has a Biblical precedent to be punished by human and national courts. Crime as an emotion can only be measured by God. Beware whenever men want God-like power.

Hate is Scriptural. God hates. Hate defines what we love. These are difficult realities, especially for non-Christian people. The Bible explains that God is love and that we should love, but it also says that there are things, actions, and even people that God hates. Lovers of God also hate what God hates. We hate the evil way especially when it manifests itself in our own lives. Love and hate are both powerful emotions that once allowed into the heart can have life altering effects. Love can be a dangerous emotion. Consider Song of Solomon 8:6-7,

"Set me as a seal upon thine heart, as a seal upon thine arm: for love is strong as death; jealousy is cruel as the grave: the coals thereof are coals of fire, which hath a most vehement flame. Many waters cannot quench love, neither can the floods drown it: if a man would give all the substance of his house for love, it would

241

utterly be contemned."

Hate is also powerful, but sometimes necessary. Consider also these verses:

- *Psalms 97:10, "Ye that love the LORD, **hate evil**: he preserveth the souls of his saints; he delivereth them out of the hand of the wicked."*
- *Psalms 101:3, "I will set no wicked thing before mine eyes: I hate the work of them that turn aside; it shall not cleave to me."*
- *Psalms 119:104, "Through thy precepts I get understanding: therefore **I hate every false way.**"*
- *Psalms 119:113, "SAMECH. **I hate vain thoughts**: but thy law do I love."*
- *Psalms 119:163, "**I hate and abhor lying**: but thy law do I love."*
- *Psalms 139:21, "Do not **I hate them, O LORD, that hate thee?** and am not I grieved with those that rise up against thee?"*
- *Psalms 139:22, "**I hate them with perfect hatred**: I count them mine enemies."*
- *Proverbs 6:16, "**These six things doth the LORD hate**: yea, seven are an abomination unto him:"*
- *Proverbs 8:13, "**The fear of the LORD is to hate evil**: pride, and arrogancy, and the evil way, and the froward mouth, do I hate."*
- *Ecclesiastes 3:8, "A time to love, and **a time to hate**; a time of war, and a time of peace."*
- *Amos 5:15, "**Hate the evil**, and love the good, and establish judgment in the gate: it may be that the LORD God of hosts will be gracious unto the remnant of Joseph."*
- *Amos 5:21, "**I hate**, I despise your feast days, and I will not smell in your solemn assemblies."*

"Hate crime" concepts prepare the culture to imprison obedient Christians who have committed no actual crime except the admission to an emotion that is sometimes Scriptural. Let it be ultimately said that those that name the name of Christ also have a spiritual ability of the highest order. While there is a time to love and to hate, there is also the high concept of loving beyond hate. Jesus said, in Matthew 5:43-44, "Ye have heard that it hath been said, Thou shalt love thy neighbour, and hate thine enemy. But I say unto you, Love your enemies, bless them that curse you, do good to them that hate you, and pray for them which despitefully use you, and persecute you;" This is not a concept for human courts to decide upon, but for the Lord that knoweth the hearts only.

Freedom of thought, conscience, and expression are American foundations. Crime should be punished, but not the crime of thought, conscience or expression. Consider the writer and observer De Tocqueville on freedom of thought in democracy and yielding to authorities and ideas as a cultural practice in America:

A man who should undertake to inquire into everything for himself, could devote to each thing but little time and attention. His task would keep his mind in perpetual unrest, which would prevent him from penetrating to the depth of any truth, or of grappling his mind indissolubly to any conviction. His intellect would be at once independent and powerless. He must therefore make his choice from amongst the various objects of human belief, and he must adopt many opinions without discussion, in order to search the better into that smaller number which he sets apart for investigation. It is true that whoever receives an opinion on the word of another, does so far enslave his mind; but it is a salutary servitude which allows him to make a good use of freedom.

A principle of authority must then always occur, under all circumstances, in some part or other of the moral and intellectual world. Its place is variable, but a place it necessarily has. The independence of individual minds may be greater, or it may be less: unbounded it cannot be. Thus the question is, not to know whether any intellectual authority exists in the ages of democracy, but simply where it resides and by what standard it is to be measured." — Alexis de Tocqueville, Democracy in America

TRANSFORMATION

10
THE WAR ON FAITH

TRANSFORMATION

NEW AGE RELIGION

"As we said before, so say I now again, If any man preach any other gospel unto you than that ye have received, let him be accursed." (Galatians 1:9)

Every culture is either created by a set of religious beliefs or spawns a set of religious beliefs. For the last 40 years, eastern mystic religions have increased in popularity in the United States. Some have taken an American flavor, using Christian terminology with new eastern mystic definitions. Others maintain their oriental trappings. They are often referred to as the "New Age movement." The New Age movement is fast becoming the religion of the "new American culture."

EASTERN MYSTIC RELIGIONS

Many Americans are curious about the number of eastern religions becoming popular and gaining followers in the United States. Zen Buddhism, Transcendental Meditation, Bahai, Hare Krishna, Sun Myung Moon's Unification Church, the Divine Light Mission and a multitude of smaller movements are attracting thousands of young Americans.

These eastern mystical religions are confusing and challenging to many Americans because of their entirely different epistemology (theory of knowledge or understanding). Classical western society is built upon the use of facts, objective truth, and reason. Ideas require rational explanations. To the eastern mystic, knowledge is entirely subjective—they cannot expect to put truth into words or expect another to understand their religious experiences. Personal inspirations and inner feelings are the basis for everything, and all truth is individual and relative.

CORRUPTION OF BIBLICAL DOCTRINES

This different approach to life and truth can be seen in the way eastern mysticism corrupts basic Christian doctrines.

Sin

To the eastern mystic, sin is the ignorance that keeps a person from being "true to himself," consistent with his inner desires and feelings. There is no moral standard outside of the individual's conscience. Failure to follow a personal moral standard is sin and the root of all discontent. This is especially attractive to many modern Americans who want to talk themselves out of the guilt their lifestyle causes them to feel. This attitude is also common among modernistic Christianity and much of modern sociology and psychology.

Since the fall of Lucifer in Isaiah 14:12-15, the essence of rebellion against God has been for one of God's created beings to insist that he will do things his own way regardless of the commandments of God. It is because individuals choose to go their own way rather than God's that the Lord Jesus had to die to provide redemption for man (Isaiah 53:6). Eastern mysticism defends and promotes this independence of spirit rather than acknowledging and trying to solve the real sin problem.

Salvation

Salvation of the eastern mystic involves the experience of "the oneness of yourself with the universe." This experience cannot be described, and only the person involved can tell whether or not he has really experienced this "oneness." Salvation does not involve changing what they are or being regenerated, but simply in realizing what they already are. The mystic recognizes that there are many ways to achieve this awareness and each of these different methods is called a Yoga (notice Galatians 1:6-9). Some of the basic yogas are:

- Jnana Yoga—intellectual discipline;
- Karma Yoga—good works;
- Tantric Yoga—sex;
- Mantra Yoga—chanting and meditation;
- Hatha Yoga—physical discipline; and
- Bhakti Yoga—devotion to a spiritual master.

The ultimate goal of all the forms of yoga (according to the mystic) is to enable the individual to hear to "Divine Voice" speak within him.

God

The eastern mystics recognize many incarnations of "god" in human history. Such leaders as Buddha, Krishna, and Mohammed are considered to be these special revelations of god upon the earth. To the mystic, Jesus Christ just another one of these manifestations—in no way the only representative of God or the visible expression of the Godhead (Hebrews 1:1-2). For all their sincerity and what are often good works, this mistake alone is enough to keep the mystic from genuine salvation (Acts 4:12). It is important that the Christian not be confused by the mystic's references to Jesus Christ—they are not talking about the Jesus Christ of the Bible.

The Scriptures

Eastern mystics recognize "scriptures" only as religious documents which help an individual realize the oneness of himself with the universe. The most common books used by the mystics are the ancient Hindu writings, the Vedas, and commentaries on the Vedas. Much of this literature deals with Bhakti Yoga. The most influential book of the Vedas is the Bhagavad Gita which deals with the supposed incarnations of Krishna. They recognize that other books have some value in helping one realize his quest for "oneness," but they do not recognize any literature as divine, infallible, revelation from God.

Meditation is a key practice in all of the eastern religions. This meditation is a far cry from Biblical meditation because it involves contemplation of oneself rather than God. This type of meditation is just another form of exalting self and ignoring the true God.

To some mystics, the use of drugs plays an important part in a religious experience. Drugs give them a personal experience that they cannot get without such chemicals, and many claim that this "expansion of their consciousness" enables them to find the ultimate experience.

There are many problems in the mystic's approach to life. They cannot truly judge mystical experience. They have no criteria for understanding what they are experiencing and being sure of its effect upon them. The mystics have no way of proving that mysticism is really the ultimate life. They must place their faith for life and eternity on something which cannot be proven or studied objectively. Is peace of mind and inner harmony a guarantee of truth and value? The mystic's eternity is staked upon his peace, but where is his assurance that his peace is real and lasting? His religion is only as perfect as his own emotions and intellect. He has nothing of the assurance of a divine verbal revelation from God that Christians have in the Bible.

Satan

The mystics are totally ignorant of the activity of Satan. They do not consider the possibility of Satan's deception or demonic activity. Satan does indeed appear to the mystic as the Angel of Light. His ignorance of the work of the devil in the midst of his spiritual search, leaves the mystic wide open to Satanic deception. Mystics fail to pass the first and basic test of Christian truth found in I John 4:1-3. They do not acknowledge Jesus as the Christ—the only incarnation of God the Father and God Himself as described in John 1:1-3. They cannot offer any objective truth as revelation from God.

The other main fallacies of mysticism are summarized as follows:

- Belief that peace is available without a Savior,
- Belief that sin is not the basis for man's problems,
- Belief in a divine spark within every man,
- Emphasis on renewal and not regeneration,
- Presentation of no clear, objective reality, and
- A total lack of any moral absolutes.

It is worth noting that these are the same basic principles of modernism and Unitarianism. It is easy to see how these could one day be combined into a one-world religion.

NEW AGE RELIGION AND AMERICAN EDUCATION

It is interesting to note that some of the same people who are deeply offended at prayer and Bible study in the public school system are promoting the use of New Age concepts in the schools.

The late Beverly Galyean developed three federally funded educational programs for the Los Angeles Public Schools using guided imagery and meditation. She described her educational philosophy:

Once we begin to see that we are all God, that we have the attributes of God, then I think the whole purpose of human life is to reown the God-likeness within us; the perfect love, the perfect wisdom, the perfect understanding, the perfect intelligence, and when we do that, we created back to that old, the essential oneness which is consciousness.

In the 1990 Spring Community School Program for Wake County Public School System of Raleigh, North Carolina, a course in Kundalini Yoga was offered for high school students and adults. The following description of the course was offered by Bob Larson in *Straight Answers on the New Age:*

According to Hindu yoga teaching, spiritual energy at the base of the spine, in the form of a serpent (Hindu goddess Shakti), that seeks ascension to the brain to form a psycho-sexual union with the Hindu god Shiva, resulting in "enlightenment."

The April, 1990, issue of the Arkansas Citizen reports the widespread use of "counseling programs said to be for the reduction of stress, New Age meditation, and visualization techniques, have been introduced . . . DUSO and Pumsy Programs are by far the most prevalent New Age curricula."

American business leaders are sucked into the New Age through corporate-sponsored "stress-reduction" seminars, retreats, and exercises.

The October, 1989, newsletter of Concerned Women for America documents how parents in Oklahoma and Maryland discovered a whole array of New Age courses in public schools promoting "the attainment of higher levels of consciousness . . . even encouraging children to go home and try with their Ouija boards."

Russell Chandler, religion editor for the Los Angeles Times, reports in his book *Understanding the New Age:*

Children in the Los Angeles City School System have been taught to imagine they are one with the sun's rays. In doing so, they are told that they are part of God, "[T]hey are one with Him."

Christians should not be fooled by New Age Religion even when Christian terminology is used. New Age religions, movements, and practices are just the religious expression of a culture in rebellion against God, demonstrating the religious angle of the Culture War.

THE OCCULT IN AMERICAN SOCIETY

"Ye are of God, little children, and have overcome them: because
greater is he that is in you, than he that is in the world."
(I John 4:4)

THE OCCULT IN MAINSTREAM AMERICAN SOCIETY

There are always those individuals in every society who practice in the "occult arts." These may involve trying to manipulate "invisible forces" for personal gain, or it may involve open witchcraft or even Satanism. When American society was predominantly Christian, such individuals were on the fringes of American society. During the Culture War, however, they have moved to the mainstream of American society.

Military chaplains are now trained to meet the spiritual needs of military personnel involved in witchcraft groups. The First Church of Satan has IRS-granted 501(c)(3) tax-exempt status (meaning that it is recognized by the government and is not required to pay taxes). Occult groups advertise and recruit openly.

Many people are lured into the occult by the promise of supernatural power and success. Advertisements promoting this appeal are common in popular magazines. These ads promise everything from "automatic mind control," to how to gain "power, wealth, and love."

The Scriptures make it clear that the Old Testament pagan culture was an occult culture. The Old Testament clearly condemns any occults activity on the part of the people of God.

Deuteronomy 18:9-14 both condemns occult activity and lists several examples of occult practices:

9 When thou art come into the land which the LORD thy God giveth thee, thou shalt not learn to do after the abominations of those nations.
10 There shall not be found among you any one that maketh his son or his daughter to pass through the fire, or that useth divination, or an observer of times, or an enchanter, or a witch.

11 Or a <u>charmer</u>, or a <u>consulter with familiar spirits</u>, or a <u>wizard</u>, or a <u>necromancer.</u>
12 For all that do these things are an abomination unto the LORD: and because of these abominations the LORD thy God doth drive them out from before thee.
13 Thou shalt be perfect with the LORD thy God.
14 For these nations, which thou shalt possess, hearkened unto observers of times, and unto diviners: but as for thee, the LORD thy God hath not suffered thee so to do.

OCCULT PRACTICES

The list of occult practices from Deuteronomy 18:9-14 is worthy of careful study.

Passing through the Fire

"There shall not be found among you any one that maketh his son or daughter to pass through the fire."

This has already been covered extensively in the chapters on the new paganism and abortion. But, this should serve as a reminder that child sacrifice is a basic occult practice, and modern-day abortion is just a sophisticated form of child sacrifice.

Divination

This refers to the concept of trying to foretell the future by contacting spirits or using supernatural power. Modern day fortune-tellers, Ouija boards, tarot cards, and kabbala are examples of divination today.

Observer of Times

This practice includes modern day astrology—the idea that certain times are somehow mystically good for some activities and somehow bad for other activities. Astrologers are referenced frequently in the book of Daniel as part of the pagan culture of Babylon. They are also mentioned in Isaiah 47:13-14:

13 Thou art wearied in the multitude of thy counsels. Let now the astrologers, the stargazers, the monthly prognosticators, stand up,

and save thee from these things that shall come upon thee.
14 Behold, they shall be as stubble; the fire shall burn them; they
shall not deliver themselves from the power of the flame: there
shall not be a coal to warm at, nor fire to sit before it.

The Lord's attitude toward astrology and other "time"-oriented "mystic arts" is clear. He is offended when people trust supernatural mystic forces instead of Him. The modern pseudo-science of "biorhythms" also fits into the category of observers of times. One only has to look at the average daily newspaper to be reminded how common astrology is in America.

Enchanters

This refers to someone who tries to "cast spells" to perform miracles. A Biblical example of "enchantment" is seen with the magicians at the court of Pharaoh (see Exodus 7:11, 22). That some of these enchantments worked and that miracles were actually performed is seen in Exodus 8:8. II Timothy 3:8 makes it clear that these magicians (two of whom were named Jannes and Jambres) were practicing demonic powers and that they were in rebellion against God: "Now as Jannes and Jambres withstood Moses, so do these also resist the truth: men of corrupt minds, reprobate concerning the faith."

The popularity of "spell casting" programs and books shows how this occult practice has influenced American culture.

Charmer

The term charm refers to the manipulation of mystic forces by using specific statements written, sung, chanted, or by specific chemical potions. Acts 19 refers to such charms among the people of Ephesus. After observing a mighty work of the Holy Spirit in Ephesus, the people destroyed their "charms." Acts 19:18-20 says:

And many that believed came, and confessed, and showed their deeds. Many of them also which used curious arts brought their books together, and burned them before all   men: and they counted the price of them, and found it fifty thousand pieces of silver. So mightily grew the word of God and prevailed.

Any public library in America today contains books of charms and spells which can be checked out by the general public.

Consulter with Familiar Spirits

This refers to a person who communicates with demonic spirits. Often the person will develop a relationship with a specific demonic spirit or spirits. These spirits and the person become "familiar" with each other, hence the term familiar spirit. This term is mentioned 16 times in the Bible, and the practice is always condemned. The Bible gives us an extended look at a woman with a familiar spirit in I Samuel 28.

King Saul, in obedience to the Lord, had "cut off" all those who openly practiced consulting with familiar spirits. This had driven the practice underground. When the Lord would no longer communicate with Saul because of his disobedience (I Samuel 28:5-7), Saul became desperate to know the future. When he discovered that some of his aides knew of a woman with a familiar spirit operating in the village of Endor, he was willing to consult with her in order to get a supernatural revelation of the future.

Saul and two other men disguised themselves and went to this woman. They asked her to bring Samuel up from the dead. The woman went into her rituals expecting to conjure up a spirit (a demon) and she went into shock when Samuel actually appeared.

The sin of consulting a familiar spirit was one of the two reasons that the Lord slew Saul, according to I Chronicles 10:13: "So Saul died for his transgression which he commited against the LORD, even against the word of the LORD, which he kept not, and also for asking counsel of one that had a familiar spirit, to inquire of it."

The modern-day channeling movement, many of the reincarnation stories, many of the ghost, UFO, and haunting stories involve familiar spirits. You do not have to look very hard to see the role of familiar spirits in modern society. They play a role in the concept of the "Force" in the Star Wars movies. The author of the popular children's book Jonathan Livingston Seagull claims that it was dictated to him by a familiar spirit.

Wizard

This particular term refers to the use of magic and sorcery. The word magic refers to two previous terms, enchanter and charmer. The word sorcery refers to the use of drugs in combination with supernatural forces (see Revelation 9:21 and 18:23). The word pharmacy is taken from one of the roots of the word sorcery. The drug menace in American society is often combined with occult activity.

Necromancer

The term necromancer refers to attempts to contact the dead.

This is the only time this term is used in the Bible. Modern-day spiritualism, séances, and Ouija boards are all a form of necromancy and are all increasingly common in America today.

The Lord is very clear in condemning all these practices. As previously stated, there have always been individuals who were in rebellion against God and involved in the occult in the United States, but they were always on the fringe of American society. For 40 years, these people have been moving into the mainstream of our society.

Many societies have developed cultures totally dominated by the occult. Ancient pagan cultures, tribal cultures, etc., are often recognized as being occult cultures. However, such cultures are not limited to ancient time. Nazi Germany was an occult society (see *The Occult Reich* by J. H. Brennan, *The Spear of Destiny* by Trevor Ravenscraft, *The Twisted Cross* by Joseph Carr, and the material on Houston Stewart Chamberlain in *Rise and Fall of the Third Reich* by William Shirer). It is entirely possible for the occult to dominate a culture in this day and age.

Of course, open Satanism is possible and on the rise in the United States. A number of Satanic organizations operate openly, and the Satanic Bible by Anton LaVey has been a best-seller. Revelation 13:4 tells about a time (the Tribulation period) when the whole world will worship the Dragon (Satan) and the anti-Christ. Revelation 13:4, "And they worshipped the dragon which gave power unto the beast: and they worshipped the beast, saying Who is like unto the beast? who is able to make war with him?" All of the occult activity today is designed to prepare the world for the worship of the dragon, the eventual one-world culture, and government in rebellion against God.

The Scripture is very clear in prescribing a test for all the spiritual activity in the world. I John 4:1-4:

1 Beloved, believe not every spirit, but try the spirits whether they are of God: because many false prophets are gone out into the world.

2 Hereby know ye the Spirit of God: Every spirit that confesseth that Jesus Christ is come in the flesh is of God:

3 And every spirit that confesseth not that Jesus Christ is come in the flesh is not of God: and this is that spirit of antichrist, whereof ye have heard that it should come; and even now already is it in the world.

4 Ye are of God, little children, and have overcome them: because greater is he that is in you, than he that is in the world.

Christians should be careful never to be confused about occult and supernatural forces. They should recognize the activity of Satan and demons. They should recognize what is happening to the culture around them.

ENVIRONISM

"Professing themselves to be wise, they became fools, And changed the glory of the uncorruptible God into an image made like to corruptible man, and to birds, and fourfooted beasts, and creeping things." (Romans 1:22-23)

The Environmental Movement as a Pagan Religion

Environism is a combination of pseudo-science, new age mysticism, paganism, and socialism which serves as a combination of political philosophy and religion. This is clearly an attempt to replace America's historic Christian culture with a new religion—a pagan religion.

The National Religious Partnership for the Environment was formed in 1993. By April, 1994, education and activity kits had been sent to 53,000 American churches. The NRPE's Executive Director Paul Gorman said, " . . . *how people of faith engage the environmental crisis will have much to do with the future well-being of the planet, and in all likelihood, with the future of religious life as well.*" The NRPE claims that the environmental movement represents a new religious enlightenment capable of uniting all religions.

The NPRE is headquartered in New York City at the Cathedral of St. John the Divine (an Episcopal Church). Also located in this church is the Gaia Institute and the Temple of Understanding. One of the recently featured speakers at this church was James Lovelock, author of The Ages of Gaia. Lovelock is credited with saying, "The earth, Gaia, is the source of life everlasting and is alive now; she gave birth to humankind, and we are a part of her." For environmentalists like Lovelock, "Mother Nature" is not an abstract concept but the living planet, a goddess to be worshipped in place of the God of the Bible.

Many other "environmentalists" offer similar religious teaching. Dr. Robert Muller, former Assistant Secretary General at the United Nations, author of the World Core Curriculum (which serves as a foundation of Goals 2000 and Outcome Based Education), and chancellor of the United Nations University of Peace in Costa Rica, has written a book entitled *New Genesis: Shaping a Global Spirituality.*

In a 1995 interview with the *World Goodwill Newsletter,* Muller said:

The UN is humanity's incipient global brain, and it is part of its global nervous system (media, NGO's, etc.). We still need a global heart . . . and we still need a global soul, namely our consciousness and fusion with the entire universe and stream of time.

What Muller means is clarified in another speech delivered to *World Goodwill.* Muller says:

We are temporary living manifestations or incarnations of this earth. We are living earth. Each of us is a cell, a perceptive nervous unit of the earth. The living consciousness of earth is beginning to operate through us.

You, as cosmic and earth cells, are part of a vast biological and evolutionary phenomenon which is of first importance at this stage, namely humanity as a whole, the whole human species, has become the brain, the heart, the soul, the expression, and the action of the earth. We now have a world brain which determines what can be dangerous or mortal for the planet: the United Nations and its agencies, and innumerable groups and networks around the world, are a part of this brain. This is our newly discovered meaning. We are a global family living in a global home. We are in the process of becoming a global civilization.

A leading theologian for the "Environist" movement is Thomas Berry, a Roman Catholic priest. *The Wanderer Forum Quarterly* says:

Father Thomas Berry, C.P., claims that it is now time for the most significant change that Christian spirituality has yet experienced. This change is part of a much more comprehensive change in human consciousness brought about by the discovery of the evolutionary story of the universe. In speaking about a new cosmology, he reminds that we are the earth come to consciousness and, therefore, we are connected to the whole living community— that is, all people, animals, plants, and the living organisms of planet earth itself.

According to *The Florida Catholic* (February 14, 1992), Berry says:

We must rethink our ideas about God; we should place less emphasis on Christ as a person and redeemer. We should put the Bible away for 20 years while we radically rethink our religious ideas. What is needed is the change from an exploitative anthropocentrism to a participative biocentrism. This change requires something more than environmentalism.

Berry is an editorial advisor to Creation magazine, which says:

The world is being called to a new post-denomonational, even a post-Christian belief system that sees the earth as a living being, mythologically, as Gaia, Mother Earth, with mankind as her consciousness. Such worship of the universe is properly called cosmolatry.

Lovelock, Muller, and Berry are convinced that the Gaia hypothesis is the inescapable, universal truth which has been distorted and forgotten by the human species. Only now, with the emergence of the Gaia hypothesis, is the world beginning to discover the truth so easily recognized by the ancient mystics, shaman [a worker with the supernatural], and pagan worshipers of the past. Berry says:

This new period in history might be called the Ecozonic era. It requires that we return to the mythic origins of the scientific venture. We feel the scientists must participate to some extent in shamanic powers. We might say that the next phase of scientific development will require above all the insight of shamanic powers.

In the environist magazine *Green Egg*, Otter Zell wrote an editorial entitled "On the Occasion of Bill and Al's Excellent Election":

We are neo-pagans—implying an eclectic reconstruction of ancient Nature religions, and combining archetypes of many cultures with

*other mystic and spiritual disciplines—and our beliefs and values
are no different from those you describe as your own.   We ask
no special favors; we wish nothing more than that you be true to
yourself, and to your own values and ideals as expressed in Earth
in the Balance [by Al Gore].   Know that there are half a million
American NeoPagans out here who support you, who   voted for
you, and who will rally to the aid of your policies for the salvation
of the Earth and the reunification of the Great Family.*

Andrea Judith supports the same concepts. She writes:

*The basic evolutionary pattern in biological organisms is
movement toward greater consciousness. When all parts of Gaia
recognize each other as participants in parallel growth heading
for an Omega point of coalescence and integrative harmony,
then the global consciousness of this planet will have awakened
to a realization of identity as a global being. Gaia's evolutionary
thrust is reflected in the spiritual goals of self-realization that
comes from acceptance of the gaia hypothesis as the reason why
human behavior must be modified to protect, preserve, and even
worship the earth goddess—Gaia.*

The Cathedral of St. John the Divine features a service called the
"Blessing of the Animals." One year the sermon was delivered by then-
Senator Al Gore. Some of the animals led down the aisle to be blessed at
the altar were: an elephant, a llama, a camel, a python so large that two
men had to carry it, birds, algae (brought in by Paul Mankiewicz, director
of the Gaia Institute), and a bowl full of worms and compost. In his
sermon, Al Gore declared that God is not separate from the earth.

Al Gore's book *Earth in the Balance* is often considered the most
important environist book in print.

Amy Elizabeth Fox, Associate Director of the NRPE, describes
their political agenda this way:

*We are required by our religious principles to look for the
links between equity and ecology. The fundamental emphasis is
on issues of environmental justice, including air pollution and*

global warming; water, food, and agriculture; population and consumption; hunger, trade, and industrial policy; community economic development; toxic pollution and hazardous waste; and corporate responsibility.

The NRPE seeks to convince its religious partners to modify their belief systems to embrace Gaia. Individual members of congregations who truly convert will not mind modifying their behavior to conform to the requirements of the new "earth ethic."

When environists say that "The planet doesn't belong to us, we belong to the planet," they are addressing a pagan concept refuted by Scripture. Scripture makes it clear that both the planet and humans belong to God. However, God has given man dominion over the earth and ordered him to subdue it. Every invention of man, from electricity to automobiles to medicines, is part of the process of subduing nature. Man does not exist for the earth; the earth was created for the glory of God and the benefit of man.

Genesis 1:26-28 says:

26 And God said, Let us make man in our image, after our likeness: and let them have dominion over the fish of the sea, and over the fowl of the air, and over the cattle, and over all the earth, and over every creeping thing that creepeth upon the earth.

27 So God created man in his own image, in the image of God created he him; male and female created he them.

28 And God blessed them, and God said unto them, Be fruitful, and multiply, and replenish the earth, and subdue it; and have dominion over the fish of the sea, and over the fowl of the air, and over every living thing that moveth upon the earth.

Scripture warns about the kind of false theology represented in environism. Romans 1:22-23, "Professing themselves to be wise, they became fools, And changed the glory of the incorruptible God into an image made like to corruptible man, and to birds, and fourfooted beasts, and creeping things."

2016:
MILLENNIALS AND GOOGLE:
THE NEW FAITH

Dr. Doug Levesque

Citizens born in the new millennium are rightly called Millennials. They know nothing of wired telephone communication, only three to four television channels, stamped or hand-written mail, or bicycle delivered newspapers. Theirs is a world of digital, wireless, instant, hand held information, communication and entertainment. They did not go to the public library, research through a card catalog or read an encyclopedia. They now have the ability to question Google out loud and get an instantaneous response based upon a pre defined set of parameters that they themselves have set. This makes the message that Google delivers to be received as a most likely satisfactory emotion, and a positive reinforcement to a vision of themselves and their own designed world. Such potential narcissism is transforming America into a myriad of little demagogues whose personal experience does not necessarily match their online profile or image. And they are OK with this arrangement. It is a living fantasy, and a made up faith. It is serving to skew Biblical faith into just another masquerade, and satanic rebellion into an understandable option.

Google is a word that represents the concept of a googleplex, or an infinite number of options. It is akin to total freedom, total confusion, total control or total slavery all at once. The company's motto was once famously "do no evil" perhaps because of the possibility of it's doing evil. If you "google" the word "evil" there are so many responses that one has to wonder if there really is such a thing. In the Millennial vernacular, to google, is to search for answers, to ponder, even in the right circumstances, to pray. This digital age phenomenon constitutes a new faith. A religion of human proportions that replaces the Bible with an online query, God with an seemingly infinite response, righteousness as any one of these responses as an accepted choice, and googling as the alternative to prayer. Mankind's corporate thought as a hive mentality is exalted into a messiah like position. Google CEO Schmidt does get ad revenues, and arbitration power over query search rules, but that doesn't seem to matter to Millennials. They are happy with the self perceptions of control. The good that Google does and the ease with which they give access to so many of life's tools is truly amazing, but it can never replace the true faith or real relationship with our creator, Jesus Christ. This transformation in our culture is alarming.

Google, Amazon, Tesla, Facebook and other 21st century technical gurus have created a new faith based upon a new concept of everlasting life. Transhumanism, teaches that by downloading one's online profile, launching it into the "cloud", and then creating a robotic version of yourself you can become your own creator. You can live forever. If the digital and synthetic can somehow merge with the biological and human, the hybrid merger would afford the savior of earth and of humanity. The Millennials technological thinking and opportunities have tempted them with these and other blasphemies. Jesus became a man, shed real blood for mankind, and died a human death in order to become a once for all and only savior. Modern transhuman ideals are a bogus religion, a war on true faith, and destructive to young minds. In this pretend faith, Biblical faith is dangerous, and should be replaced, with all Christian adherents removed from interference. The "Climate Change" dogma of the UN is really about this new faith. They want to create a world where only the truly transhuman can survive an earth without livable breathable air. The Millennials are the first generation capable of being guinea pigs in this devilish experiment.

The transformation now at hand is the end of the road for America. The archaic and self-defeating concept of religion will be removed along with the simplistic notion of nationhood. The darkest part of darkness is now being imagined.

Consider Romans 1:21, "Because that, when they knew God, they glorified him not as God, neither were thankful; but became vain in their imaginations, and their foolish heart was darkened."

TRANSFORMATION

11
THE WAR ON ENTERTAINMENT

TRANSFORMATION

ROCK MUSIC

"Let the word of Christ dwell in you richly in all wisdom; teaching and admonishing one another in psalms and hymns and spiritual songs, singing with grace in your hearts to the Lord."
(Colossians 3:16)

CULTURE AND MUSIC

Just as every culture develops its own religion (or is developed from a religion), every culture develops its own distinctive music. The new American culture of rebellion against God is no exception. In fact, some would say that the music developed first, and the rest of the new American culture came from this new music: rock music.

Allan Bloom comments on the role of rock music in the American culture in *The Closing of the American Mind*. He says:

> *This is the significance of rock music. I do not suggest that it has any high intellectual sources. But it has risen to current heights in the education of the young on the ashes of classical music, and in an atmosphere where there is no intellectual resistance to attempts to tap the rawest passions. Modern-day rationalists, such as economists, are indifferent to it and what it represents. The irrationalists are all for it. There is no need to fear that "the blond beasts" are going to come forth from the bland souls of our adolescents. But rock music has one appeal only, a barbaric appeal, to sexual desire—not love, not eros, but sexual desire undeveloped and untutored. It acknowledges the first emanations of children's emerging sensuality and addresses them seriously, eliciting them and legitimating them, not as little sprouts that must be carefully tended in order to grow into gorgeous flowers, but as the real thing. Rock gives children, on a silver platter, with all the public authority of the entertainment industry, everything their parents always used to tell them they had to wait for until they grew up and would understand later.*

THREE BASIC DRIVES

Every human being is motivated by three basic drives:

- Physical,
- Social, and
- Spiritual.

How one meets his needs and decides which drive is most important determines what kind of life he will lead.

Each part of music corresponds to one of these basic drives:

- Melody is the spiritual part of music,
- Harmony is the social part, and
- Rhythm is the physical part of music.

Any one of these three parts of music can be the dominant theme in a musical piece. Music in which the physical (rhythm) is dominant is called ROCK music. It was given the name "Rock and Roll" because of its ability to relate to physical movement. Margaret Sears, musical therapist, says "In rock, the rhythm, rather than the melody, ebbs and flows and has an hypnotic effect."

THE INFLUENCE OF MUSIC

It is important to remember that the influence of music is subtle and not always obvious to the one being influenced. Crowded restaurants play fast music to get their customers to eat faster. Very rarely does the customer realize he is hurrying to keep pace with the music. It is also important to note that music LEADS; it does not FORCE. Melodious music encourages spiritual growth but does not demand it. Rhythm-dominated music leads to physical response, but the listener does not always respond immediately and fully to the message of the music.

Plato recognized the importance of music when he said, "Musical training is a more potent instrument than any other." Henry David Thoreau recognized it when he prophesied the doom of western civilization: "Even music may be intoxicating. Such apparently slight causes destroyed

Greece and Rome, and will destroy England and America." Conductor Laszlo Gati of the Victoria, British Columbia Symphony warned:

I am really worried that one hundred or three hundred years from now when they try to analyze why the rest of civilization has demised the reason will not be the atomic bomb but the kind of music we have listened to!

ROCK MUSIC AND SEX

Rock musicians claim that rock music leads to sexual activity. Frank Zappa (Mothers of Invention) said, "Rock music is sex, the big beat matches the body's rhythms." Mick Jagger (Rolling Stones) said, "Rock is sex and you have to hit them in the face with it." Mike Quarto (a rock music show producer) said, "The heavy rock music now in style motivates you internally, gives you a sensual feeling. A girl can be turned on by the music. It releases her inhibitions."

Any casual examination of much rock music will show that many of the lyrics are clearly obscene and suggestive. Rock musicians claim that the music itself has the same message. Who can argue with them?

ROCK MUSIC AND DRUGS

Yale sociologist Charles Reich feels that rock music is vitally connected with the drug scene. He said, "An enormous number of the young listeners had instruments or even bands and played the new music themselves, and both bands and listeners considered drugs to be an integral part of the music experience." Newspaperman Fred Sparks of the Detroit News agrees and said this about America's rock groups, "They are guilty for all the revolutionary talk in this nation, they are guilty for all the drug abuse, and for much of the sexual immorality." Many rock stars are famous for their involvement with drugs, and drugs have led to the deaths of such rock stars as Janis Joplin and Jimi Hendrix. During the time that rock music has been prominent in our country, the drug menace has increased tremendously.

Musical therapist Adam Knieste warns:

Rock is not a harmless pastime but a dangerous drug on

which our children are hooked; rock is more deadly than heroin because it is generally thought to be harmless and therefore does its damage unchallenged.

Rock music is part of a physically oriented culture that ignores spiritual truth. Rock music is vitally connected with both the beginning and the continuation of the Culture War.

ROCK MUSIC AND REVOLUTION

Revolutionary Jerry Reuben said, "Rock and roll marked the beginning of the revolution." He also credited Elvis Presley with starting the sexual revolution—the Culture War—with his lewd on-stage behavior and the message of is music. The Beatles declared that their own music is "capable of causing emotional instability, disorganized behavior, riot, and eventually revolution." Time magazine reported, "All rock is revolutionary." Billboard magazine declared, "Rock and roll has been feeding the fire of the second American revolution." The appeal of rock music to physical action, ignoring spiritual truth, inevitably leads to rebellious attitudes and self indulgence.

Rock musicians make no secret of how important they feel their music is. Mick Jagger said, "We are moving after the minds, so are most of the new groups." Arthur Brown said, "Rock is the most underestimated infiltration of modern systems today." Rolling Stone magazine reported, "Rock and roll is more than just music. It is the energy center of the new culture and youth revolution."

PHYSICAL EFFECTS OF ROCK

Another important matter related to rock music is the physical effect is has on hearing. The International Safety Institute of California, Pennsylvania, measured the sound of hundreds of performances of rock music. They warn of the health hazard that such loud music provides. Most of these performances exceed the legal limit of 115 decibels for 15 minutes which is the maximum standard protecting industrial employees. For two years, Mrs. Dorothy Retallock of Denver, Ohio, played rock music to various plants, and the noise and vibration killed them.

One good way to judge rock music is to ask what the rock concerts and festivals have produced. Was Woodstock noted for its peaceful gathering of people serious about doing right, or for its nudity, immorality, homosexuality, and drugs? Are rock concerts places of spiritual refreshment for America's young people, or places where drugs and alcohol flow freely and sin is glorified?

Christians have the Biblical responsibility to prove that the things they involve themselves with are acceptable to the Lord (Ephesians 5:10). What evidence is there that rock music is acceptable to the Lord? What spiritual blessing does it produce? What benefits does it provide? Any Christian who wishes to listen to rock music has the responsibility to answer these questions.

Galatians 6:8 warns that the person who sows to the flesh (the old Adamic nature) reaps of the flesh corruption. Just as daily vitamins over a period of time produce benefits, worldly, fleshly, physical music over a period of time will produce at least some form of sinful corruption.

A Christian ought to have his spiritual drive controlling the physical and social drives. "But seek ye first the kingdom of God, and his righteousness; and all these things shall be added unto you." (Matthew 6:33)

Because it is important that we concentrate our energies and thoughts on being right spiritually, we receive the command of Philippians 4:8, "Finally, brethren, whatsoever things are true, whatsoever things are honest, whatsoever things are just, whatsoever things are pure, whatsoever things are lovely, whatsoever things are of good report; if there be any virtue, and if there be any praise, think on these things." What we think about has the greatest influence in determining what we are like. The Bible says, "As he thinketh in his heart, so is he." (Proverbs 23:7) Everything that influences our thoughts has the greatest impact on determining our spiritual character.

Recognizing the importance of music to the Christian, Johann Sebastian Back said, "The aim and final reason of all music should be nothing else but the glory of God and the refreshment of the spirit." Every Christian should seek to increase his own personal purity by avoiding rock music and should encourage others to do so as well.

This is why the Bible puts such emphasis on the right kind of music:

"Speaking to yourselves in psalms and hymns and spiritual songs, singing and making melody in your heart to the Lord." (Ephesians 5:19)

"Let the word of Christ dwell in you richly in all wisdom; teaching and admonishing one another in psalms and hymns and spiritual songs, singing with grace in your hearts to the Lord." (Colossians 3:16)

THE ENTERTAINMENT MEDIA

"Finally, brethren, whatsoever things are true, whatsoever things
are honest, whatsoever things are just, whatsoever things are pure,
whatsoever things are lovely, whatsoever things are of good report;
if there be any virtue, and if there be any praise,
think on these things." (Philippians 4:8)

Media analyst Michael Medved began his famous book on the entertainment media, Hollywood vs. America, this way:

America's long-running romance with Hollywood is over.

As a nation, we no longer believe that popular culture enriches our lives. Few of us view the show business capital as a magical source of uplifting entertainment, romantic inspiration, or even harmless fun. Instead, tens of millions of Americans now see the entertainment industry as an all-powerful enemy, an alien force that assaults our most cherished and corrupts our children. The dream factory has become the poison factory.

Network television officials are adamant that TV and the movies do not influence people's behavior and that the entertainment media is in no way responsible for modern cultural problems. After all, studies authorized and paid for by ABC, NBC, and CBS have concluded (surprise) that there is no relationship between what people watch and what they do! But if TV does not influence both the thinking and behavior of people, why is television advertising a billion-dollar business?

The truth is that of over 3,000 research projects and scientific studies between 1960 and 1992, 86% have concluded that there is a relationship between entertainment and behavior. Warnings have been issued by the Surgeon General of the United States, the American Medical Association, American Academy of Pediatrics, the American Medical Association, National Institute of Mental Health, U.S. Public Health Service, the National PTA, and the National Education Association.

A number of surveys show that the American people are concerned about the moral quality of the entertainment media. A 1993 Times-Mirror poll showed that 73% of viewers thought there was way too much violence on TV. A 1994 survey conducted by Scripps-Howard News Service and Ohio State University indicated that 64% of viewers felt that movies promoted real-life violence.

While television is still a major contributor to American culture, viewer dissatisfaction is being felt. Over the last 15 years, the three major networks have lost 33% of their evening viewers.

Even Hillary Clinton has expressed concern about the quality of programming on TV:

There has been a reinforcement by popular culture of the undermining of social values and institutions. I, personally, worry more about television than other forms of media, because it's so pervasive, and it's a primary baby-sitter and value-transmitter for many children.

I think, on both the actual substance of entertainment and the process by which it's delivered, there are grounds to worry about its impact—particularly on children.

More and more attention is being focused on the role of television and movies. Before 1970, 38% of all shows that depicted non-marital sexuality clearly condemned it. In 1993, only seven percent of programs that referred to such material presented it in a disapproving light. Before 1969, references to moral impurity occurred in only one out of 30 TV episodes. In 1993, it was one out of six. A typical teenager watching TV today hears or sees almost 40 mentions of moral impurity daily. By the time the average child graduates from elementary school, they will have seen 8,000 murders and 100,000 other acts of violence on TV.

Many in Hollywood clearly understand the importance of their influence. Michael Hudson, vice president of the Hollywood-funded "People for the American Way," said, "We are in the midst of a culture war."

ANTI-CHRISTIAN BIAS

Movies bashing evangelical Christians are common in Hollywood. There are films depicting them as sexual perverts, serial killers, members

276

of killer cults, and demon-possessed. Christian ministers have been portrayed as hypnotists using TV to take over the world, seductors who prey on teenaged girls, or as completely immoral and financially dishonest. A favorite theme is to show Christians as hypocrites. One film has a Nazi-like Christian fundamentalist character who enslaves people, enforcing public accommodation to religion while living in private immorality. Another is about a woman who lives a life of immorality, makes a profession of faith, and joins an evangelical church. This leads her to kill her daughter and to commit suicide. Still another movie is about psychotic, mean-spirited, repressed Protestant missionaries in the Amazon. When not attacking Christians, Hollywood enjoys making fun of the concept of a true and living God, with special attention being given to blaspheming the Lord Jesus Christ.

Actress Amanda Donahoe, referring to a scene she played in the movie "The Lair of the White Worm," said, "I'm an atheist, so it actually was a joy. Spitting on Christ was a great deal of fun." The anti-Christian bias is not found only in movies. Television is also guilty of vast amounts of such material and, of course, movies are often rebroadcast on television for in-home prime time viewing.

"THE LAST TEMPTATION OF CHRIST"

The 1988 release of the film, "The Last Temptation of Christ," illustrates much of Hollywood's attitude toward Christianity and Jesus Christ. Many evangelicals, as well as Roman Catholics, expressed their offense and asked Universal Films to withdraw the film.

It is hard to imagine a movie creating more controversy than was caused by "The Last Temptation of Christ." Christian leaders publicly attacked the movie and called for a strong public Christian reaction. Roman Catholic bishops urged their parishioners to boycott the movie. Campus Crusade leader Bill Bright offered to raise $10 million (an estimate of the production costs) to give Universal in exchange for all the copies of the film. They refused.

The movie, "The Last Temptation of Christ," was based upon a fictional novel of the same name by Nikos Kazantzakis. This novel was a major factor in his being censured by the Greek Orthodox Church. The screenplay was written by Paul Schrader, and the movie was produced by Martin Scorsese (who once wanted to be a Roman Catholic priest).

This movie presents a most unorthodox interpretation of the nature, life, and ministry of Jesus Christ and was an unveiled attack upon the Savior. The Lord Jesus was presented as a lustful, adulterous, instable revolutionary, and apostle Paul was a liar and a hypocrite, while Judas Iscariot is set forth as the hero. Even secular media commented on the extremely unorthodox portrayals in the movie. Patrick O'Driscoll of USA Today called it "Scorsese's cinematic vision of a sometimes weak, doubting, even lustful Jesus." He quotes the producers' main aim as creating "a psychological portrait of Jesus as a man learning to accept his divinity." The August 15, 1988, issue of Time magazine contained an article entitled "A Holy Furor" in which the blasphemy was described. Time concluded, "Such an approach to explaining Christ goes beyond even films such as 'Jesus Christ Superstar' and 'Godspell,' which offended believing Christians."

Many critics accused believing Christians of being "afraid" that his film would destroy the faith of Christians. They completely misunderstood the issue. Presenting Christ as a mentally incompetent, unsure religious reformer, overwhelmed by dreams of lust and adultery is insulting to those who know Jesus Christ as the sinless Son of God and who place their faith in Him as their personal Savior.

We would not react calmly if someone produced such vicious attacks on the character of anyone that we love. Evangelicals are especially incensed when such misrepresentation is made toward Jesus Christ.

Telling the story of Christ apart from the historical and theological truth has no possible value. It would be the same with ordinary human beings.

Such stories would tell you a lot about the fantasies of those who wrote and produced such stories.

Scorsese spent 16 years trying to get this film to the public. He was given a copy of the novel in 1972 by Barbara Hershey, who played Mary Magdalene in the film. He says that the movie "is my way of getting closer to God."

Amidst the furor caused by their insistence upon releasing the controversial film, Universal Studios responded by attacking those who said they were offended and aggressively releasing and promoting the film. When everything was said and done, they ended up losing $10 million on the project.

The role of modern rock music, movies, and (increasingly) television in promoting moral impurity, mocking the traditional family, promoting illegitimacy, focusing on the bizarre and perverted, and glorifying irresponsibility is well known. Even Hollywood insider Steve Allen (a clear liberal in most areas) said the following:

Humans can do without roller skates or TV but they literally cannot long survive, as a rational, emotionally healthy species, without a secure family structure.

The reason, to belabor the obvious, is that the family is the soil in which each year's new crop of humans grow. It is mostly the failed family therefore, which has produced our present millions of prison inmates, rapists, drug addicts, burglars, muggers, sexual psychopaths.

It is no wonder that so many parents are concerned about the message of television.

ENTERTAINMENT MEDIA AND VIOLENCE

The relationship between the entertainment media and violence has been the subject of a great deal of study. Particularly disturbing in the discussion is the lack of separation of self-defense of freedom from mindless violence. In many movies, it is increasingly hard to tell the heroes from the villains.

Another influence of television on popular culture is the way that adults and children are exposed to the same information. In The Disappearance of Childhood, 1990, author Neil Postman, professor of media and communications at New York University, asserts that TV has erased the boundary that once separated childhood from adulthood. This boundary, according to Postman, was only possible to maintain through a culture that communicates primarily through the print media.

Children and adults read different literature, but they often watch the same TV shows.

As a result, children are pushed into adult experiences before they are ready. The innocence of childhood is gone for most children. The teenage years were once thought to be a bridge between childhood and the adult years. Now children often act the way that teens used to and teens engage in activity once reserved for adults.

Finally, in the most recent trend in the entertainment media's unabashed attacks in the concept of family, more and more television programs and movies are being introduced where the homosexual movement is presented as a completely normal, alternate lifestyle. This subtle, "normalized" presentation will certainly have an even greater effect on public opinion in the future than it already has.

Television programming presents a perverted view of men. Sit-coms routinely bash men, especially fathers, who are presented as indecisive, weak, simple-minded, and naïve. They are shown as people who need their wives and kids to help them through life and who are "clueless" when it comes to teenage issues. All of this contributes to a breakdown in male leadership in the family, as well as in society.

Christians must learn to be very careful about the entertainment media. They must be aware that many of the people involved in the entertainment media are engaged in a Culture War against Christianity. Christians should be very wary of the potential for the entertainment media to spoil their spiritual life. Philippians 4:8, "Finally, brethren, whatsoever things are true, whatsoever things are honest, whatsoever things are just, whatsoever things are pure, whatsoever things are lovely, whatsoever things are of good report; if there be any virtue, and if there be any praise, think on these things."

2016:
NETFLIX, BINGE TV AND THE CLOUD

Dr. Doug Levesque

The average American watches almost five hours of TV per day. That is close to 35 hours a week! It is almost a full time job these days. In fact with cable and streaming services the choices are endless. American culture almost has an on-demand access to every TV show and movie ever made all at once. We are close to such a media fete. That means modern watchers can now set the goal of watching everything that was ever broadcast! Add to this list the endless programming uploaded by Youtube and other self promoting web services. Maybe watching it all is now impossible? There are approximately 80 milion videos available through Youtube comprising over 800 million hours of viewing. If we live to be 75 years old we would only have 675,000 hours of viewing. Apparently, you can now officially waste your entire life watching TV and movies. The culture war on entertainment is now simply a tsunami of programming meant to inundate you with images and information. Some of the content is helpful or entertaining, but most is without a premise of virtue, and much is now against the concept of God. Beware the idolatry of TV.

Like most new innovations, Netflix started out as a great way to pull away from broadcast and cable TV choices. Older, cleaner TV was making a comeback. Families could find a friendly show, and then order it up on any night they had time. Presto! Family friendly TV. Twenty first century technologies have given TV watchers a myriad of new ways to pick and deliver entertainment. Unfortunately, poor programming abounds as does purely evil programming. The promise of better choices quickly turned into more choices. The flood tide of anything and everything is now overwhelming the soul with an anxiety that "we are missing something." Netflix, Hulu, Amazon and other "new media" are now producing original programming with modern dogmas akin with current social trends. Bible preaching pulpits no longer compete with a show or a channel. It is not even a competition with an industry. It is now a multi channel, multi industry, multi media fight for the minds and hearts of Americans. Church attendance is suffering. Christians, like most Americans are watching too much TV.

A new word has come on the scene, "binge" watching. "Binge" used to be a word associated with the loss of all restraint. Binge drinking, binge eating, binge drug using and even binge fornicating were all deemed dangerous, bad for your health and a destroyer of society. Today "binge" is a sales point. Advertisers sell the "binge" worthy aspects of their products, especially when it comes to media consumption. It seems the "more is better" crowd is winning out. Do you like watching the news? Try 24 hour news channels. There are at least a half dozen of them. Pick a cultural slant, liberal or conservative, there will be a dedicated news channel for you. How about sports? Pick a sport and there is a channel for it. When did our culture leave the pleasure of fishing in order to WATCH fishing? And if you like programming uniquely adjusted to your social likes, there are channels just for men, just for women, just for children, just for nature lovers, just for foodies, and, yes, just for homosexuals. It seems the vanity fair of Pilgrim's Progress has arrived and is offering a dainty for just about every soul. Even so called Christian programming is a damning prospect. Put down the remote, turn off the screen, get off the couch. How else can one turn down the volume of the world and listen intently to the "small still voice of God"?

As if the constant onslaught of entertainment was not enough, the added prospect of watching this imagery anywhere and everywhere is also now on the menu. With the introduction of the "cloud" or digital and wireless connectivity, the full slate of media offerings are available to stream into your phone, your vehicle, or your office at a moment's notice. Total TV superpowers now allow children, housewives, students and men at work the god like purview of a million worlds all at once. Everywhere you look there is a person plugged into a device watching, communicating, involving themselves in some drama. Children riding the bus, teens walking the mall, mom's on their daily power walk and dad's at their desks watching, watching, watching . . .everything, and . . . nothing of importance. Furthermore, most of what is being watched is also being recorded by some automatic process. Data is collected in order to psychologically diagnose everyone at some future point for some unknown reason. The prospect of all this media has to be serving the

Devil's own purpose of programming minds and hearts to reject the Lord and receive a phony messiah. Wholesome moments of entertainment are not worth the cost to society that infinite digital indoctrination can bring. Wage war on media by turning it off.

Consider the hard bargain of the world with God's people found in 1 Samuel 11:2, "And Nahash the Ammonite answered them, On this condition will I make a covenant with you, that I may thrust out all your right eyes, and lay it for a reproach upon all Israel."

TRANSFORMATION

12

FIGHTING THE CULTURE WAR

TRANSFORMATION

SPIRITUAL WARFARE

"For the weapons of our warfare are not carnal, but mighty through
God to the pulling down of strong holds."
(2 Corinthians 10:4)

The Scriptures make it clear that Christians should expect to find
themselves in the middle of serious spiritual warfare. Notice the terms of
violence and combat used in II Corinthians 10:3-6 (used here in a spiritual
sense):

3 For though we walk in the flesh, we do not war after the flesh:
4 (For the weapons of our warfare are not carnal, but mighty
through God to the pulling down of strong holds;)
5 Casting down imaginations, and every high thing that exalteth
itself against the knowledge of God, and bringing into captivity
every thought to the obedience of Christ;
6 And having in a readiness to revenge all disobedience, when
your obedience is fulfilled.

This passage clearly refers to a spiritual battle and to spiritual weapons
available to the believer. Evil imaginations are seen as the opposing
weapons that Christians must overcome. The battlefield is seen to be the
hearts and minds of men (not a physical battlefield or even a legislative
one). The battle is won when people are persuaded into obedience to
Christ.

Ephesians 6:10-18 describes the spiritual weapons available to
Christians as they fight the Culture War:

10 Finally, my brethren, be strong in the Lord, and in the power
of His might.
11 Put on the whole armour of God, that ye may able to stand
against the wiles of the devil.
12 For we wrestle not against flesh and blood, but against
principalities, against powers, against the rulers of the darkness

of this world, against spiritual wickedness in high places.
13 Wherefore take unto you the whole armour of God, that ye may be able to withstand in the evil day, and having done all, to stand.
14 Stand therefore, having your loins girt about with truth, and having on the breastplate of righteousness;
15 And your feet shod with the preparation of the gospel of peace;
16 Above all, taking the shield of faith, wherewith ye shall be able to quench all the fiery darts of the wicked.
17 And take the helmet of salvation, and the sword of the Spirit, which is the word of God:
18 Praying always with all prayer and supplication in the Spirit, and watching thereunto with all perseverance and supplication for all saints;

Sometimes Christians seem overwhelmed as they look at the cultural forces arrayed against them. Government agencies with taxing and regulating power, most of the entertainment media (movies, music, TV, and magazines), most of the public education establishment, the overwhelming majority of the news media, and modern peer pressure seem like formidable forces in the war against our Christian culture. However, Christians possess weapons more powerful than the forces against them. Ephesians 6:10 makes it clear that the issue is the Lord's strength and the power of His might, not our strength or power.

Verse 11 makes it clear that the issue is not the strength of our enemies, or even the power and trickery of the Devil. This is confirmed in I John 4:4, "Ye are of God, little children, and have overcome them: because greater is he that is in you, than he that is in the world."

The rest of this passage (Ephesians 6) begins to list specific weapons available to the Christian. They are all considered important and make up the whole armor of God. No sensible warrior would want to go into battle missing parts of his armor.

Verse 12 reminds us again that this ultimately is a spiritual battle. The demonic origin of this conflict is clearly seen here. The words "principalities and powers" clearly refers to demonic spirits. Bible students debate the meaning of the phrase "rulers of the darkness of this world" and "spiritual wickedness in high places." Some believe that these are also phrases that refer to demonic spirits, others believe that they refer to human rulers under demonic influence. Either way, it is clearly a spiritual battle.

Verse 13 refers again to the whole armor of God and the importance of Christians taking a clear stand for the Lord.

MORAL RESPONSIBILITY

The first spiritual weapon is referred to in verse 14. The phrase "having your loins girt about with truth," is a reference to moral responsibility. The principle is simple: do not do anything with your loins that you cannot afford to be honest about. A spouse should not do anything that he cannot afford to tell his/her spouse. Teens should not do anything they cannot afford to tell their parents they are doing. At first, moral responsibility might not seem like much of a weapon in the Culture War, so it deserves a closer look. The lure of moral impurity is the primary temptation that draws people into rebellion against God and into paganism. Maintaining a pure moral life is a real barrier against being drawn into the attitude of rebellion. Furthermore, some Christians who make important contributions in the public debate have lost their opportunity to be a voice for the Lord because of their lack of personal responsibility. Every Christian who maintains God's moral standards is taking a big step toward refusing to have his spiritual life "spoiled."

KEEPING YOUR HEART RIGHT

The second weapon is also referred to in verse 14, "Having on the breastplate of righteousness." The breastplate covers the chest and protects the heart. Keeping your heart right with the Lord keeps those who have declared war on Christianity from "spoiling" your spiritual life. Proverbs 4:23 makes the same point: "Keep thy heart with all diligence; for out of it are the issues of life."

Moral responsibility and a heart right with the Lord are powerful defensive weapons against a culture in rebellion against the Lord. Such weapons have allowed men like Daniel and Joseph and women like Esther to live in spiritual triumph and victory even in pagan cultures like Babylon, Egypt, and Persia.

SOULWINNING

The third weapon is in verse 15: "feet shod with the preparation of the gospel of peace." Feet and the gospel are also connected together in Romans 10:15, "And how shall they preach, except they be sent? as it is written, How beautiful are the feet of them that preach the gospel of peace, and bring glad tidings of good things!" The principle is clear: feet are connected with the gospel of peace because the gospel of peace is something we are to take to people. The power of the gospel is a power that the Culture War against Christianity cannot overcome. No one ever waged a more violent or vicious Culture War against Christianity that Saul of Tarsus. But the gospel of peace turned Saul into Paul the Apostle. Look at what the gospel did to pagan King Nebuchadnezzar (Daniel 4).

It is a terrible mistake for Christians to become so involved in fighting political or legislative battles (though these need to be fought) that they forget their responsibility to get the gospel out. Soulwinning is fighting the Culture War in the most powerful way.

FAITH IN THE WORD OF GOD

A fourth weapon is introduced in verse 16 with the words, "above all." This weapon is the "shield of faith." The faith referred to here is our faith in the Word of God. Just as we trusted what the Bible says about salvation and eternal life, we must trust what it says about all the details of Christian living. The fiery darts of the wicked are the philosophies, vain deceits, traditions, and worldly ideas that are designed to spoil the spiritual life and Christian values of believers. The shield of faith (simply trusting what God says) protects the Christian from these fiery darts hurled by government agencies, the entertainment and news media, and some professional educators. God's Word must never be subjected to the whims of the moment or the social pressures of the day. Worldly philosophies come and go but the Word of God stands forever.

RENEWING OUR MINDS

A fifth weapon is mentioned in verse 17: "the helmet of salvation." This refers to thinking like a saved person—the Biblical process of renewing our minds. When a person trusts Christ, a brand new potential becomes available to him. The thought patterns of the old nature and the worldly principles are replaced with the doctrines of the Word of God. This process of growth will ultimately become complete and total when we meet the Lord. How fast individual Christians grow now depends upon their openness to the Lord. Learning to think like a saved person protects the believer from all the principles of vain deceit and evil imagination that are used to try to "spoil" the believers.

THE PREACHING OF THE WORD OF GOD

A sixth weapon is also mentioned in verse 17. It is "the Sword of the Spirit." The Lord's primary offensive weapon is clearly the Word of God. His kingdom is not built by physical force but by the preaching of the Word of God. "For the word of God is quick, and powerful, and sharper than any twoedged sword, piercing even to the dividing asunder of soul and spirit, and of the joints and marrow, and is a discerner of the thoughts and intents of the heart." (Hebrews 4:12).

Many Christians are hesitant to refer to Scriptures in the public debates of the day. They have been told to refrain from doing this. But who authorized special interest groups to legislate the Bible out of public life? The Founders of our country constantly referred to the Bible in the public debates of the day—indeed our system of government could not have been designed without reference to the Scriptures. The power of the Scriptures speaks for itself, and Christians must realize the power of this weapon that the Lord has entrusted to us. "Is not my word like as a fire? saith the Lord; and like a hammer that breaketh the rock in pieces?" (Jeremiah 23:29).

PRAYER

A seventh weapon is in verse 18. The weapon of prayer is mentioned in great detail. "Praying always with all prayer and supplication in the Spirit, and watching thereunto with all perseverance and supplication for all saints." Prayer is tragically underrated even among long-time Christians. Think of the effect of Stephen's prayer upon Saul of Tarsus, of Samson's prayer in the Philistine temple, of Daniel's prayer in the lions' den. Prayer is God's way of allowing us to communicate to Him and request His specific activity. Prayer frightens those who are in rebellion against God, and they campaign endlessly against public prayer. Someone has suggested that if the modern ACLU had its way, they would have to build lions' dens in all our public schools.

Phrases like "all prayer and supplication" and "always" are used to describe the prayer life of concerned Christians. There is no way to over-estimate the importance of prayer in the modern Culture War. No Christian is ever weaponless. Even when the Word of God has been taken from him, he can still pray. When his God-given freedom has been stolen from him, he can still pray. The Christian can intercede with God for and about those who would "spoil" his faith. God hears the prayers of His saints, "Let us therefore come boldly unto the throne of grace, that we may obtain mercy, and find grace to help in time of need." (Hebrews 4:16). "The effectual fervent prayer of a righteous man availeth much." (James 5:16).

Ephesians 6:18 also refers to "watching" in connection with prayer. Christians must learn to pay close attention to what is going on around them. They must learn to be prayerful as they face the challenges of the day. The verse also mentions "supplication for all saints." As individual Christians each face a unique set of cultural challenges, they should pray for one another and call down the blessings of God upon one another.

There has been much talk in the United States about people being afraid that the churches will take over the government. But who has all the bazookas, machine guns, missiles, airplanes, explosives, and atomic bombs? The churches of America are no threat to force the government into anything.

What those in rebellion against God are really afraid of is that Christians will persuade people to follow the Lord. Preaching, prayer, personal morality, and witnessing are all weapons that they cannot compete with on equal terms. The new pagans all want to advance their agenda with the force of government.

- They want the force of government to remove the Bible from public life.
- They want the force of government to prevent public prayer.
- They want the force of government to make Christians pay for their neighbors' abortions.
- They want the force of government to make everyone express approval of homosexuality.

- They want the force of government to teach all children, including the children of Christians, Joycelyn Elders-style bizarre theories about teenage moral impurity.

Christians must stand up to these attacks with the weapons provided by the Lord. Moral responsibility, hearts right with the Lord, sharing the gospel, trusting and using the Word of God, thinking like Christians, and prayer are the most powerful weapons in the Culture War.

Those who wish to destroy Christianity are under-equipped. Laws, prisons, weapons of physical warfare, brain-washing, control of education, and the media have never been able to destroy the work of God. The testimony of the Scriptures, as well as of church history is clear: Christian are better armed. It is our responsibility to avail ourselves of our spiritual weapons in the spiritual warfare.

CHRISTIANS AND PUBLIC POLICY

"Then Peter and the other apostles answered and said, We ought
to obey God rather than men." (Acts 5:29)

THE CHALLENGE TO AMOS (Amos 7:12-13):

*Also Amaziah said unto Amos, O thou seer, go, flee thee away into
the land of Judah, and there eat bread, and prophesy there: But
prophesy not again any more at Bethel: for it is the king's chapel,
and it is the king's court.*

Amaziah's point was simple. Bethel was a center for the calf-cult
started by King Jeroboam I. While this worship took place in the name
of Jehovah, it was designed to fuse together Egyptian paganism with
the worship of Jehovah. Jeroboam had feared that worship centered
in Jerusalem would lead the people of the northern ten tribes back to
allegiance to Rehoboam. So, he simply declared this to be the "politically
correct" way to worship Jehovah.

This cult competed with Baal worship throughout the history of
the Northern Kingdom. Jeroboam II had officially restored this cult to
favor. It was the official public policy of his administration of support
this religion while rejecting both Baal worship and Scriptural worship of
Jehovah.

Amaziah was claiming the king's right to regulate the worship of
Jehovah. It was his "chapel" as well as his "court." Because it was his
chapel, nothing should be said or done there that was contrary to the
public policy of his administration. By prophesying judgment, Amos
had violated the public policy of the king's chapel. Public policy was to
assure the people that they were in the will of God.

Every government has a "public policy." This term simply refers
to the aims and goals of the administration and their methods for
accomplishing those goals. Public policy may reflect long-standing law
and cultural traditions, but it also includes the specific goals of a particular

leader or administration. Every totalitarian government expects religious assemblies (as well as educational organizations and social groups) to support public policy.

Throughout the Scriptures, preachers (and other principled believers) have had to pick between public policy and the revealed will of God. Examples of believers who chose to "obey God rather than men" are abundant.

- The Egyptian midwives rebelled against the public policy of Pharaoh (and lied to the government) when they saved the children of the Hebrews (Exodus 15-20). God rewarded them for this.
- Moses and Aaron challenged the public policy of Pharaoh when they led the children of Israel out of Egypt (Exodus chapters 1-15).
- Rahab violated the public policy of Jericho when she aided the two spies (Joshua 2:1-4).
- Samuel openly rebuked the public policy of Saul when Saul took upon himself, as King, the role of Priest (I Samuel 15).
- David rebelled against the public policy of Saul when he gathered a private army to defend the children of Israel (I Samuel 22).
- Nathan exposed the sin of David—covering it up would have been public policy—when he declared "thou art the man" (II Samuel 12).
- An unnamed man of God preached against the public policy of Jeroboam I when the king started a new calf-cult in the name of Jehovah (I Kings 13:1-4).
- The prophet Hanani withstood the public policy of King Asa and was thrown in jail as a result (II Kings 16:7-10)/
- The prophet Jehu preached against the public policy of wicked King Baasha (I Kings 16) and even against the public policy of good King Jehosaphat (II Chronicles 19).
- Both the prophets Elijah and Micaiah preached against the public policy of Ahab's administration (I Kings 18, 22).
- The prophet Eliezer rebuked Jehosaphat for supporting King Ahaziah (II Chronicles 20:35-37).
- Elijah defied the agents of King Ahaziah and, thus, his public policy (II Kings 1).
- Elisha preached against the king of Israel when the king tried to

blame the preacher for the problems his administration caused (II Kings 6).

- Jehoiada rebelled against the public policy of Athaliah and saved Joash alive and hid him (II Chronicles 24).
- When Joash later rebelled against God, Jehoida's son Zechariah challenged his public policy and, as a result, Zechariah was stoned to death (II Chronicles 24).
- When Uzziah the king tried to take control over the temple worship, Azariah the priest and 80 valiant men withstood his public policy and refused him entrance (II Chronicles 26:16-18)
- Jeremiah was accused of treason when his preaching contradicted the public policy of King Zedekiah, who had him imprisoned (Jeremiah 37).
- Daniel and his three friends challenged "the public nutrition policy" of Babylon (Daniel 1).
- Shadrach, Meshach, and Abednego refused to obey the order to worship the golden image of King Nebuchadnezzar (Daniel 3).
- Daniel refused to obey King Darius' attempt to institute public policy prayer guidelines (Daniel 6).
- Zerubbabel and the elders in Jerusalem defied the public building permit policy of the Persian Empire and started rebuilding the temple in defiance of the instruction of King Artaxerxes (Ezra 4, 5).
- John the Baptist was disobeying public policy when he preached against the wickedness of King Herod (Luke 3). He was arrested and later killed because of it.
- The Sanhedrin ordered Peter and John to stop preaching and teaching about Jesus (thus creating a new public policy). Peter and John refused declaring, "Whether it be right in the sight of God to hearken unto you more than unto God, judge ye. For we cannot but speak the things which we have seen and heard" (Acts 4:1-19).
- When the Sanhedrin repeated the new public policy to all of the apostles, they replied, "We ought to obey God rather than man" (Acts 5:29).
- Stephen continued to defy the public policy of the Sanhedrin until they had him stoned to death (Acts 6, 7).

- After Herod determined to enforce the public policy of the Sanhedrin by killing James, the entire church continued to defy public policy, resulting in the arrest of Peter (Acts 12).
- Paul and Barnabas preached the gospel in defiance of the public policy of authorities in Iconium (Acts 14).
- Paul and Silas preached the gospel in defiance of the public policy of Philippi (Acts 15).

Throughout church history, believers have often had to choose between "public policy" and the revealed will of God. Millions of faithful believers have faced persecution and even death rather than to obey the public policy of governments in rebellion toward God.

As our government and culture grow farther and farther from our heritage, American Christians may have to make the choice between public policy and Scripture.

CHRISTIANS AS SALT AND LIGHT

"That ye may be blameless and harmless, the sons of God, without
rebuke, in the midst of a crooked and perverse nation,
among whom ye shine as lights in the world."
(Philippians 2:15)

Ye are the salt of the earth: but if the salt have lost its savour,
wherewith shall it be salted? It is thenceforth good for nothing, but
to be cast out, and to be trodden under foot of men. Ye are the
light of the world. A city that is set on an hill cannot be hid. Neither
do men light a candle, and put it under a bushel, but on a candlestick; and it giveth light unto all that are in the house. Let your light
so shine before men, that they may see your good works
and glorify your Father which is in heaven.
(Matthew 5:13-16).

THE SALT PRINCIPLE

There are two clear principles stated for Christians in this passage. The first in the Salt Principle, which, simply stated, is salt preserves from corruption. When the New Testament was written, salt was the primary preservative for meat. God's people are left in this world to witness against iniquity and to set an example for righteousness. Christians are to be the moral conscience of society. If Christians are comparable to salt which has lost its saltiness;, they are good for nothing (in terms of their value to society).

THE LIGHT PRINCIPLE

The second principle is the Light Principle. Christ designated Himself as the "light of the world" (John 9:5). In His physical absence, His disciples are to witness for Him in the darkness of this world. The Bible also refers to this principle in Philippians 2:15, "That ye may be blameless and harmless, the sons of God, without rebuke, in the midst of a crooked and perverse nation, among whom ye shine as lights in the world." Simply put, Christians should see to it that the light of revelation is made available to everyone.

As we have seen earlier, some truths are self-evident—creation, the Creator, morality, and judgment, for example. However, the glorious gospel of grace is not self-evident. Left to themselves, men always devise a system of salvation by works. The gospel of salvation by grace is made known unto men solely by the light of revelation.

The Scripture makes it clear that carrying out these two responsibilities is not optional for Christians. These responsibilities are commands. It is not that we could be salt and light—it is that we are salt and light. We may be salt that has lost its savour, or we may be a light hid under a bushel, but we are still the salt and light of society. In other words, we may be failures in these two areas, but Christians are still the only salt and the only light that society has.

The effectiveness of Christians as salt and light will determine the nature of the civilization in which our children and grandchildren will grow up. The following are three ways that every Christian should be carrying out the salt and light principles in our society.

STRONG FAMILIES

First, every Christian should be helping to build a strong family. God has designed that families should be the building-blocks of society. It is not God's plan that all of society function as one big, happy family, but that each child should have his or her own parents that belong uniquely to that child. Each husband belongs to his own wife and each wife with a husband who is uniquely hers. Strong families build individuals who are not molded to the collective will of society but to the values of that family. Nothing is a greater threat to the plans of those who have declared a Culture War against Christian values than strong families.

A common quote today among those who want to change American culture is, "It takes a whole village to raise a child." In fact, in 1996, First Lady Hillary Clinton published a book on children entitled It Takes a Village, taking her title from this old African tribal proverb. In the days when American culture was primarily Christian, it did not take all of society to raise children. It only took responsible parents. In homes that honor Christian principles, this is all it takes today.

STRONG LOCAL CHURCHES

A second way to be salt and light in our society is to help build a strong local church. Every Christian should be involved in this. The church is God's way of uniting people for shining forth the light of God's revelation. "Not forsaking the assembling of yourselves together, as the manner of some is; but exhorting one another: and so much the more, as ye see the day approaching." (Hebrews 10:25) The church is designed that Christians may carry out the Great Commission, encourage one another, and be God's means for carrying out His work.

Just as God illustrates individual Christians with the picture of the candle, He pictures the local church with the image of the candlestick— several candles together (see Revelation 2:5). In fact, the same passage that tells us not to hide our candle under a bushel tells us to put it on a candlestick. Several lights together shine so much more brightly than one individual light.

As our civil government becomes increasingly pagan, our schools, entertainment, and news media join the Culture War against Christian truth. The independent, Bible-believing, local church remains the primary vehicle for maintaining any of America's Christian culture and heritage. This is precisely why the church so often comes under attack by government agencies.

PRAYER

A third way all Christians are to function as salt and light is prayer. I Timothy 2:1-3:

> *I exhort therefore, that, first of all, supplications, prayers, intercessions, and giving of thanks, be made for all men; For kings, and for all that are in authority; that we may lead a quiet and peaceable life in all godliness and honesty. For this is good and acceptable in the sight of God our Saviour.*

Notice that the primary purpose of praying for the leaders of civil government is that they will leave us alone to live quietly and peaceably. This passage does not imply that you pray for God's blessings and wisdom upon leaders who are in rebellion against God. God cannot bless such leaders in that way. Believers can pray that God will bless leaders according to their faithfulness to Him, that He will convict and save those who do not know Him, and that He will block the wicked plans of those who are in rebellion against Him.

Every American believer should pray for the President, the Vice President, the Cabinet, the Governor, state legislators, and mayor or county commissioners each day.

EXERCISING THE SALT AND LIGHT PRINCIPLES

The following are some ways that Christians can exercise the salt and light principles. No one could do all of these things (and some are controversial even among good Christians).

Voting

All American Christians should be consistent, careful, and prayerful about voting. When someone reaches voting age, he should make his right to vote count.

Christians should be careful in evaluating candidates and campaign promises. Candidates who promise that government can do what God should do or that government can take the place of families and churches should be rejected. Unfortunately, evangelical Christians have the reputation of being a segment of society that (percentage-wise) does not vote very heavily. If evangelicals want their voice to be heard by their elective representatives, they need to vote consistently.

Campaigning

Christians can volunteer to campaign for candidates who reflect their concerns. The outcomes of Presidential elections, or campaigns for U.S. Senator or Congressman, state lawmakers, county officials, state Governors, school boards, etc., affect the lives of Christians. Contributions of time and money are appropriate and welcome.

Running for Office

Some Christians should consider running for office. In spite of the complaints of those who feel threatened by Christians in public life, Christians have the same rights as anyone else. Godly, dedicated public officials are very important to any improvements in American life.

Community Involvement

Christians can serve in good community organizations and neighborhood associations. These organizations often greatly influence local communities, and Godly influence can mean much.

Donating good Christian and conservative books to school libraries and public libraries can make a great impact. There is no telling how often these books will be read. If the only information available to those who use the library is non-Christian or anti-Christian, you cannot expect the general public to get the answers they need.

Public meetings on community issues should be well attended by Christians. A small number of people often decide issues. Those who are not involved cannot expect their views to be heard.

Christians should regularly attend school board meetings (even those who educate their children in private schools or at home still pay taxes for the public school system). Can you imagine the effect on local school boards if they knew that every Bible-believing church in their community was represented at every school board meeting?

Letters to the editor of local and city newspapers are often a good way to keep Christian truth and conservative values in front of the public. Intelligent callers to radio and TV call-in shows can also keep good information in front of the public.

Voicing Opinions

Christians should regularly write or call their elected representatives and communicate their views. The homosexual population (less than two percent) puts such pressure on government officials that they regularly hear their agenda. If the 34% of Americans that who are professing evangelical Christians (according to a Gallup poll) communicated their views as earnestly as the homosexual population, their concerns would be the most important political agenda in America.

Many national organizations promote values or focus on one specific Christian or conservative theme. Financial support and activity make these programs stronger and help to spread their message.

There are a number of good radio and TV programs spreading the traditional, conservative, Christian worldview that deserve to be listened to, watched, and financially supported.

Grassroots activity in distributing literature and information has influenced many issues in America—and is the one form of communication that the forces opposed to Christian values cannot influence or regulate.

Protests and Boycotts

Many Christians have protested the tragedy of abortion at abortion clinics. These protests take a variety of forms, but many feel that they raise a standard of righteousness against this horror.

Some dedicated Christians have protested and picketed outside places that distribute pornographic material. In many communities, these protests and boycotts have made a big difference.

Other Ways

When Christians serve as foster parents or adopt children, they have precious opportunities to communicate life-changing values.

Another very important way that Christians can be salt and light is by supporting one another. During this Culture War, Christians are often spoken against, harassed, persecuted, and sometimes even falsely prosecuted and imprisoned. This is what the Scripture refers to in passages such as, "Yea, and all that will live godly in Christ Jesus shall suffer persecution" (II Timothy 3:12) and, "Remember them that are in bonds, as bound with them; and them which suffer adversity, as being yourselves also in the body" (Hebrews 13:3). At such times, suffering believers really need the support of fellow Christians. Sadly, sometimes Christians falsely judge each other during these times. Even Paul had to endure being misunderstood during his imprisonment for Christ (see Philippians 1:13-18).

The story of William Wilberforce is a prime example of the salt and light principles at work. Wilberforce was a member of the British House of Commons in 1785. After trusting Christ as his Saviour, he became concerned about how he should serve the Lord as a political leader. He became burdened about seeing slavery abolished in England. Ending slavery would be no easy task. Slavery had long been a part of English tradition. Wilberforce began to campaign for legislation to restrict and then outlaw slavery. His speeches and motions in Parliament met with a great deal of opposition. For 20 years, the battle continued in Parliament. Wilberforce had to take his case to the public. He had to endure criticism and repeated attempts to blacken his reputation. He was mocked as the leader of a hopeless cause, but, after 20 years of campaigning, the English Parliament finally outlawed slavery, setting an entirely new public moral tone in England. In the United States 600,000 people died in a bloody Civil War to accomplish the same purpose.

2016:
RELIGIOUS LIBERTY
VS. RELIGIOUS PLURALISM

Dr. Doug Levesque

Religious liberty in early America meant the freedom from a state sponsored, nationally mandated church. Roman Catholicism and the Church of England were examples of such religious authorities ultimately persecuting other forms of Christian expression. Biblical Christianity that differed from the state endorsed expressions of faith was often deemed heresy, dissent and dangerous. True believers were banished, burned, or imprisoned. Underground churches were formed. Separatists fled to frontiers and wilderness regions in order to gain freedom of religion. Many of the first American pilgrims were simply religious and therefore political refugees. Our forefathers ensured through the first amendment that such tyranny would not be possible in their new country. Unfortunately, the freedom to obey the Scriptures without state interference had morphed in the freedom to not only reject the Scriptures, but alienate all true gospel mandates from government offices. Re-defined, religious liberty has become a Babylonian type of religious pluralism.

At the time of this writing, President Elect Trump has won 80% of the so called evangelical vote while at the same time touting a dedication to "religious pluralism". Real threats to the original concept of religious liberty are coming from both the left and right. The threat may seem like a simple misunderstanding or mistaken vocabulary, but more often the new pluralism is a scheme to overthrow the culture of Christianity and it's voice in the halls of power.

Make no mistake, Pluralism is the political lowering of Biblical faith to the mandated level of every other opinion or religion. It puts shackles on preachers to proclaim sin or the "only Jesus saves" message. It defines and punishes Christian opinion as "hate", points out true believers as the problem in American culture, and subtly re-creates a state religion.

If the Biblical role of women is misogynistic, if warnings against accepting homosexuality as a civil right are deemed threats, if rejection of

Islam is called racist, then Christians under religious pluralism are only one step from civil disobedience or worse . . .prison. An even greater danger of accepting the pluralism or tolerance mantra over true religious liberty is the voluntary quieting of churches in regards to their evangelistic mission in the world. Gospel witnessing is our chief activism, and without it all other attempts to affect society will be watered down. Patrick Henry said it best, "Give me liberty or give me death!" It was a command statement, a didactic sentence, and a prophetic truth all at once.

Consider these current headlines:

"What Are the Limits of 'Religious Liberty?'"
-July 7, 2015, *The New York Times Magazine*

"Civil rights or religious liberty - what's on top?"
-September 9, 2016, *The Washington Post*

"'Religious freedom,' 'liberty' just 'code words' for intolerance,
U.S. Civil Rights chairman says"
-September 8, 2016, *Washington Times*

These articles all reference the battle between backing religious liberty advocates, who wish to live in a reality that rejects homosexuality as normal, and the LGBTQ community that wants to mandate its views as a civil right forcing American conscience to reject the clear admonishments of Scripture. Obviously, this cultural and legal conundrum has no real way of coexistence, therefore the cultural tide turning to pluralism is a form of compromise.

The greatest way to preserve true religious liberty is to practice it. Preach the Word in season, and out of season. Proclaim the truth of Jesus Christ when it is fashionable AND when it is illegal. Call out sin when the culture backs it, and when all of the courts condemn it. We are living in a surreal time in America when political activism and pulpit exposition will be deemed the same thing, despised by elected officials and religious panhandlers alike. To reform our truth in order to comply with pluralistic expectations or to quiet our voices in order not to offend is not an option that our Biblical examples or American forefathers would consider. This scenario is not the beginning of America's Transformation but the death throes of a journey into darkness. It is not the politician's job to lead in this particular cultural wrestling match, but pastors and Christians honor to stand and face the darkness.

TRANSFORMATION

CONCLUSION

DR. DOUG LEVESQUE

TRANSFORMATION

It has taken hundreds of years to transform America. We started as a virtuous people, grounded in the Bible and though a republic, dedicated to one king, Jesus Christ. Though not all were true Christians, most were overwhelmingly compliant to the beautiful life of a Christian culture. Even the skeptics knew that a Christian America was the best prospect for everyone. Only an adherence to a national persona, painted by the Scripture itself, could produce our Declaration, Constitution and other formative rules of order. But from the beginning of our nation, the timeless battle between Satan and God raged on. While the Lord gave a land of freedom where the greatest Bible printing, missionary sending, jew supporting force for good in the world could operate, Lucifer began an insidious campaign of usurpation that has lasted hundreds of years. He wanted the mechanics of our nation for his own nefarious purposes. The journey toward darkness began almost immediately, but the foundations were strong and lasting. They are still here, barely, but against all odds, still alive. It is up to us to continue to be wise, noble and dedicated to fighting this insurrection of evil in our day.

Paul wrote in his day, 2 Corinthians 2:11, "Lest Satan should get an advantage of us: for we are not ignorant of his devices."

Besides defending the original intent of our founders and their documents, we should know our corporate history and see the working of God in it. We do not just have Christian origins and heritage, but a continuous believing culture. The battle for a Biblical culture can be charted alongside the richest histories of American events. A clear delineation of this cultural war and a basic understanding of our losses and gains with each battle is helpful when trying to plan for the warfare of today. God is truly on our side, it is a simple prospect that we should also be on His side. Picking sides becomes clear when both history and the Bible are well known. The idea that we have to find middle ground in the culture is a satanic one. It is true that we are sheep, but we are not without the great shepherd. The valleys of culture war do not make us afraid, for the spirit of a lion is in us. "Ye are of God, little children, and have overcome them: because greater is he that is in you, than he that is in the world." (I John 4:4) That one can be meek and yet maintain a warrior mentality seems foreign in today's churches, but this idea must be recalled in every generation.

That Christ is our Captain, who came to bring a cultural sword, and calls upon us to fight the good fight must not be forgotten or fade in the American psyche. The Devil must feel like he is close to the transformation of American society. Indeed, prophecy tells of a time when his fallacy seems very close at hand. But let nothing of the sort be realized without a real contest of wills. Christians are "more than conquerors" when they want to be. The spiritual armor, so wonderfully explained by Dr. Stringer in this volume is still available and effectual. Remember that the "gates of hell shall not prevail against the church", and that nothing short of a rapture of saints, will allow the final transformational showdown. The previous chapters are by no means meant to offer capitulation to the enemy. They are an intelligence gathering, a rally for resolve, and a pre game pep talk. This information is meant to be a challenge and an inspiration. Share it with your circle of influence and add to it in the battle to come. Cataloging the evil is a sign of the good guys amassing. We are awake. The victors write the history and define the vocabulary. Transformation, Americas Journey Toward the Darkness was a trumpet call to battle when first published. Today, it is a hundred trumpets or more, like Gideon's blast at the darkest of midnights amidst the throng of enemies. May it serve to steel your soul, commence your inner fight, and begin yet another victory in the battle for American culture.

Face the darkness!

CONCLUSION

TRANSFORMATION

ABOUT THE AUTHOR

Dr. Phil Stringer

Dr. Phil Stringer is the Vice President for Church Relations at the Dayspring Bible College (Quentin Road Baptist Church). He was formerly the pastor of Ravenswood Baptist Church of Chicago.

He has been in full-time ministry for 41 years and has served as youth pastor, evangelist, college professor and administrator, and pastor. He was ordained by the Lifegate Baptist Church in 1975.

Pulpit Ministry
He has spoken at over 400 churches, schools and colleges. He has spoken in 48 states, as well as Washington D.C. and Puerto Rico and several foreign countries including Canada, Mexico, Vietnam, Syria, The Philippines, The Bahamas, Barbados, Trinidad, Suriname, Guatemala, South Korea, Grenada, Singapore, India, Columbia, St. Lucia, England, Wales and Japan.

Teaching Ministry
Every year Dr. Stringer teaches as a visiting professor at several colleges. He has taught full courses at 21 colleges, 11 in the United States, and 10 in other countries. He has spoken at nine other colleges.

Boards
He serves on the Advisory Councils for First Light Baptist Mission, the Graceway Bible Society (Canada), the Bible Nation Society and the Shalom Native Mission. He is the Vice President of the King James Bible Research Council. He serves on the Board of Directors for the Center for the Study and Preservation of the Majority Text. He is on the Board of Trustees for the Dayspring Bible College.

Author

He is the author of several books and booklets including: *The Faithful Baptist Witness, The Transformation, Fifty Demonstrations of America's Christian Heritage, The Bible and Government, Biblical English, The Real Story of King James, The Means of Inspiration, A History of the English Bible, In Defense of 1 John 5:7, Misidentified Identity, Many Infallible Proofs, The Westcott and Hort Only Controversy, The Scripture Cannot Be Broken, Ready Answers, The Da Vinci Code Controversy, The Messianic Claims of Gail Riplinger, the Received Text for the Whole World, Majestic Legacy, The Occult connection of Gail Riplinger, The Foundations of Our World Vol. 1 and Vol. 2, The Heaven Rescued Land, and The Heaven Rescued Land Vol. 2.*

Education

He graduated with a Bachelor of Science in Bible degree from Indiana Baptist College in 1975. He received a Masters degree in Christian Education from Freedom University in 1980. He received a Doctor of Philosophy degree in English Bible from Landmark Baptist College in 1997. He received a Doctor of Religious Education degree from the American Bible College in 2004.

Awards

Dr. Stringer was awarded the honorary degree of Doctor of Divinity by the Asia Baptist Bible College in 2002. He was awarded the honorary degree of Doctor of Literature by the American Bible College in 2002. In 2007, he was awarded the Heritage Baptist University alumni educator of the year award. In 2008, he received the Hoosier Hill Baptist Camp pastor of the year award.

He can be contacted at:

Dayspring Bible College & Seminary
27875 N. Fairfield Road
Mundelein, IL 60060
224-677-7800
Email: philstringer@att.net

ABOUT THE AUTHOR

Dr. Doug Levesque

Dr. Levesque is the founder of The Bible Nation Society. He is also the Pastor Emeritus of Immanuel Baptist Church in Corunna, Michigan where he planted and led that body for over 20 years. He has been married to his wife, Amy, for 24 years. They have five sons and all enjoy backpacking, basketball, and reading. Dr. Levesque's books and articles may be found at BibleNation. org.

The Bible Nation Society is a non-profit organization dedicated to increase and diffuse knowledge about the Bible and promote its positive effects upon society. To that end, Bible Nation has engaged the culture with Biblical thought through many forms of media.

Print
Bible Nation began it's media efforts with Bible Nation magazine running multiple print issues. Dr. Levesque has recently launched BNS Press, a publishing arm of Bible Nation for his own writings as well as other worthy titles. Dr. Levesque first published *Surviving this Babylon* in 2015, quickly followed by his second work *The Confident Shepherd* in 2016. BNS Press has now grown an taken on multiple authors.

Video
Dr. Levesque has produced dozens of DVD's with the *Bible in Culture* Series. This series offers Biblical perspective on a wide range of cultural issues including marriage, religious liberty, abortion, evolution, economics, education, technology, and foreign policy.

Online
BibleNation.org is home to all BNS print and video resources as well as Dr. Levesque's articles engaging current events and cultural issues.

OTHER TITLES FROM DR. LEVESQUE

Surviving This Babylon

Dr. Doug Levesque

Babylon never really died. Its pervasive influence fades and reappears like an unruly evil. Every mighty empire has been enticed by its attractive smile and ancient promises. America is no different. Inside such bait is always a hook. The United States is currently in the grips of "mystery, Babylon." Her lies are changing the heart and soul of this fine country. Good men and women are being deceived and drawn into perdition. Christians are suffering a modern day lions' den. The lions of Babylon are fierce but the ancient secrets revealed in Scripture will help you to roar back with a perfect boldness.

The Confident Shepherd

Dr. Doug Levesque

Sheep without a shepherd get fearful, scattered, sick and lost. Without a true and properly confident shepherd, the flock gets targeted by predators, stolen, and even killed. Shepherds are important to the general welfare and direction of society's flocks. It is possible to be a faithful shepherd. Multiple shepherds practicing the same skill set as the LORD Himself can turn society around.

Titles Available on Amazon.com and BibleNation.org

MORE FROM BNS PRESS

When Israel Stands Alone

Charles E. Lang, Sr.

The Middle East conflict has plagued the world for centuries, and nations, perhaps greater than ours, have tried and failed to solve the Jewish question. The difficult answer can be found in understanding one man, his family, and his covenant with God.

Is the ancient history about Abraham's descendants relevant to our circumstances in the world as we know it today? Should the story of Abraham's life have been better left alone to decay in some museum or dusty archive? Not a good idea. Does it bring anything worthwhile to bear on our present day worldwide issues? Yes, it certainly does.

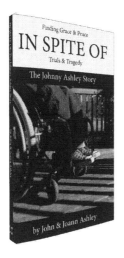

In Spite Of:
The Johnny Ashley Story

John Ashley

Finding grace and peace in spite of trials and tragedy. Johnny came into this world with multiple congenital malformations. He endured over forty surgeries including two heart valve replacements and a kidney transplant. At the age of two and a half we discovered Johnny was also profoundly deaf. "In Spite of" is how our son Johnny lived his life. Despite the many challenges he faced, he was an inspiration to all who knew him.

Titles Available on Amazon.com and BibleNation.org

BibleNation.org

Your source of Biblical thought online

Visit the newly redesigned BibleNation.org and discover a bold and compelling Biblical perspective on current events and cultural issues.

Expert-written articles and videos engage the national and global culture with Biblical thought on news and topics including:

Morality & Ethics | Religion | Media & Arts | Science | Economics

This great resource is now online with new content and features.

 New Articles   Video Series   Article Submission   Expert Authors   BNS Store

Make BibleNation.org part of your regular online experience.

 BibleNationSociety   @BibleNation   BibleNation

320

Made in the USA
Middletown, DE
02 December 2022

16447680R00179